Elements of Literature

Sixth Course

The Holt Reader

HOLT, RINEHART AND WINSTON
A Harcourt Education Company
Orlando • Austin • New York • San Diego • London

Printed in the United States of America

ISBN 978-0-03-099631-3
ISBN 0-03-099631-7

1 2 3 4 5 179 11 10 09 08

Contents

To the Student

A Book for You

Teachers open the door, but you must enter by yourself.
—Chinese Proverb

The more you put into reading, the more you get out of it. This book is designed to do just that—help you interact with the selections you read by marking them up, asking your own questions, taking notes, recording your own ideas, and responding to the questions of others.

A Book Designed for Your Success

The Holt Reader goes hand in hand with *Elements of Literature*. It is designed to help you interact with the selections and master important language arts skills.

The Holt Reader has three types of selections: literature, informational texts, and documents that you may encounter in your various activities. All the selections include the same basic preparation, support, and review materials. Vocabulary previews, skill descriptions, graphic organizers, review questions, and other tools help you understand and enjoy the selections. Moreover, tips and questions in the side margins ensure that you can apply and practice the skills you are learning as you read.

A Book for Your Own Thoughts and Feelings

Reading is about *you*. It is about connecting your thoughts and feelings to the thoughts and feelings of the writer. Make this book your own. The more you give of yourself to your reading, the more you will get out of it. We encourage you to write in this book. Jot down how you feel about the selection. Write down questions you have about the text. Note details you think need to be cleared up or topics that you would like to investigate further.

A Walk Through the Book

The Holt Reader is arranged in collections, just like *Elements of Literature*, the book on which this one is based. Each collection has a theme or basic idea. The stories, poems, articles, or documents within the collection follow that theme. Let's look at how the arrangement of *The Holt Reader* helps you enjoy a collection as a whole and the individual selections within the collection.

Unit Opener Pages

Key Concepts

The Fifth Course of *Elements of Literature* focuses on American literature and its role in our country's history. The Sixth Course traces the development of British and world literature. Each unit in the Fifth and Sixth Course books highlights a historical period and some of the works written during that period. Key Concepts from the student edition unit introductions are included in *The Holt Reader* so that you have a better idea of how history and literature are connected.

Academic Vocabulary

Academic vocabulary refers to the specialized language that is used to talk about books, tests, and formal writing. Academic vocabulary for each unit is introduced here. Pronunciations, definitions, and sentences using the terms are provided.

Before Reading the Selection

Preparing to Read

From experience, you know that you understand something better if you have some idea of what's going to happen. So that you can get the most from the reading, this page previews the skills and vocabulary that you will see in the reading.

Literary Focus

For fiction selections—stories, poems, and plays—this feature introduces the literary skill that is the focus for the selection. Examples and graphic elements help explain the literary skill.

Reading Focus

Also in fiction selections, this feature highlights a reading skill you can apply to the story, poem, or play. The feature points out why this skill is important and how it can help you become a better reader.

Informational Text Focus

For informational, or nonfiction, selections, this feature introduces you to the format and characteristics of nonfiction texts. Those texts may be essays, newspaper articles, Web sites, employment regulations, application forms, or other similar documents.

Selection Vocabulary

This feature introduces you to selection vocabulary that may be unfamiliar. Each entry gives the pronunciation and definition of the word as well as a sentence in which the word is used correctly.

Word Study

Various activities reinforce what you have learned about the selection's vocabulary.

While Reading the Selection

Background gives you basic information on the selection, its author, or the time period in which the story, essay, poem, or article was written.

Side-Column Notes

Each selection has notes in the side column that guide your reading. Many notes ask you to underline or circle in the text itself. Others provide lines on which you can write your responses to questions.

Types of Notes

Several different types of notes throughout the selection provide practice for the skills introduced on the Preparing to Read pages. The notes help you with various strategies for understanding the text. The types of side-column notes are

- **Quick Check** notes ask you to pause at certain points so that you can think about basic ideas before proceeding further. Your teacher may use these notes for class discussions.
- **Literary Focus** notes practice the skill taught in the Literary Focus feature on the Preparing to Read page. Key words related to the specific skill are highlighted.
- **Reading Focus** notes practice the reading skill from the Preparing to Read page.
- **Literary Analysis** notes take basic comprehension one step further and ask you to think more deeply about what you have read.
- **Language Coach** notes reinforce the language skill found in the Preparing to Read pages of *Elements of Literature*.
- **Vocabulary** notes examine selection vocabulary, academic vocabulary, and topics related to how words are used.

After Reading the Selection

Skills Practice

For some selections, graphic organizers reinforce the skills you have practiced throughout the selection.

Applying Your Skills

This feature helps you review the selection. It provides additional practice with selection vocabulary and literary, reading, and informational text focus skills.

After Reading the Collection

Skills Review

This page provides for a review of the collection through practice using language, writing, and oral skills.

Language Coach

These activities draw on the Language Coach skills in the *Elements of Literature* Preparing to Read pages. This feature asks you to apply those skills to texts from throughout the collection.

Writing Activity

You may have found that you need more practice writing. These short writing activities challenge you to apply what you have learned to you own ideas and experiences.

Oral Language Activity

Writing Activities alternate with Oral Language Activities. These features are designed to help you express your thoughts clearly aloud. The features are particularly helpful if you are learning English or if you need practice with Standard English.

Unit Closer Pages

Academic Vocabulary Review

At the end of the unit, you can review the Academic Vocabulary. Some vocabulary terms from the selections are also included.

Applying the Unit Key Concepts

This feature challenges you to apply the unit's Key Concepts to the selections you have read.

Unit 1

The Anglo-Saxon Period and the Middle Ages 449–1485

Houses of Parliament, Westminster, London/Bridgeman Art Library

Key Concepts

THE ANGLO-SAXON LEGACY

History of the Times The end of the Roman Empire left Britain, the Roman province farthest to the north, unprotected. German peoples invaded and ruled Britain for about 600 years. These Anglo-Saxons had a warrior culture. They were divided into clans but later united under King Alfred the Great.

Literature of the Times Anglo-Saxon literature shares common themes and ideals of conduct. The epic poem *Beowulf* describes a society that valued loyalty, strength, and courage. The Anglo-Saxons thought that to die in battle was the best end for a warrior.

THE NORMANS INVADE BRITAIN

History of the Times In 1066, a nobleman from northern France called William the Conqueror led an invasion of England and defeated the Anglo-Saxons. This event is called the Norman invasion. As king, William divided the land among his followers. This system created a social structure in which every person had a place in a fixed hierarchy.

Literature of the Times Under King Alfred, a history titled the *Anglo-Saxon Chronicle* had helped make English a respected language. After 1066, literature was usually written in Latin or Norman French. The use of French shows the division between the British people and their Norman rulers.

LIFE IN MEDIEVAL SOCIETY

History of the Times Under the feudal system, medieval society was made up of clearly defined social classes. The classes included the nobles, knights, peasants, clergy, and merchants.

Literature of the Times Although monks wrote scholarly works in Latin and French, other medieval writers began to use the language of the common people. Works written in English, such as ballads and romances, helped to define England's national identity.

ACADEMIC VOCABULARY

concept (KAHN SEHPT) *n.:* notion or idea. *The concept of courage was very important to the Anglo-Saxons.*

diverse (DY VURS) *adj.:* varied. *A person of diverse interests can talk on many subjects.*

emphasis (EHM FUH SIHS) *n.:* stress; importance. *When writing your essay, give special emphasis to your own views.*

status (STAT UHS) *n.:* social or professional rank. *What was the status of women in medieval society?*

attribute (UH TRIHB YOOT) *v.:* regard as being caused by something. *We attribute the core values of* Beowulf *to Anglo-Saxon traditions.*

Collection 1

The Anglo-Saxons: Songs of Ancient Heroes

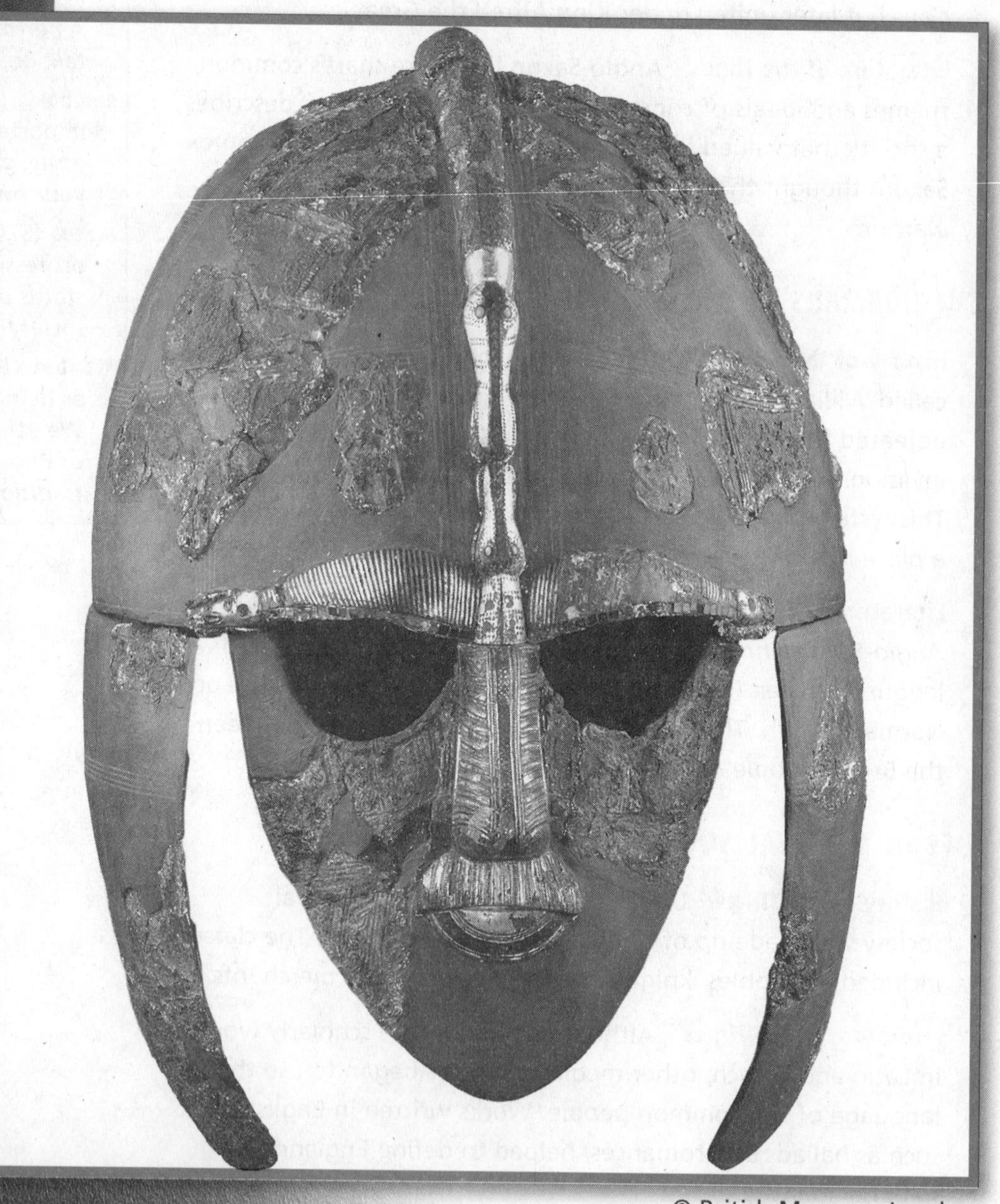

© British Museum, London

Preparing to Read

from Beowulf: The Battle with Grendel *and* The Final Battle

LITERARY FOCUS: ARCHETYPE—THE EPIC HERO

In literature, **archetypes** are models of things that appear over and over in stories from many cultures throughout time. An archetype can be a character, a plot, an image, or a setting. One character archetype is the **epic hero**, the main character in a myth or an epic, which is a long poem that tells a story. These heroes reflect the highest values of the societies that create their stories.

READING FOCUS: PARAPHRASING

Poets often use literary devices and unusual word orders to create a rhythmic or musical quality in their poems. Sometimes, however, these methods can make it hard for readers to understand what is happening in the poem. **Paraphrasing** can help you understand passages of poetry that might be hard to read. When you paraphrase a passage, try to group nouns, verbs, and phrases that support an idea. Then rewrite the passage in your own words.

Use the Skill As you read the following selections from *Beowulf*, pause occasionally to paraphrase the complex, poetic text to be sure that you understand what's happening. One example of paraphrasing is provided below.

Original text	Paraphrase
"And his [Grendel's] heart laughed, he relished the sight, / Intended to tear the life from those bodies / By morning; the monster's mind was hot / With the thought of food and the feasting his belly / Would soon know." (lines 21–25)	Grendel looked happily at the sleeping soldiers he planned to kill. He was excited to be getting something to eat.

Literary Skills Understand the epic hero archetype.

Reading Skills Paraphrase a text.

Vocabulary Development

from Beowulf: The Battle with Grendel *and* The Final Battle

SELECTION VOCABULARY

vehemently (VEE UH MUHNT LEE) *adv.:* violently.

The villain vehemently attacked the hero.

infallible (IHN FAL UH BUHL) *adj.:* unable to fail or be wrong.

She was very good at her job, but was not infallible.

extolled (EHK STOHLD) *v.:* praised.

The teacher extolled the student's hard work.

WORD STUDY

DIRECTIONS: Many English words come from Latin root words. Understanding the root can help you remember the meaning of words with prefixes and suffixes. In the following exercise, identify the vocabulary word that uses the given Latin root. Then circle the root in the vocabulary word.

1. *tollere:* to lift up

   Vocabulary word: ____________________

2. *vemen:* violent

   Vocabulary word: ____________________

3. *fallo:* mistaken

   Vocabulary word: ____________________

THE BATTLE WITH GRENDEL

from Beowulf
translated by Burton Raffel

BACKGROUND

At the beginning of this epic, King Hrothgar, ruler of the Danes, has recently built the great hall Herot to commemorate his many victories. However, a monster called Grendel lurks in the swamps nearby, seething with hatred for humans. Eventually, Grendel attacks Herot and kills thirty of Hrothgar's men. This marks the beginning of Grendel's reign of terror over the Danes, which lasts for 12 years.

Beowulf, a great warrior who comes from the land of the Geats (Sweden), travels to Denmark with some of his strongest men to battle Grendel. Beowulf meets King Hrothgar and announces that he will fight the monster that night without weapons. After a celebration feast, Beowulf and his men take the place of Hrothgar's followers and lie down to sleep in Herot. Beowulf is awake, however, and eager to meet his enemy. He is not kept waiting long.

8

Out from the marsh, from the foot of misty
Hills and bogs, bearing God's hatred,
Grendel came, hoping to kill
Anyone he could trap on this trip to high Herot.
He moved quickly through the cloudy night,
Up from his swampland, sliding silently
Toward that gold-shining hall. (A) He had visited Hrothgar's
Home before, knew the way—
But never, before nor after that night,
Found Herot defended so firmly, his reception
So harsh. He journeyed, forever joyless,
Straight to the door, then snapped it open,
Tore its iron fasteners with a touch,

Circle the words that describe the setting.

A VOCABULARY

Word Study

Based on the conext of this sentence, what do you think a *threshold* is?

B READING FOCUS

Paraphrase lines 15–20.

And rushed angrily over the threshold. A
He strode quickly across the inlaid
Floor, snarling and fierce: His eyes
Gleamed in the darkness, burned with a gruesome
Light. Then he stopped, seeing the hall
Crowded with sleeping warriors, stuffed
With rows of young soldiers resting together. B
And his heart laughed, he relished the sight,
Intended to tear the life from those bodies
By morning; the monster's mind was hot
With the thought of food and the feasting his belly
Would soon know. But fate, that night, intended
Grendel to gnaw the broken bones
Of his last human supper. Human
Eyes were watching his evil steps,
Waiting to see his swift hard claws.
Grendel snatched at the first Geat

© British Museum, London

He came to, ripped him apart, cut
His body to bits with powerful jaws,
Drank the blood from his veins, and bolted
Him down, hands and feet; death
And Grendel's great teeth came together,
Snapping life shut. **C** Then he stepped to another
Still body, clutched at Beowulf with his claws,
Grasped at a strong-hearted wakeful sleeper
—And was instantly seized himself, claws
Bent back as Beowulf leaned up on one arm.
    That shepherd of evil, guardian of crime,
Knew at once that nowhere on earth
Had he met a man whose hands were harder;
His mind was flooded with fear—but nothing
Could take his talons and himself from that tight
Hard grip. Grendel's one thought was to run
From Beowulf, flee back to his marsh and hide there:
This was a different Herot than the hall he had emptied.
But Higlac's follower[1] remembered his final
Boast and, standing erect, stopped
The monster's flight, fastened those claws
In his fists till they cracked, clutched Grendel
Closer. The infamous killer fought
For his freedom, wanting no flesh but retreat,
Desiring nothing but escape; his claws
Had been caught, he was trapped. **D** That trip to Herot
Was a miserable journey for the writhing monster!
    The high hall rang, its roof boards swayed,
And Danes shook with terror. Down
The aisles the battle swept, angry
And wild. Herot trembled, wonderfully
Built to withstand the blows, the struggling
Great bodies beating at its beautiful walls;
Shaped and fastened with iron, inside
And out, artfully worked, the building

1. **Higlac's follower:** Beowulf. Higlac is Beowulf's leader.

C LITERARY ANALYSIS

Underline the verbs in this sentence. What do Grendel's actions suggest about his character and about the task facing Beowulf?

D LITERARY FOCUS

What qualities does Beowulf possess that might make him an **epic hero**?

A LANGUAGE COACH

A words's **connotations** are the emotions or ideas attached to the word. For example, *defeat* can have sad, angry, or other negative connotations. Underline at least four words on this page that have a connotation of fear.

B LITERARY FOCUS

One characteristic of **epic heroes** is their willingness to risk their lives for the benefit of society. Why do you think Beowulf risked his life to fight Grendel?

C READING FOCUS

Paraphrase what's happening at this point in the fight between Beowulf and Grendel.

Stood firm. Its benches rattled, fell
To the floor, gold-covered boards grating
As Grendel and Beowulf battled across them.
Hrothgar's wise men had fashioned Herot
To stand forever; only fire,
They had planned, could shatter what such skill had put
Together, swallow in hot flames such splendor
Of ivory and iron and wood. Suddenly
The sounds changed, the Danes started
In new terror, cowering in their beds as the terrible
Screams of the Almighty's enemy sang
In the darkness, the horrible shrieks of pain
And defeat, the tears torn out of Grendel's
Taut throat, hell's captive caught in the arms
Of him who of all the men on earth
Was the strongest. **A**

9

That mighty protector of men
Meant to hold the monster till its life
Leaped out, knowing the fiend was no use
To anyone in Denmark. **B** All of Beowulf's
Band had jumped from their beds, ancestral
Swords raised and ready, determined
To protect their prince if they could. **C** Their courage
Was great but all wasted: They could hack at Grendel
From every side, trying to open
A path for his evil soul, but their points
Could not hurt him, the sharpest and hardest iron
Could not scratch at his skin, for that sin-stained demon
Had bewitched all men's weapons, laid spells
That blunted every mortal man's blade.
And yet his time had come, his days
Were over, his death near; down
To hell he would go, swept groaning and helpless

To the waiting hands of still worse fiends.
Now he discovered—once the afflictor
Of men, tormentor of their days —what it meant (D)
To feud with Almighty God: Grendel
Saw that his strength was deserting him, his claws
Bound fast, Higlac's brave follower tearing at
His hands. The monster's hatred rose higher,
But his power had gone. He twisted in pain,
And the bleeding sinews deep in his shoulder
Snapped, muscle and bone split
And broke. The battle was over, Beowulf
Had been granted new glory: Grendel escaped,
But wounded as he was could flee to his den,
His miserable hole at the bottom of the marsh,
Only to die, to wait for the end
Of all his days. And after that bloody
Combat the Danes laughed with delight.
He who had come to them from across the sea,
Bold and strong-minded, had driven affliction
Off, purged Herot clean. (E) He was happy,
Now, with that night's fierce work; the Danes
Had been served as he'd boasted he'd serve them; Beowulf,

© British Museum, London

(D) VOCABULARY

Word Study

Afflictor is a noun based on the Latin verb *afflictare*, meaning "to injure." Based on this and the word's context, what does *afflictor* mean?

(E) QUICK CHECK

Who wins the battle? Where does Grendel go after the battle?

A prince of the Geats, had killed Grendel,
Ended the grief, the sorrow, the suffering
Forced on Hrothgar's helpless people
By a bloodthirsty fiend. No Dane doubted
The victory, for the proof, hanging high
From the rafters where Beowulf had hung it, was the monster's
Arm, claw and shoulder and all. **A**

10

And then, in the morning, crowds surrounded
Herot, warriors coming to that hall
From faraway lands, princes and leaders
Of men hurrying to behold the monster's
Great staggering tracks. They gaped with no sense
Of sorrow, felt no regret for his suffering,
Went tracing his bloody footprints, his beaten
And lonely flight, to the edge of the lake
Where he'd dragged his corpselike way, doomed
And already weary of his vanishing life. **B**
The water was bloody, steaming and boiling
In horrible pounding waves, heat
Sucked from his magic veins; but the swirling
Surf had covered his death, hidden
Deep in murky darkness his miserable
End, as hell opened to receive him. **C**
Then old and young rejoiced, turned back
From that happy pilgrimage, mounted their hard-hooved
Horses, high-spirited stallions, and rode them
Slowly toward Herot again, retelling
Beowulf's bravery as they jogged along.
And over and over they swore that nowhere
On earth or under the spreading sky
Or between the seas, neither south nor north,
Was there a warrior worthier to rule over men.

A LITERARY ANALYSIS

Beowulf hangs Grendel's torn-off shoulder and arm high in the rafters of Herot. Why do you think he does this?

B LITERARY FOCUS

The actions of **epic heroes** often reflect the values of their cultures. What does the Danes' celebration of Grendel's defeat say about them?

C VOCABULARY

Academic Vocabulary

Why do you think so much *emphasis*, or importance, is put on the details of Grendel's death?

(But no one meant Beowulf's praise to belittle
Hrothgar, their kind and gracious king!) . . . D

WHAT HAPPENS NEXT After celebrating Grendel's death, Hrothgar and his men sleep in Herot. Grendel's mother arrives and kills Hrothgar's best warrior in revenge for her son's death. Hrothgar, Beowulf, and their men find Grendel's mother's lair in a strange lake. Wearing armor and carrying a sword, Beowulf dives into the lake. At once, Grendel's mother attacks Beowulf. When she is unable to injure him through his armor, Grendel's mother pulls Beowulf to the bottom of the lake. There, in a cave containing the bodies of Grendel and many men the two monsters have killed, Grendel's mother and Beowulf fight a terrible battle. At first, Grendel's mother has the upper hand, but Beowulf's armor protects him from blows that would otherwise kill him. When Beowulf realizes that his sword cannot hurt his opponent, he throws it down. Taking one of Grendel's mother's swords, a mighty weapon, he cuts off her head. When he comes upon the corpse of Grendel, Beowulf severs the head, then swims to the surface. Beowulf returns to Herot, where Hrothgar praises him.

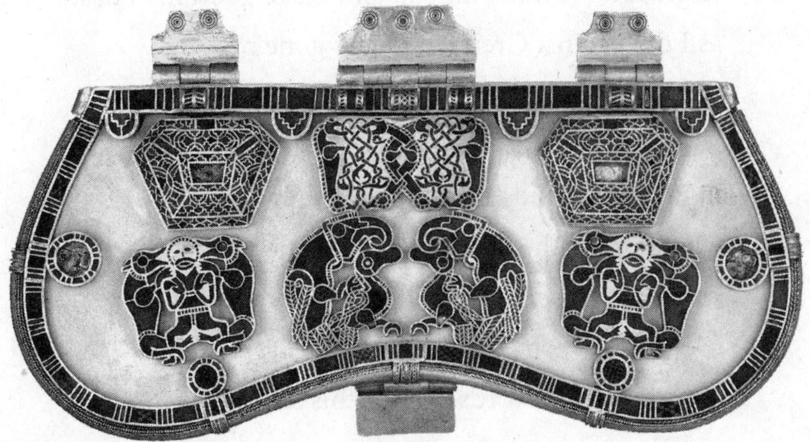

© British Museum, London

D READING FOCUS

How does "The Battle with Grendel" end? **Paraphrase** the last six lines.

THE FINAL BATTLE

from Beowulf
translated by Seamus Heaney

BACKGROUND

Beowulf carries Grendel's head to King Hrothgar and then returns with gifts to the land of the Geats, where he becomes king. After fifty winters pass, Beowulf, now an old man, faces his final task: he must fight a dragon who, angry because a thief has stolen a jeweled cup from the dragon's stash of gold, is destroying the Geats' land. Beowulf and eleven warriors are guided to the dragon's lair by the thief who stole the cup.

A READING FOCUS

Paraphrase what Beowulf has said so far.

14

Then he addressed each dear companion
one final time, those fighters in their helmets,
resolute and high-born: "I would rather not
use a weapon if I knew another way
to grapple with the dragon and make good my boast
as I did against Grendel in days gone by.
But I shall be meeting molten venom
in the fire he breathes, so I go forth
in mail-shirt and shield. I won't shift a foot
when I meet the cave-guard: what occurs on the wall
between the two of us will turn out as fate,
overseer of men, decides. I am resolved.
I scorn further words against this sky-borne foe. **A**

"Men at arms, remain here on the barrow,[1]
safe in your armour, to see which one of us

1. **barrow** (BAR OH): a hill.

is better in the end at bearing wounds
in a deadly fray. This fight is not yours,
nor is it up to any man except me
to measure his strength against the monster
or to prove his worth. I shall win the gold
by my courage, or else mortal combat,
doom of battle, will bear your lord away." **B**

Then he drew himself up beside his shield.
The fabled warrior in his warshirt and helmet
trusted in his own strength entirely
and went under the crag. No coward path.
Hard by the rock-face that hale[2] veteran,
a good man who had gone repeatedly
into combat and danger and come through,
saw a stone arch and a gushing stream

2. **hale:** healthy and energetic.

B LITERARY FOCUS

What characteristics of an **epic hero** does Beowulf show in this speech?

© Museum of Cultural History-University of Oslo, Norway/Photo: Eirik Irgens Johnsen

A QUICK CHECK

Why does Beowulf shout at the dragon instead of going into its cave?

B VOCABULARY

Selection Vocabulary

To do something *vehemently* means to do it strongly or violently. Write a sentence of your own using *vehemently*.

C LANGUAGE COACH

The nouns *fear* and *terror* have similar meanings, but they have different **connotations**—the feelings and ideas carried with a word. Which word has a stronger connotation, *fear* or *terror*? Why?

that burst from the barrow, blazing and wafting
a deadly heat. It would be hard to survive
unscathed near the hoard, to hold firm
against the dragon in those flaming depths.
Then he gave a shout. **A** The lord of the Geats
unburdened his breast and broke out
in a storm of anger. Under grey stone
his voice challenged and resounded clearly.
Hate was ignited. The hoard-guard recognized
a human voice, the time was over
for peace and parleying.[3] Pouring forth
in a hot battle-fume, the breath of the monster
burst from the rock. There was a rumble under ground.
Down there in the barrow, Beowulf the warrior
lifted his shield: the outlandish thing
writhed and convulsed and vehemently **B**
turned on the king, whose keen-edged sword,
an heirloom inherited by ancient right,
was already in his hand. Roused to a fury,
each antagonist struck terror in the other. **C**
Unyielding, the lord of his people loomed
by his tall shield, sure of his ground,
while the serpent looped and unleashed itself.
Swaddled in flames, it came gliding and flexing
and racing towards its fate. Yet his shield defended
the renowned leader's life and limb
for a shorter time than he meant it to:
that final day was the first time
when Beowulf fought and fate denied him
glory in battle. So the king of the Geats
raised his hand and struck hard
at the enamelled scales, but scarcely cut through:
the blade flashed and slashed yet the blow
was far less powerful than the hard-pressed king

3. **parlaying:** discussing.

had need of at that moment. The mound-keeper
went into a spasm and spouted deadly flames:
when he felt the stroke, battle-fire
billowed and spewed. Beowulf was foiled[4]
of a glorious victory. The glittering sword,
infallible before that day,
failed when he unsheathed it, as it never should have. **D**
For the son of Ecgtheow, it was no easy thing
to have to give ground like that and go
unwillingly to inhabit another home
in a place beyond; so every man must yield
the leasehold of his days.

It was not long
until the fierce contenders clashed again.
The hoard-guard took heart, inhaled and swelled up
and got a new wind; he who had once ruled
was furled[5] in fire and had to face the worst.
No help or backing was to be had then
from his high-born comrades; that hand-picked troop
broke ranks and ran for their lives
to the safety of the wood. **E** But within one heart
sorrow welled up: in a man of worth
the claims of kinship cannot be denied.

15

His name was Wiglaf, a son of Weohstan's,
a well-regarded Shylfing warrior
related to Aelfhere. When he saw his lord
tormented by the heat of his scalding helmet,
he remembered the bountiful gifts bestowed on him,
how well he lived among the Waegmundings,
the freehold[6] he inherited from his father before him.

4. **foiled:** prevented from.
5. **furled:** rolled up.
6. **freehold:** estate.

D VOCABULARY

Selection Vocabulary
Infallible means to be unable to fail. Knowing this, what do you think the word *fallible* means? How does the prefix *in–* change the word?

E QUICK CHECK

How do most of Beowulf's men react to the sight of the dragon succeeding in defeating their leader?

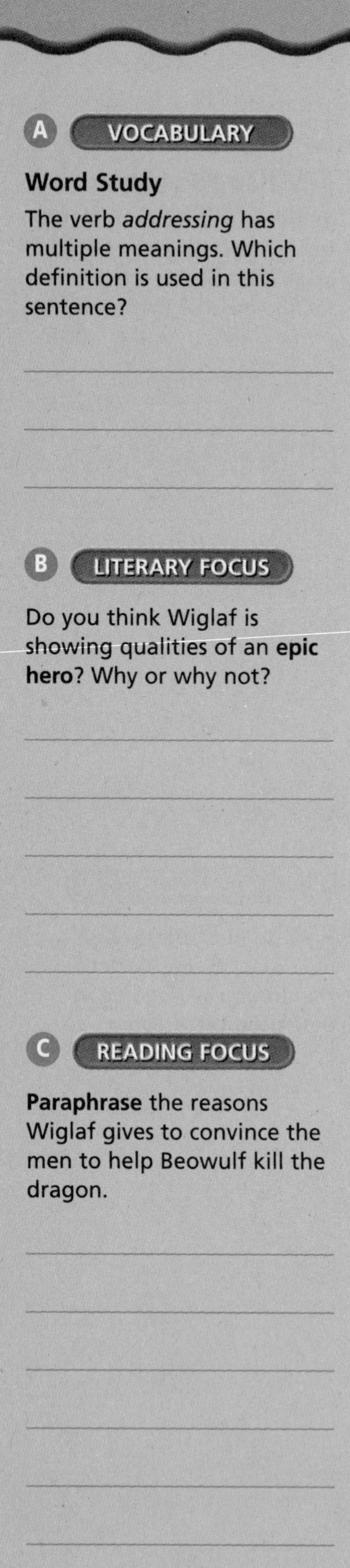

A VOCABULARY

Word Study

The verb *addressing* has multiple meanings. Which definition is used in this sentence?

B LITERARY FOCUS

Do you think Wiglaf is showing qualities of an **epic hero**? Why or why not?

C READING FOCUS

Paraphrase the reasons Wiglaf gives to convince the men to help Beowulf kill the dragon.

He could not hold back: one hand brandished
the yellow-timbered shield, the other drew his sword— . . .

Sad at heart, addressing his companions,
Wiglaf spoke wise and fluent words: (A)
"I remember that time when mead was flowing,
how we pledged loyalty to our lord in the hall,
promised our ring-giver we would be worth our price,
make good the gift of the war-gear,
those swords and helmets, as and when
his need required it. He picked us out
from the army deliberately, honoured us and judged us
fit for this action, made me these lavish[7] gifts—
and all because he considered us the best
of his arms-bearing thanes.[8] (B) And now, although
he wanted this challenge to be one he'd face
by himself alone—the shepherd of our land,
a man unequaled in the quest for glory
and a name for daring—now the day has come
when this lord we serve needs sound men
to give him their support. Let us go to him,
help our leader through the hot flame
and dread of the fire. As God is my witness,
I would rather my body were robed in the same
burning blaze as my gold-giver's body
than go back home bearing arms.
That is unthinkable, unless we have first
slain the foe and defended the life
of the prince of the Weather-Geats. I well know
the things he has done for us deserve better.
Should he alone be left exposed
to fall in battle? We must bond together,
shield and helmet, mail-shirt and sword." (C)

7. **lavish** (LAV IHSH): extravagant.
8. **thanes** (THAYNZ): In Anglo-Saxon England, a group of men who held land of the king in exchange for military service.

© National Museum of Denmark

Together Beowulf and the young Wiglaf kill the dragon, but the old king is fatally wounded. Beowulf, thinking of his people, asks to see the monster's treasure. Wiglaf enters the dragon's cave and finds a priceless hoard of jewels and gold.

16

. . . Wiglaf went quickly, keen to get back,
excited by the treasure; anxiety weighed
on his brave heart, he was hoping he would find
the leader of the Geats alive where he had left him
helpless, earlier, on the open ground.
So he came to the place, carrying the treasure,
and found his lord bleeding profusely,
his life at an end; again he began
to swab his body. The beginnings of an utterance
broke out from the king's breast-cage.
The old lord gazed sadly at the gold.

"To the everlasting Lord of All,
to the King of Glory, I give thanks
that I behold this treasure here in front of me,
that I have been thus allowed to leave my people
so well endowed on the day I die. D

D VOCABULARY

Academic Vocabulary

To what does Beowulf *attribute*, or regard as being caused by, his thanks?

A LITERARY FOCUS

The **archetype** of the death of a hero in literature often includes a symbolic passing on of duties. How does Beowulf pass on his heroic duties?

B QUICK CHECK

What is Beowulf's last request?

C LITERARY ANALYSIS

What do the items that Beowulf gives to Wiglaf represent?

Now that I have bartered my last breath
to own this fortune, it is up to you
to look after their needs. I can hold out no longer. (A)
Order my troop to construct a barrow
on a headland on the coast, after my pyre[9] has cooled.
It will loom on the horizon at Hronesness
and be a reminder among my people—
so that in coming times crews under sail
will call it Beowulf's Barrow, as they steer
ships across the wide and shrouded waters." (B)

Then the king in his great-heartedness unclasped
the collar of gold from his neck and gave it
to the young thane, telling him to use
it and the warshirt and the gilded helmet well.

"You are the last of us, the only one left
of the Waegmundings. Fate swept us away,
sent my whole brave high-born clan
to their final doom. Now I must follow them." (C)
That was the warrior's last word.
He had no more to confide. The furious heat
of the pyre would assail[10] him. His soul fled from his breast
to its destined place among the steadfast ones.

Wiglaf berates the faithless warriors who did not go to the aid of their king. With sorrow the Geats cremate the corpse of their greatest king. They place his ashes, along with all of the dragon's treasure, in a huge burial tower by the sea, where it can be seen by voyagers.

9. **pyre** (PY UHR): pile of wood used for cremating, or burning, a dead body as part of a funeral.
10. **assail** (UH SAYL): attack.

© British Museum, London

17

Then twelve warriors rode around the tomb,
chieftains' sons, champions in battle,
all of them distraught, chanting in dirges,
mourning his loss as a man and a king.
They extolled his heroic nature and exploits
and gave thanks for his greatness; which was the proper thing,
for a man should praise a prince whom he holds dear
and cherish his memory when that moment comes
when he has to be convoyed from his bodily home. D
So the Geat people, his hearth companions,
sorrowed for the lord who had been laid low.
They said that of all the kings upon the earth
he was the man most gracious and fair-minded,
kindest to his people and keenest to win fame. E

D VOCABULARY

Selection Vocabulary

Use context clues to figure out the meaning of *extolled*. Write its meaning below and underline the clues in this sentence that help you find the definition.

E LITERARY FOCUS

According to the last lines of the poem, what qualities made Beowulf an **epic hero**?

Applying Your Skills

from Beowulf: The Battle with Grendel *and* The Final Battle

VOCABULARY DEVELOPMENT

DIRECTIONS: Complete the paragraph with vocabulary words from the Word Box.

Word Box

vehemently
infallible
extolled

Beowulf was an epic hero who (1) ______________ fought evil creatures such as the monster Grendel. Although people (2) ______________ his bravery, he was not (3) ______________. His desire to fight alone eventually led to his death.

LITERARY FOCUS: ARCHETYPE: THE EPIC HERO

DIRECTIONS: Based on what you have read, list four personality traits that you think are typical of the **archetype** of an **epic hero**.

1. ______________________________
2. ______________________________
3. ______________________________
4. ______________________________

READING FOCUS: PARAPHRASING

DIRECTIONS: Complete the chart below by **paraphrasing** the following passages from *Beowulf*:

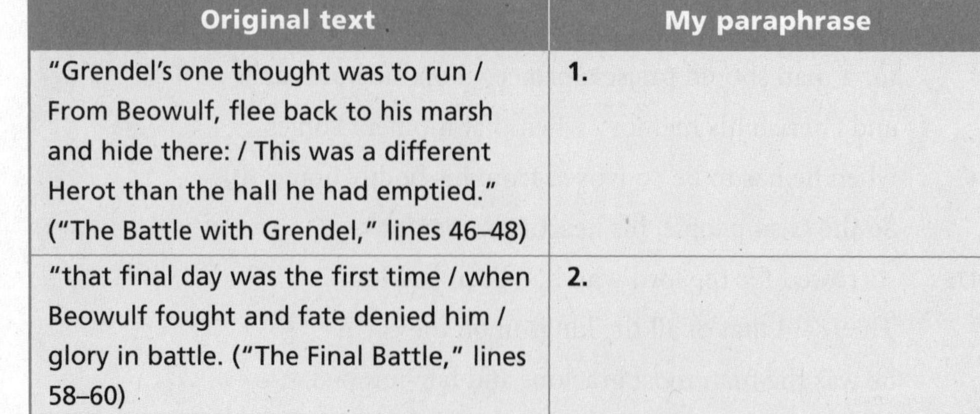

Original text	My paraphrase
"Grendel's one thought was to run / From Beowulf, flee back to his marsh and hide there: / This was a different Herot than the hall he had emptied." ("The Battle with Grendel," lines 46–48)	1.
"that final day was the first time / when Beowulf fought and fate denied him / glory in battle. ("The Final Battle," lines 58–60)	2.

SKILLS FOCUS

Literary Skills Understand the epic hero archetype.

Reading Skills Paraphrase a text.

Collection 1

LANGUAGE COACH

Some words have similar meanings but different **connotations**—the things you think about when you use a word. For example, *extol* means "to praise," but it has a more positive connotation than the word *praise*. If you *extol* someone's good qualities, you praise them with great enthusiasm.

DIRECTIONS: Look at the pairs of synonyms (words with similar meanings) in the chart below. In the second column, describe how the connotation of each word differs from its synonym.

Synonyms	How Connotations Differ
happy, ecstatic	1.
mournful, sad	2.
worry, agonize	3.
infallible, perfect	4.
tired, exhausted	5.

WRITING ACTIVITY

DIRECTIONS: With a partner, choose one long passage from *Beowulf*. Each of you should paraphrase the passage. Then, compare how you both paraphrased the passage. What are the similarities and differences?

Collection 2

The Middle Ages: The Tales They Told

© British Museum, London

from The Prologue to The Canterbury Tales

by Geoffrey Chaucer

LITERARY FOCUS: CHARACTERIZATION

Characterization is the process by which an author reveals a character's personality. In "The Canterbury Tales," Chaucer develops his characters by:

- directly stating what the characters are like.
- describing their looks and clothing.
- telling what the characters say and do.
- revealing their thoughts and feelings.
- showing how others react to the characters.

READING FOCUS: ANALYZING STYLE: KEY DETAILS

With so many pilgrims in the story, Chaucer could not describe any one character at great length. Instead, he uses **key details** to help the reader visualize and understand the characters traveling to Canterbury. As you read, analyze what Chaucer is trying to say about a character by including these details. Use a chart like the one below to note details about each character.

Character and description	My analysis
The Wife of Bath: "Her hose were of the finest scarlet red/ And gartered tight; her shoes soft and new." (lines 238–239)	Red is often associated with passion, or possibly lust in this case. Chaucer could be criticizing her for not dressing more modestly.
The Miller: "He could heave any door off hinge and post . . . /His mighty mouth was like a furnace door . . ." (lines 316, 325)	The Miller is a strong and intimidating man. Chaucer does not seem to think too highly of him though, as he compares him to a furnace.

Literary Skills Understand characterization.

Reading Skills Analyze style using key details.

Vocabulary Development

from The Prologue to The Canterbury Tales

SELECTION VOCABULARY

guile (GYL) *n.:* sly dealings; skill in deceiving.

The thief used his guile to steal things before his victims could notice.

benign (BIH NYN) *adj.:* kind; gracious.

The benign Knight was always willing to lend a helping hand.

obstinate (AHB STUH NIHT) *adj.:* unreasonably stubborn.

An obstinate man, the Pardoner will never admit when he's wrong.

WORD STUDY

DIRECTIONS: Complete the following exercise by deciding if the words listed after each vocabulary word are antonyms or synonyms of that word. Underline synonyms and circle antonyms. Remember that a synonym is a word with nearly the same definition as another word, and an antonym is a word with the opposite definition of another word. For instance, *pleased* and *satisfied* are synonyms, while *forbidden* and *allowed* are antonyms.

1. guile

- **a.** honesty
- **b.** trickiness
- **c.** deviousness

2. benign

- **a.** caring
- **b.** hostile
- **c.** sympathetic

3. obstinate

- **a.** inflexible
- **b.** cooperative
- **c.** unyielding

from THE PROLOGUE TO THE CANTERBURY TALES

by Geoffrey Chaucer, translated by Nevill Coghill

BACKGROUND

"The Canterbury Tales" is a collection of stories told by people traveling together on a pilgrimage, a religious journey made to a holy place. The group of pilgrims is making the 55-mile journey on horseback, from London to the burial place of the martyr Saint Thomas à Becket at Canterbury Cathedral in southeastern England. These pilgrims are of different ages, occupations, and economic means. Their stories give us a fascinating picture of life during the Middle Ages.

"The Canterbury Tales" begins with a Prologue. The host of the inn suggests that the pilgrims exchange stories to pass the time on their long journey. This sets up the main story of the pilgrimage that includes each pilgrim's story. In the Prologue, the pilgrim narrator (whom many consider to be Chaucer himself) describes his fellow pilgrims.

Only portions of the Prologue are included here.

The Prologue

When in April the sweet showers fall
And pierce the drought of March to the root, and all
The veins are bathed in liquor of such power
As brings about the engendering of the flower, A
When also Zephyrus[1] with his sweet breath
Exhales an air in every grove and heath
Upon the tender shoots, and the young sun
His half-course in the sign of the *Ram*[2] has run,
And the small fowl are making melody
That sleep away the night with open eye

A 

Word Study

Engendering is based on the Latin verb *ingenerare,* meaning "to beget," and is related to the verb *generate*, meaning "to produce or bring into existence." Using this knowledge and the word's context, write what you think *engendering* means.

1. **Zephyrus** (ZEF EHR UHS): in Greek mythology, god of the west wind.
2. **Ram:** Aries, first sign of the zodiac. The time is mid-April.

A QUICK CHECK

According to the narrator, who has arrived at the inn?

B LITERARY FOCUS

How will the narrator **characterize** each traveler?

(So nature pricks them and their heart engages)
Then people long to go on pilgrimages
And palmers[3] long to seek the stranger strands
Of far-off saints, hallowèd in sundry lands,
And specially, from every shire's end
Of England, down to Canterbury they wend[4]
To seek the holy blissful martyr, quick
To give his help to them when they were sick.
It happened in that season that one day
In Southwark, at *The Tabard*, as I lay
Ready to go on pilgrimage and start
For Canterbury, most devout at heart,
At night there came into that hostelry
Some nine and twenty in a company
Of sundry folk happening then to fall
In fellowship, and they were pilgrims all
That towards Canterbury meant to ride. **A**
The rooms and stables of the inn were wide:
They made us easy, all was of the best.
And, briefly, when the sun had gone to rest,
I'd spoken to them all upon the trip
And was soon one with them in fellowship,
Pledged to rise early and to take the way
To Canterbury, as you heard me say.
But none the less, while I have time and space,
Before my story takes a further pace,
It seems a reasonable thing to say
What their condition was, the full array
Of each of them, as it appeared to me,
According to profession and degree,
And what apparel they were riding in; **B**
And at a Knight I therefore will begin.

3. **palmers:** people who had visited the Holy Land and wore palm fronds to show it.
4. **wend:** go; travel.

The Knight

There was a *Knight*, a most distinguished man,
Who from the day on which he first began
To ride abroad had followed chivalry,
Truth, honor, generousness, and courtesy. **C**
He had done nobly in his sovereign's war
And ridden into battle, no man more,
As well in Christian as in heathen[5] places,
And ever honored for his noble graces.
When we took Alexandria,[6] he was there.
He often sat at table in the chair
Of honor, above all nations, when in Prussia.
In Lithuania he had ridden, and Russia,
No Christian man so often, of his rank.
When, in Granada, Algeciras sank
Under assault, he had been there, and in
North Africa, raiding Benamarin;
In Anatolia he had been as well
And fought when Ayas and Attalia fell,
For all along the Mediterranean coast
He had embarked with many a noble host.
In fifteen mortal battles he had been
And jousted for our faith at Tramissene
Thrice in the lists, and always killed his man.
This same distinguished knight had led the van
Once with the Bey of Balat, doing work
For him against another heathen Turk; **D**
He was of sovereign value in all eyes.
And though so much distinguished, he was wise
And in his bearing modest as a maid.
He never yet a boorish thing had said

5. **heathen:** pagan. Chaucer uses the term to describe non-Christians.
6. **Alexandria:** city in Egypt captured by the Crusaders in 1365. In the next few lines, Chaucer is indicating the Knight's distinguished and extensive career.

C QUICK CHECK

Chivalry refers to a code of conduct by which knights should live. Circle the qualities associated with chivalry that the Knight possesses.

D LITERARY FOCUS

The narrator describes the knight's military service. What does this **characterization** tell us about the Knight's personality?

A VOCABULARY

Word Study

In Chaucer's day, the word *gentle* meant "well bred and considerate." What term similar to *gentle-knight* is still used today to refer to a courteous, well-mannered man?

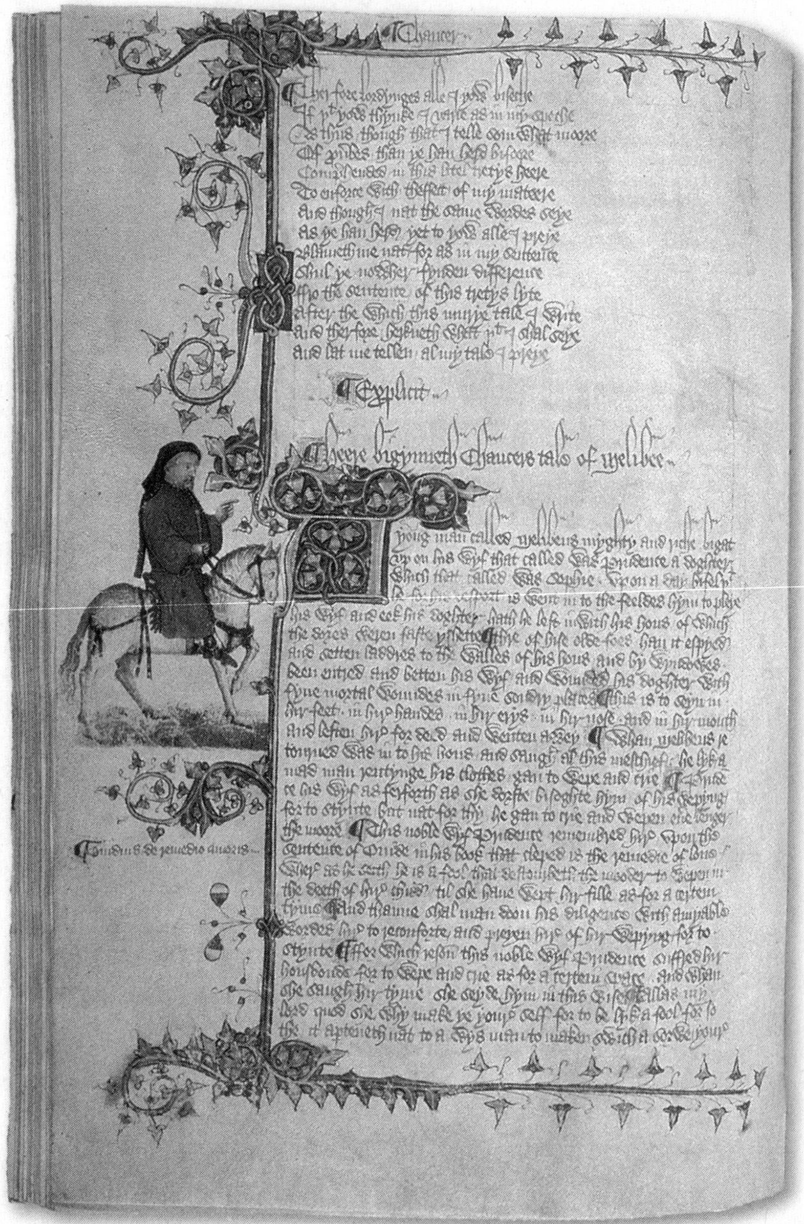

© Hungtinton Library and Art Gallery, San Marino, CA/The Bridgeman Art Library

In all his life to any, come what might;
He was a true, a perfect gentle-knight. A
    Speaking of his equipment, he possessed
Fine horses, but he was not gaily dressed.
He wore a fustian[7] tunic stained and dark
With smudges where his armor had left mark;
Just home from service, he had joined our ranks
To do his pilgrimage and render thanks. . . .

---

7. **fustian** (FUHS CHUHN): made of coarse cloth woven from linen and cotton.

The Nun

There also was a *Nun*, a Prioress,
Her way of smiling very simple and coy.
Her greatest oath was only "By St. Loy!"[8]
And she was known as Madam Eglantyne.[9]
And well she sang a service, with a fine
Intoning through her nose, as was most seemly,
And she spoke daintily in French, extremely,
After the school of Stratford-atte-Bowe[10]
French in the Paris style she did not know. **B**
At meat her manners were well taught withal;
No morsel from her lips did she let fall,
Nor dipped her fingers in the sauce too deep;
But she could carry a morsel up and keep
The smallest drop from falling on her breast.
For courtliness she had a special zest,
And she would wipe her upper lip so clean
That not a trace of grease was to be seen
Upon the cup when she had drunk; to eat,
She reached a hand sedately for the meat. **C**
She certainly was very entertaining,
Pleasant and friendly in her ways, and straining
To counterfeit a courtly kind of grace,
A stately bearing fitting to her place,
And to seem dignified in all her dealings.
As for her sympathies and tender feelings,
She was so charitably solicitous
She used to weep if she but saw a mouse
Caught in a trap, if it were dead or bleeding.
And she had little dogs she would be feeding
With roasted flesh, or milk, or fine white bread.

---

8. **St. Loy:** Saint Eligius, known for his perfect manners.
9. **Eglantyne:** a kind of a rose and also the name of several romantic heroines. The Nun herself is a romantic.
10. **Stratford-atte-Bowe:** Benedictine convent near London where inferior French was spoken.

B READING FOCUS

What **details** about the Nun has the narrator given so far to suggest that he thinks that she is trying to appear more refined and "high class" than she really is?

C LITERARY ANALYSIS

What do the table manners of the Nun tell you about her character?

A READING FOCUS

Considering the **details** the narrator uses to describe the nun's face, do you think she's attractive? Circle one detail to support your answer.

B QUICK CHECK

What sort of activities does the Monk enjoy?

And bitterly she wept if one were dead
Or someone took a stick and made it smart;
She was all sentiment and tender heart.
Her veil was gathered in a seemly way,
Her nose was elegant, her eyes glass-gray;
Her mouth was very small, but soft and red,
Her forehead, certainly, was fair of spread,
Almost a span[11] across the brows, I own;
She was indeed by no means undergrown. **A**
Her cloak, I noticed, had a graceful charm.
She wore a coral trinket on her arm,
A set of beads, the gaudies tricked in green,[12]
Whence hung a golden brooch of brightest sheen
On which there first was graven a crowned A,
And lower, *Amor vincit omnia.*[13]

The Monk

A *Monk* there was, one of the finest sort
Who rode the country; hunting was his sport.
A manly man, to be an Abbott able;
Many a dainty horse he had in stable. **B**
His bridle, when he rode, a man might hear
Jingling in a whistling wind as clear,
Aye, and as loud as does the chapel bell
Where my lord Monk was Prior of the cell.
The Rule of good St. Benet or St. Maur[14]
As old and strict he tended to ignore;
He let go by the things of yesterday

11. **span:** nine inches.
12. **a set of beads . . . green:** Beads are a rosary, or prayer beads and a crucifix on a string or chain. Every eleventh bead is a gaud, a large bead indicating when the Lord's Prayer is to be said.
13. ***Amor vincit omnia*** (AH MAWR WIHN KIHT AWM NEE UH): Latin for "Love conquers all."
14. **St. Benet** [Benedict] or **St. Maur** [Maurice]: Saint Benedict (c. 480–c. 547) was an Italian monk who founded numerous monasteries and wrote a famous code of regulations for monastic life. Saint Maurice was a follower of Benedict.

And took the modern world's more spacious way. **C**
He did not rate that text at a plucked hen
Which says that hunters are not holy men
And that a monk uncloistered is a mere
Fish out of water, flapping on the pier,
That is to say a monk out of his cloister.
That was a text he held not worth an oyster;
And I agreed and said his views were sound;
Was he to study till his head went round
Poring over books in cloisters? Must he toil
As Austin[15] bade and till the very soil?
Was he to leave the world upon the shelf?
Let Austin have his labor to himself.
This Monk was therefore a good man to horse;
Greyhounds he had, as swift as birds, to course.[16]
Hunting a hare or riding at a fence
Was all his fun, he spared for no expense.
I saw his sleeves were garnished at the hand
With fine gray fur, the finest in the land,
And on his hood, to fasten it at his chin
He had a wrought-gold, cunningly fashioned pin;
Into a lover's knot it seemed to pass. **D**
His head was bald and shone like looking-glass;
So did his face, as if it had been greased.
He was a fat and personable priest;
His prominent eyeballs never seemed to settle.
They glittered like the flames beneath a kettle;
Supple his boots, his horse in fine condition.
He was a prelate fit for exhibition,
He was not pale like a tormented soul.
He liked a fat swan best, and roasted whole.
His palfrey[17] was as brown as is a berry.

15. **Austin:** Saint Augustine (354–430), bishop of Hippo in North Africa. He criticized lazy monks and suggested they do some hard manual labor.
16. **course:** to cause to chase game.
17. **palfrey:** horse.

C LITERARY FOCUS

How does the narrator **characterize** the monk in lines 136–137? Is this the behavior you would expect from a monk? Explain.

D LITERARY ANALYSIS

In Chaucer's day, monks took a vow of poverty. Does it seem like this monk takes this vow seriously? Why or why not?

A READING FOCUS

Describe the picture the narrator is painting of the Oxford Cleric with the **details** he's using so far.

B QUICK CHECK

How does the Cleric thank his friends for the money they give him?

C LITERARY FOCUS

How does the narrator immediately **characterize** the Doctor? Based on that information, what else can you infer about the Doctor?

The Oxford Cleric

An *Oxford Cleric,* still a student though,
One who had taken logic long ago,
Was there; his horse was thinner than a rake,
And he was not too fat, I undertake,
But had a hollow look, a sober stare;
The thread upon his overcoat was bare.
He had found no preferment in the church
And he was too unworldly to make search
For secular employment. By his bed
He preferred having twenty books in red
And black, of Aristotle's[18] philosophy,
Than costly clothes, fiddle, or psaltery.[19] **A**
Though a philosopher, as I have told,
He had not found the stone for making gold.[20]
Whatever money from his friends he took
He spent on learning or another book
And prayed for them most earnestly, returning
Thanks to them thus for paying for his learning. **B**
His only care was study, and indeed
He never spoke a word more than was need,
Formal at that, respectful in the extreme,
Short, to the point, and lofty in his theme.
A tone of moral virtue filled his speech
And gladly would he learn, and gladly teach.

The Doctor

A *Doctor* too emerged as we proceeded;
No one alive could talk as well as he did
On points of medicine and of surgery, **C**
For, being grounded in astronomy,

18. Aristotle's (AR IH STAHT UHL): Aristotle (384–322 B.C.) was a Greek philosopher.

19. psaltery (SAWL TUHR EE): a stringed instrument that is plucked.

20. stone . . . gold: Alchemists at the time were searching for a stone that was supposed to turn ordinary metals into gold.

He watched his patient closely for the hours
When, by his horoscope, he knew the powers
Of favorable planets, then ascendent,
Worked on the images for his dependent.
The cause of every malady you'd got
He knew, and whether dry, cold, moist, or hot;[21]
He knew their seat, their humor and condition.
He was a perfect practicing physician.
These causes being known for what they were,
He gave the man his medicine then and there. **D**
All his apothecaries in a tribe
Were ready with the drugs he would prescribe
And each made money from the other's guile;
They had been friendly for a goodish while. **E**
He was well-versed in Aesculapius[22] too
And what Hippocrates and Rufus knew
And Dioscorides, now dead and gone,
Galen and Rhazes, Hali, Serapion,
Averroes, Avicenna, Constantine,
Scotch Bernard, John of Gaddesden, Gilbertine.
In his own diet he observed some measure;
There were no superfluities for pleasure,
Only digestives, nutritives and such.
He did not read the Bible very much.
In blood-red garments, slashed with bluish gray
And lined with taffeta, he rode his way;
Yet he was rather close as to expenses
And kept the gold he won in pestilences.
Gold stimulates the heart, or so we're told.
He therefore had a special love of gold.

21. dry . . . hot: the four humors, or fluids. People of the time believed that one's physical and mental conditions were influenced by the balance of four major fluids in the body—blood (hot and wet), yellow bile (hot and dry), phlegm (cold and wet), and black bile (cold and dry).

22. Aesculapius (EHS KYUH LAY PEE UHS): in Greek and Roman mythology, the god of medicine. The names that follow were early Greek, Roman, Middle Eastern, and medieval medical authorities.

D READING FOCUS

What **details** in lines 202–206 tell you that the Doctor is efficient at his job?

E VOCABULARY

Selection Vocabulary

The word *guile* means "sly dealings; skill in deceiving." What does the use of this word here tell you about the Doctor and the apothecaries?

A QUICK CHECK

What is the Wife's profession?

B READING FOCUS

Circle **details** in lines 227–240 that help you visualize the Wife of Bath.

C READING FOCUS

What generalization can you make about the Wife of Bath from the **details** the narrator provides in lines 245–250? Which details helped you come to this conclusion?

The Wife of Bath

A worthy *woman* from beside *Bath* city
Was with us, somewhat deaf, which was a pity.
In making cloth she showed so great a bent
She bettered those of Ypres and of Ghent.[23] **A**
In all the parish not a dame dared stir
Towards the altar steps in front of her,
And if indeed they did, so wrath was she
As to be quite put out of charity.
Her kerchiefs were of finely woven ground;[24]
I dared have sworn they weighed a good ten pound,
The ones she wore on Sunday, on her head.
Her hose were of the finest scarlet red
And gartered tight; her shoes were soft and new.
Bold was her face, handsome, and red in hue. **B**
A worthy woman all her life, what's more
She'd had five husbands, all at the church door,
Apart from other company in youth;
No need just now to speak of that, forsooth.
And she had thrice been to Jerusalem,
Seen many strange rivers and passed over them;
She'd been to Rome and also to Boulogne,
St. James of Compostella and Cologne,
And she was skilled in wandering by the way.
She had gap-teeth,[25] set widely, truth to say. **C**
Easily on an ambling horse she sat
Well wimpled[26] up, and on her head a hat
As broad as is a buckler or a shield;
She had a flowing mantle that concealed
Large hips, her heels spurred sharply under that.
In company she liked to laugh and chat

23. **Ypres** (EE PR) **and of Ghent:** Flemish centers of the wool trade.
24. **ground:** type of cloth.
25. **gap-teeth:** In Chaucer's time, gap-teeth on a woman were considered a sign of boldness and were said to indicate an aptitude for love and travel.
26. **wimpled:** a linen covering for the head and neck.

And knew the remedies for love's mischances,
An art in which she knew the oldest dances. . . .

The Parson

A holy-minded man of good renown
There was, and poor, the *Parson* to a town,
Yet he was rich in holy thought and work.
He also was a learned man, a clerk,
Who truly knew Christ's gospel and would preach it
Devoutly to parishioners, and teach it. D
Benign and wonderfully diligent,[27]
And patient when adversity was sent
(For so he proved in much adversity)
He hated cursing to extort a fee,
Nay rather he preferred beyond a doubt
Giving to poor parishioners round about
Both from church offerings and his property;
He could in little find sufficiency. E
Wide was his parish, with houses far asunder,
Yet he neglected not in rain or thunder,
In sickness or in grief, to pay a call
On the remotest, whether great or small,
Upon his feet, and in his hand a stave.[28]
This noble example to his sheep he gave
That first he wrought, and afterward he taught;
And it was from the Gospel he had caught
Those words, and he would add this figure too,
That if gold rust, what then will iron do?
For if a priest be foul in whom we trust
No wonder that a common man should rust;
And shame it is to see—let priests take stock—
A shitten shepherd and a snowy flock.
The true example that a priest should give
Is one of cleanness, how the sheep should live.

27. **diligent** (DIHL UH JUHNT): careful and persistent in work.
28. **stave:** staff.

D **LITERARY FOCUS**

Underline the words in lines 259–264 that the narrator uses to directly **characterize** the Parson.

E **VOCABULARY**

Selection Vocabulary

Considering what you've learned about the Parson so far, what might the word *benign* (line 265) mean?

A LITERARY ANALYSIS

Why doesn't the Parson take advantage of opportunities to make money?

B VOCABULARY

Selection Vocabulary

The word *obstinate* means "stubborn." What did the Parson do when a person was obstinate?

C QUICK CHECK

What are the two ways the Miller can knock down a door?

He did not set his benefice to hire[29]
And leave his sheep encumbered in the mire
Or run to London to earn easy bread
By singing masses for the wealthy dead,
Or find some Brotherhood and get enrolled.[30]
He stayed at home and watched over his fold
So that no wolf should make the sheep miscarry.
He was a shepherd and no mercenary. **A**
Holy and virtuous he was, but then
Never contemptuous of sinful men,
Never disdainful, never too proud or fine,
But was discreet[31] in teaching and benign.
His business was to show a fair behavior
And draw men thus to Heaven and their Savior,
Unless indeed a man were obstinate;
And such, whether of high or low estate,
He put to sharp rebuke, to say the least.
I think there never was a better priest. **B**
He sought no pomp or glory in his dealings,
No scrupulosity had spiced his feelings.
Christ and His Twelve Apostles and their lore
He taught, but followed it himself before.

The Miller

The *Miller* was a chap of sixteen stone,[32]
A great stout fellow big in brawn and bone.
He did well out of them, for he could go
And win the ram at any wrestling show.
Broad, knotty, and short-shouldered, he would boast
He could heave any door off hinge and post,
Or take a run and break it with his head. **C**
His beard, like any sow or fox, was red

29. **benefice to hire:** He did not hire someone else to perform his duties.
30. **find . . . enrolled:** He did not take a job as a paid chaplain to a guild.
31. **discreet** (DIHS KREET): cautious about one's words or actions.
32. **sixteen stone:** 224 pounds.

© British Library Board, Roy.18 D 11 f.148

And broad as well, as though it were a spade;
And, at its very tip, his nose displayed
A wart on which there stood a tuft of hair
Red as the bristles in an old sow's ear.
His nostrils were as black as they were wide.
He had a sword and buckler at his side,
His mighty mouth was like a furnace door.
A wrangler and buffoon, he had a store
Of tavern stories, filthy in the main.
His was a master-hand at stealing grain.
He felt it with his thumb and thus he knew
Its quality and took three times his due—
A thumb of gold, by God, to gauge an oat![33]
He wore a hood of blue and a white coat.
He liked to play his bagpipes up and down
And that was how he brought us out of town. . . . D

The Summoner

There was a *Summoner* with us at that Inn, E
His face on fire, like a cherubim,[34]

---

33. thumb . . . oat: In other words, he pressed on the scale with his thumb to increase the weight of the grain.

34. cherubim: in medieval art, a little angel with a rosy face.

D READING FOCUS

Do the narrator's **details** portray the Miller in a positive or negative way? Explain your answer.

E VOCABULARY

Word Study

A *summoner* was a low-ranking official who called people to appear in a church court. What verb, which is the root of *summoner*, means "to call."

A **LANGUAGE COACH**

Because they have similar spellings, *except* ("with the exclusion of; but") is often mistaken for the word *accept* ("to take or receive something offered"). Correctly use each word in two sentences of your own.

For he had carbuncles.[35] His eyes were narrow,
He was as hot and lecherous as a sparrow.
Black scabby brows he had, and a thin beard.
Children were afraid when he appeared.
No quicksilver, lead ointment, tartar creams,
No brimstone, no boracic, so it seems,
Could make a salve that had the power to bite,
Clean up, or cure his whelks[36] of knobby white
Or purge the pimples sitting on his cheeks.
Garlic he loved, and onions too, and leeks,
And drinking strong red wine till all was hazy.
Then he would shout and jabber as if crazy,
And wouldn't speak a word except in Latin
When he was drunk, such tags as he was pat in; **A**
He only had a few, say two or three,
That he had mugged up out of some decree;
No wonder, for he heard them every day.
And, as you know, a man can teach a jay[37]
To call out "Walter" better than the Pope.
But had you tried to test his wits and grope
For more, you'd have found nothing in the bag.
Then "*Questio quid juris*"[38] was his tag.
He was a noble varlet[39] and a kind one,
You'd meet none better if you went to find one.
Why, he'd allow—just for a quart of wine—
Any good lad to keep a concubine
A twelvemonth and dispense him altogether!
And he had finches of his own to feather:[40]
And if he found some rascal with a maid

35. **carbuncles** (KAHR BUHNG KUHLS): pus-filled skin inflammations, something like boils.
36. **whelks:** pus-filled sores.
37. **jay:** type of bird.
38. ***Questio quid juris*** (KWEST EE OH KWID YOO RIHS): Latin for "I ask what point of the law [applies]." The Summoner uses this phrase to stall and dodge the issue.
39. **varlet** (VAHR LIHT): scoundrel.
40. **finches . . . feather:** a maxim that means roughly the same as "feathering one's nest"—taking care of one's own interests.

He would instruct him not to be afraid
In such a case of the Archdeacon's curse
(Unless the rascal's soul were in his purse)
For in his purse the punishment should be. **B**
"Purse is the good Archdeacon's Hell," said he.
But well I know he lied in what he said;
A curse should put a guilty man in dread,
For curses kill, as shriving brings, salvation.
We should beware of excommunication.
Thus, as he pleased, the man could bring duress
On any young fellow in the diocese.
He knew their secrets, they did what he said.
He wore a garland set upon his head
Large as the holly-bush upon a stake
Outside an ale-house, and he had a cake,
A round one, which it was his joke to wield
As if it were intended for a shield.

The Pardoner

He and a gentle *Pardoner* rode together,
A bird from Charing Cross of the same feather,
Just back from visiting the Court of Rome.
He loudly sang "*Come hither, love, come home!*"
The Summoner sang deep seconds[41] to this song,
No trumpet ever sounded half so strong. **C**
This Pardoner had hair as yellow as wax,
Hanging down smoothly like a hank of flax.
In driblets fell his locks behind his head
Down to his shoulders which they overspread;
Thinly they fell, like rat-tails, one by one.
He wore no hood upon his head, for fun;
The hood inside his wallet had been stowed,
He aimed at riding in the latest mode;
But for a little cap his head was bare

41. deep seconds: harmonies.

B QUICK CHECK

What does the Summoner do when he catches people sinning?

C QUICK CHECK

How are the Pardoner and the Summoner alike?

A **READING FOCUS**

How do the **details** of the Pardoner's appearance affect your perception of his personality?

B **LITERARY ANALYSIS**

How does the Pardoner make a lot of money in a short amount of time?

And he had bulging eye-balls, like a hare. A
He'd sewed a holy relic[42] on his cap;
His wallet lay before him on his lap,
Brimful of pardons[43] come from Rome, all hot.
He had the same small voice a goat has got.
His chin no beard had harbored, nor would harbor,
Smoother than ever chin was left by barber.
I judge he was a gelding, or a mare.
As to his trade, from Berwick down to Ware
There was no pardoner of equal grace,
For in his trunk he had a pillow-case
Which he asserted was Our Lady's veil.
He said he had a gobbet[44] of the sail
Saint Peter had the time when he made bold
To walk the waves, till Jesu Christ took hold.
He had a cross of metal set with stones
And, in a glass, a rubble of pigs' bones.
And with these relics, any time he found
Some poor up-country parson to astound,
In one short day, in money down, he drew
More than the parson in a month or two,
And by his flatteries and prevarication[45]
Made monkeys of the priest and congregation. B
But still to do him justice first and last
In church he was a noble ecclesiast.[46]
How well he read a lesson or told a story!
But best of all he sang an Offertory,[47]
For well he knew that when that song was sung
He'd have to preach and tune his honey-tongue

---

42. relic: remains of a saint.
43. pardons: small strips of parchment with papal seals attached. They were sold as indulgences (pardons for sins), with the proceeds supposedly going to a religious house.
44. gobbet: fragment.
45. prevarication (PRIH VAR IH KAY SHUHN): telling lies.
46. ecclesiast (EH KLEE ZEE AST): practitioner of church ritual.
47. Offertory: hymn sung while offerings are collected in church.

And (well he could) win silver from the crowd.
That's why he sang so merrily and loud. **C**
Now I have told you shortly, in a clause,
The rank, the array, the number, and the cause
Of our assembly in this company
In Southwark, at that high-class hostelry
Known as *The Tabard*, close beside *The Bell.*
And now the time has come for me to tell
How we behaved that evening; I'll begin
After we had alighted at the Inn,
Then I'll report our journey, stage by stage,
All the remainder of our pilgrimage.
But first I beg of you, in courtesy,
Not to condemn me as unmannerly
If I speak plainly and with no concealings
And give account of all their words and dealings,
Using their very phrases as they fell.
For certainly, as you all know so well,
He who repeats a tale after a man
Is bound to say, as nearly as he can,
Each single word, if he remembers it,
However rudely spoken or unfit,
Or else the tale he tells will be untrue,
The things pretended and the phrases new. **D**
He may not flinch although it were his brother,
He may as well say one word as another.
And Christ Himself spoke broad in Holy Writ,
Yet there is no scurrility[48] in it,
And Plato says, for those with power to read,
"The word should be as cousin to the deed."
Further I beg you to forgive it me
If I neglect the order and degree
And what is due to rank in what I've planned.
I'm short of wit as you will understand.

48. scurrility (SKUH RIHL UH TEE): indecency.

C QUICK CHECK

According to lines 424–428, what is the Pardoner good at?

D LITERARY ANALYSIS

According to the narrator, who is to blame if some of the tales offend his readers? Why?

A VOCABULARY

Word Study

Victuals can be a noun meaning "food or provisions" or it can be a verb meaning "to supply with food." Which part of speech is *victuals* being used as in this line?

B QUICK CHECK

What is the Host going to reveal to the pilgrims?

The Host

Our *Host* gave us great welcome; everyone
Was given a place and supper was begun.
He served the finest victuals you could think, [A]
The wine was strong and we were glad to drink.
A very striking man our Host withal,
And fit to be a marshal in a hall.
His eyes were bright, his girth a little wide;
There is no finer burgess in Cheapside.[49]
Bold in his speech, yet wise and full of tact,
There was no manly attribute he lacked,
What's more he was a merry-hearted man.
After our meal he jokingly began
To talk of sport, and, among other things
After we'd settled up our reckonings,
He said as follows: "Truly, gentlemen,
You're very welcome and I can't think when—
Upon my word I'm telling you no lie—
I've seen a gathering here that looked so spry,
No, not this year, as in this tavern now.
I'd think you up some fun if I knew how.
And, as it happens, a thought has just occurred
To please you, costing nothing, on my word.
You're off to Canterbury—well, God speed!
Blessed St. Thomas answer to your need!
And I don't doubt, before the journey's done
You mean to while the time in tales and fun.
Indeed, there's little pleasure for your bones
Riding along and all as dumb as stones.
So let me then propose for your enjoyment,
Just as I said, a suitable employment. [B]
And if my notion suits and you agree
And promise to submit yourselves to me
Playing your parts exactly as I say

49. **Cheapside:** district of medieval London.

Tomorrow as you ride along the way,
Then by my father's soul (and he is dead)
If you don't like it you can have my head!
Hold up your hands, and not another word."
    Well, our opinion was not long deferred,
It seemed not worth a serious debate;
We all agreed to it at any rate
And bade him issue what commands he would.
"My lords," he said, "now listen for your good,
And please don't treat my notion with disdain.
This is the point. I'll make it short and plain.
Each one of you shall help to make things slip
By telling two stories on the outward trip
To Canterbury, that's what I intend,
And, on the homeward way to journey's end
Another two, tales from the days of old;
And then the man whose story is best told,
That is to say who gives the fullest measure
Of good morality and general pleasure,
He shall be given a supper, paid by all,
Here in this tavern, in this very hall,
When we come back again from Canterbury. **C**
And in the hope to keep you bright and merry
I'll go along with you myself and ride
All at my own expense and serve as guide.
I'll be the judge, and those who won't obey
Shall pay for what we spend upon the way.
Now if you all agree to what you've heard
Tell me at once without another word,
And I will make arrangements early for it." **D**
    Of course we all agreed, in fact we swore it
Delightedly, and made entreaty[50] too
That he should act as he proposed to do,
Become our Governor in short, and be

C QUICK CHECK

How will the best story be determined?

D LITERARY FOCUS

How is the Host **characterized** here?

50. entreaty: urgent request.

A QUICK CHECK

How do the pilgrims react to the Host's offer?

Judge of our tales and general referee,
And set the supper at a certain price.
We promised to be ruled by his advice
Come high, come low; unanimously thus
We set him up in judgment over us.
More wine was fetched, the business being done;
We drank it off and up went everyone
To bed without a moment of delay. **A**
    Early next morning at the spring of day
Up rose our Host and roused us like a cock,
Gathering us together in a flock,
And off we rode at slightly faster pace
Than walking to St. Thomas' watering-place;
And there our Host drew up, began to ease
His horse, and said, "Now, listen if you please,
My lords! Remember what you promised me.
If evensong and matins will agree[51]

51. **If . . . agree:** in other words, if you feel the same way in the evening (at evensong, or evening prayers) as you do in the morning (at matins, or morning prayers).

© Private Collection/The Bridgeman Art Libra

Let's see who shall be first to tell a tale.
And as I hope to drink good wine and ale
I'll be your judge. The rebel who disobeys,
However much the journey costs, he pays.
Now draw for cut[52] and then we can depart;
The man who draws the shortest cut shall start." B

B VOCABULARY

Academic Vocabulary

Choose two of the characters from "The Prologue to The Canterbury Tales." Of the two, which character do you think has the higher *status*, or social or professional rank? Explain your answer.

52. **draw for cut:** in other words, draw straws.

Applying Your Skills

from The Prologue to The Canterbury Tales

VOCABULARY DEVELOPMENT

DIRECTIONS: Write "Yes" after each sentence below if the italicized vocabulary word is being used correctly. Write "No" if it is being used incorrectly.

1. The *benign* Miller frequently cheated when dealing grain. ________
2. The narrator frowns upon the Pardoner's use of *guile* to steal from the unsuspecting poor. ________
3. The Wife of Bath earned money by working as an *obstinate*. ________

LITERARY FOCUS: CHARACTERIZATION

DIRECTIONS: Complete the chart below by explaining the method or methods the author uses in each **characterization**.

Quote	Characterization methods
The Knight: "He had done nobly in his sovereign's war / And ridden into battle, no man more, / As well in Christian as in heathen places, / And ever honored for his noble graces." (lines 47–50)	**1.**
The Parson: "Yet he neglected not in rain or thunder, / In sickness or in grief, to pay a call / On the remotest, whether great or small" (lines 274–276)	**2.**

Literary Skills Understand characterization.

Reading Skills Analyze style using key details.

READING FOCUS: ANALYZING DETAILS

DIRECTIONS: Select one traveler introduced in "The Prologue." On a separate sheet of paper, write a brief paragraph discussing how the use of **details** enhanced your understanding of that character.

Preparing to Read

Lord Randall

LITERARY FOCUS: BALLAD

Ballads are songs or songlike poems that tell stories in simple, rhythmic language. Ballads are meant to be read or sung aloud. Most ballads include certain common features, such as a sad story, missing details, or mysterious events. Ballads also usually include a **refrain**, or a repeated word, line, or group of lines.

Use the Skill As you read this ballad, look for examples of the features listed below, and record them in the chart.

Ballad features	Example from "Lord Randall"
Sad story	
Missing details	
Mysterious events	
Refrain	

Literary Skill Understand ballads.

Preparing to Read

Lord Randall

READING FOCUS: UNDERSTANDING PURPOSE

We do not know who wrote "Lord Randall," but we can still figure out the author's purpose from details in the text. A **purpose** is the reason that an author writes something. Details such as dialogue, images, or repeated words can help us guess the purpose. For example, in "Lord Randall," the mother repeats the words "my son" and "my handsome young man" in each section, or stanza. We can guess that she loves her boy and that she is upset about his condition. Based on this information, what do you think might be one purpose for this ballad?

Use the Skill In the chart below, write what you think the author's purpose might be for each example of literature listed.

Type of literature	Author's purpose
an autobiography by a woman who grew up in poverty and became a successful business owner	**1.**
a children's book about a rabbit who travels in space	**2.**
a collection of Native American myths	**3.**
a consumer guide about the different types of cars that are on the market this year	**4.**
a book about American soldiers who fought in World War II	**5.**

Reading Skill
Examine an author's purpose.

LORD RANDALL

BACKGROUND

This ballad was written in the Middle Ages. In the ballad, a young man and his loyal hunting dogs get sick after eating dinner. Food poisoning and stomach illnesses were very common problems in the Middle Ages. No refrigeration and unclean habits made it hard to keep foods as safe as we can today.

"Oh where hae ye been, Lord Randall my son?
O where hae ye been, my handsome young man?"
"I hae been to the wild wood; mother, make my bed soon,
For I'm weary wi' hunting, and fain[1] wald lie down." (A)

"Where gat ye your dinner, Lord Randall my son?
Where gat ye your dinner, my handsome young man?"
"I din'd wi' my true-love; mother, make my bed soon,
For I'm weary wi' hunting, and fain wald lie down."

---

1. **fain:** gladly

(A) **QUICK CHECK**

What is happening in this opening section, or stanza?

© British Library Board f.5 Add 18850

A LANGUAGE COACH

This poem is written in an old Scottish version of English, which means it is different from the English language you are used to. Some of the words may look incomplete. List any incomplete words in the first three stanzas and write their modern English spellings.

B LITERARY FOCUS

What is one **refrain** in this ballad?

C READING FOCUS

What do you think is the author's **purpose** for writing this poem?

"What gat ye to[2] your dinner, Lord Randall my son?
What gat ye to your dinner, my handsome young man?"
"I gat eels boil'd in broo;[3] mother, make my bed soon,
For I'm weary wi' hunting, and fain wald lie down." **A**

"What became of your bloodhounds, Lord Randall my son?
What became of your bloodhounds, my handsome young man?"
"O they swell'd and they died; mother, make my bed soon,
for I'm weary wi' hunting, and fain wald lie down."

"O I fear ye are poison'd, Lord Randall my son!
O I fear ye are poison'd, my handsome young man!"
"O yes, I am poison'd: mother, make my bed soon,
For I'm sick at the heart, and I fain wald lie down." **B** **C**

2. **gat ye to:** did you have for
3. **broo:** old term for "broth"

Lord Randall

USE A COMPARISON TABLE

DIRECTIONS: Many ballads include **refrains**, or repeated words, lines, or groups of lines. Use the table below to analyze refrains in "Lord Randall." In the left column, write the refrains. In the right column, explain why you think the author chose to repeat those particular lines.

Refrains in "Lord Randall"	Explanation
	1.
	2.
	3.
	4.
	5.

Lord Randall

LITERARY FOCUS: BALLAD

DIRECTIONS: Write a short paragraph that explains what makes "Lord Randall" a **ballad**. Be sure to discuss the elements of a ballad and give examples of these elements from the poem.

____
____
____
____
____
____
____
____

READING FOCUS: UNDERSTANDING PURPOSE

DIRECTIONS: In the concept web below, write the **purpose** or purposes of this ballad. Write supporting details from the text in the outside ovals.

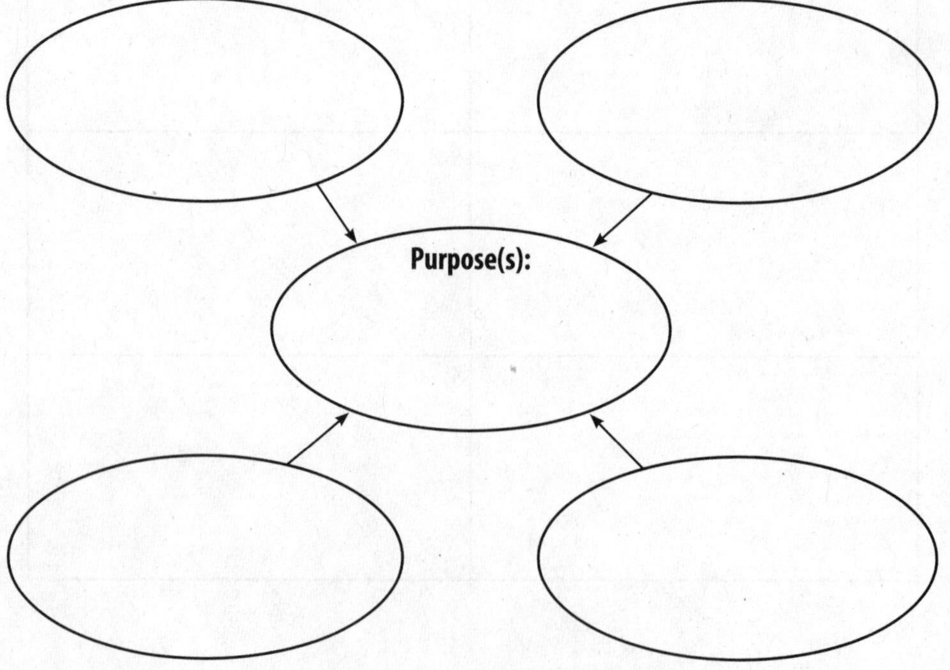

Literary Skills Understand ballads.

Reading Skills Examine an author's purpose.

Preparing to Read

from Sir Gawain and the Green Knight

translated by John Gardner

LITERARY FOCUS: THE ROMANCE

During medieval times (from about 500 to 1400), **romance** stories became very popular. Medieval romance stories can be told in poetry or prose. The romances may involve romantic love, or ideals like heroic bravery and loyalty. The romance always features a hero who goes on a quest and overcomes danger for the sake of a noble lady or for a high ideal. Along the way, the hero faces challenges and adventures, which often involve magical beings. The most famous romances from this period are about King Arthur and his Knights of the Round Table. Sir Gawain was one of King Arthur's knights.

READING FOCUS: UNDERSTANDING CAUSE AND EFFECT

A **cause** is the event that makes something happen. An **effect** is the result of that event. Recognizing causes and effects will help you understand the relationship between events in a story. Sometimes one action follows another, but is not caused by it. Two events that are incorrectly labeled as cause and effect create a **logical fallacy**.

Use the Skill As you read, use the diagram below. List major events in the second column and their causes in the first column.

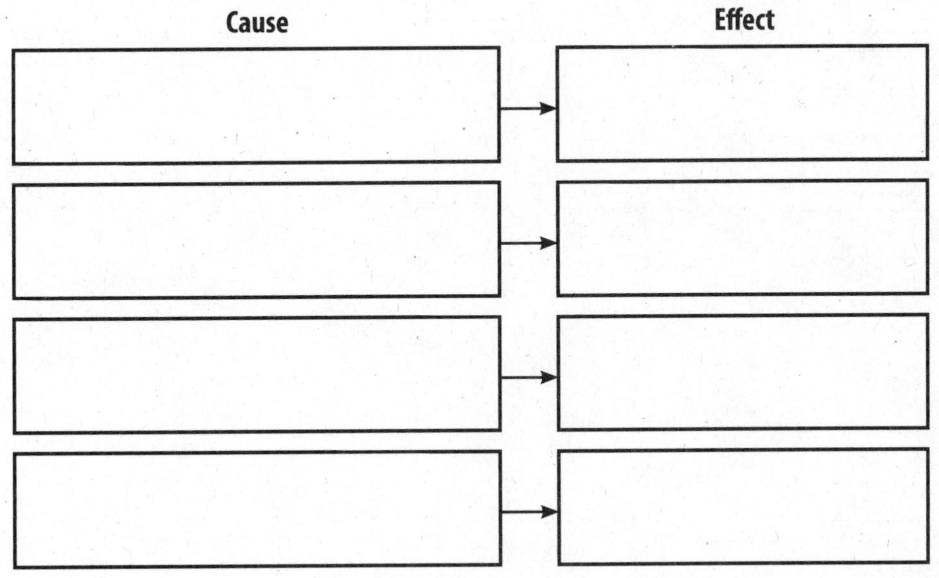

Literary Skills Analyze a medieval romance story.

Reading Skills Understand cause and effect.

Vocabulary Development

from Sir Gawain and the Green Knight

SELECTION VOCABULARY

whetting (HWEHT IHNG) *v.* used as *adj.:* the act of sharpening a blade on a stone made for the purpose.
He sharpened the blade on a whetting stone.

daunted (DAWNT IHD) *v.* used as *adj.:* made to lose courage.
Gawain had never before been daunted by anything.

shied (SHYD) *v.:* shrank or flinched away.
Gawain shied from the blow of the ax.

efficacious (EF UH KAY SHUS) *adj.:* effective or useful.
Gawain's brave voice proves to be efficacious in his confrontation with the Green Knight.

covetousness (KUHV UH TUHS NIHS) *n.:* desire for what belongs to others.
Gawain accused himself of covetousness.

WORD STUDY

DIRECTIONS: List one synonym (word with a similar meaning) and one antonym (word with the opposite meaning) for each vocabulary word listed below. Use a thesaurus if you need help.

1. *shied*

   synonym: ______________________

   antonym: ______________________

2. *efficacious*

   synonym: ______________________

   antonym: ______________________

from SIR GAWAIN AND THE GREEN KNIGHT

translated by John Gardner

BACKGROUND

"Sir Gawain and the Green Knight" was probably written around 1375. The author is unknown. The following part of the story takes place a year after Sir Gawain accepted a challenge from the Green Knight to try to strike him down with one blow. Gawain beheaded the Knight, who picked up his head and left. Now Gawain is traveling to the Green Chapel to accept a return blow from the Knight. Along his journey, he stayed at a castle. Gawain promised the castle lord that he would pass along any gift he received while the lord was away. Each day the lord's wife tempted Gawain by kissing him. True to his word, Gawain passed the kisses of friendship on to the lord. On the last day of his stay, the wife gave Gawain a green sash that she claimed would protect him from harm. Fearing for his life, Gawain kept the sash and left for the Green Chapel.

He put his spurs to Gringolet,[1] plunged down the path,
Shoved through the heavy thicket grown up by the woods
And rode down the steep slope to the floor of the valley;
He looked around him then—a strange, wild place,
And not a sign of a chapel on any side
But only steep, high banks surrounding him,
And great, rough knots of rock and rugged crags
That scraped the passing clouds, as it seemed to him.
He heaved at the heavy reins to hold back his horse
And squinted in every direction in search of the Chapel,
And still he saw nothing except—and this was strange—
A small green hill all alone, a sort of barrow,[2]
A low, smooth bulge on the bank of the brimming creek 

A QUICK CHECK

Describe the landscape that Sir Gawain encounters in the opening lines.

1. **Gringolet:** Gawain's horse.
2. **barrow:** grave mound.

© Blue Lanterns Studio/Corbis

A VOCABULARY

Word Study

Reins are leather straps used to control a horse. List two other words that have the same pronunciation but different spellings as *reins*. What are the definitions of these two words?

That flowed from the foot of a waterfall,
And the water in the pool was bubbling as if it were boiling.
Sir Gawain urged Gringolet on till he came to the mound
And lightly dismounted and made the reins secure **A**
On the great, thick limb of a gnarled and ancient tree;
Then he went up to the barrow and walked all around it,
Wondering in his wits what on earth it might be.
It had at each end and on either side an entrance,
And patches of grass were growing all over the thing,
And all the inside was hollow—an old, old cave
Or the cleft of some ancient crag, he couldn't tell which
it was.
"Whoo, Lord!" thought the knight,
"Is this the fellow's place?
Here the Devil might
Recite his midnight mass.

"Dear God," thought Gawain, "the place is deserted enough!

And it's ugly enough, all overgrown with weeds!
Well might it amuse that marvel of green
To do his devotions here, in his devilish way!
In my five senses I fear it's the Fiend himself
Who's brought me to meet him here to murder me. B
May fire and fury befall this fiendish Chapel,
As cursed a kirk[3] as I ever yet came across!"
With his helmet on his head and his lance in hand
He leaped up onto the roof of the rock-walled room
And, high on that hill, he heard, from an echoing rock C
Beyond the pool, on the hillside, a horrible noise.
Brrrack! It clattered in the cliffs as if to cleave them,
A sound like a grindstone grinding on a scythe![4]
Brrrack! It whirred and rattled like water on a mill wheel!
Brrrrrack! It rushed and rang till your blood ran cold.
And then: "Oh God," thought Gawain, "it grinds, I think,
For me—a blade prepared for the blow I must take
as my right!
God's will be done! But here!
He may well get his knight,
But still, no use in fear;
I won't fall dead of fright!"

And then Sir Gawain roared in a ringing voice,
"Where is the hero who swore he'd be here to meet me?
Sir Gawain the Good is come to the Green Chapel!
If any man would meet me, make it now,
For it's now or never, I've no wish to dawdle here long."
"Stay there!" called someone high above his head,
"I'll pay you promptly all that I promised before."
But still he went on with that whetting noise a while, D
Turning again to his grinding before he'd come down.
At last, from a hole by a rock he came out into sight,
Came plunging out of his den with a terrible weapon,

3. **kirk:** Scottish word for "church."
4. **scythe** (SYTH): long-handled cutting tool.

B READING FOCUS

What **caused** Sir Gawain to go to the Green Chapel? Why does he stay if it is as awful as it seems?

C LITERARY FOCUS

In **romances**, the authors use vivid imagery to create certain moods. What is the mood of this scene? Underline words that support this mood.

D VOCABULARY

Selection Vocabulary

How is the grinding noise that Sir Gawain hears related to the word *whetting*?

A LITERARY FOCUS

The Green Knight had told Sir Gawain to meet him at the Green Chapel a year later to take a blow from an ax. Based on what you know about **romantic** heroes, why does Gawain keep this agreement even though it endangers his life?

B READING FOCUS

The Green Knight is going to give Gawain an ax blow to the neck. What would you expect the **effect** of this action to be?

A huge new Danish ax to deliver his blow with,
With a vicious swine of a bit bent back to the handle,
Filed to a razor's edge and four foot long,
Not one inch less by the length of that gleaming lace.
The great Green Knight was garbed as before,
Face, legs, hair, beard, all as before but for this:
That now he walked the world on his own two legs,
The ax handle striking the stone like a walking-stave.[5]
When the knight came down to the water he would not wade
But vaulted across on his ax, then with awful strides
Came fiercely over the field filled all around
with snow.
Sir Gawain met him there
And bowed—but none too low!
Said the other, "I see, sweet sir,
You go where you say you'll go!

"Gawain," the Green Knight said, "may God be your guard!
You're very welcome indeed, sir, here at my place;
You've timed your travel, my friend, as a true man should.
You recall the terms of the contract drawn up between us:
At this time a year ago you took your chances,
And I'm pledged now, this New Year, to make you my payment.
And here we are in this valley, all alone,
And no man here to part us, proceed as we may; **A**
Heave off your helmet then, and have here your pay;
And debate no more with me than I did then
When you severed my head from my neck with a single swipe."
"Never fear," said Gawain, "by God who gave
Me life, I'll raise no complaint at the grimness of it;
But take your single stroke, and I'll stand still
And allow you to work as you like and not oppose
you here." **B**
He bowed toward the ground

5. **walking-stave:** walking stick or staff.

© Clive Barda/The Arena Pal Picture Library

And let his skin show clear;
However his heart might pound,
He would not show his fear.

Quickly then the man in the green made ready,
Grabbed up his keen-ground ax to strike Sir Gawain;
With all the might in his body he bore it aloft
And sharply brought it down as if to slay him;
Had he made it fall with the force he first intended
He would have stretched out the strongest man on earth.
But Sir Gawain cast a side glance at the ax
As it glided down to give him his Kingdom Come,[6]
And his shoulders jerked away from the iron a little,
And the Green Knight caught the handle, holding it back, C

6. **his Kingdom Come:** life after death.

C READING FOCUS

What **caused** the Green Knight to stop his ax from striking Gawain?

And mocked the prince with many a proud reproof:[7]
"You can't be Gawain," he said, "who's thought so good,
A man who's never been daunted on hill or dale!
For look how you flinch for fear before anything's felt!
I never heard tell that Sir Gawain was ever a coward!
I never moved a muscle when *you* came down;
In Arthur's hall I never so much as winced.
My head fell off at my feet, yet I never flickered;
But you! You tremble at heart before you're touched!
I'm bound to be called a better man than you, then,
my lord." **A**
Said Gawain, "I shied once: **B**
No more. You have my word.
But if my head falls to the stones
It cannot be restored.

"But be brisk, man, by your faith, and come to the point!
Deal out my doom if you can, and do it at once,
For I'll stand for one good stroke, and I'll start no more
Until your ax has hit—and that I swear."
"Here goes, then," said the other, and heaves it aloft
And stands there waiting, scowling like a madman;
He swings down sharp, then suddenly stops again,
Holds back the ax with his hand before it can hurt,
And Gawain stands there stirring not even a nerve;
He stood there still as a stone or the stock of a tree
That's wedged in rocky ground by a hundred roots.
O, merrily then he spoke, the man in green:
"Good! You've got your heart back! Now I can hit you.
May all that glory the good King Arthur gave you
Prove efficacious now—if it ever can—
And save your neck." In rage Sir Gawain shouted, **C**
"*Hit* me, hero! I'm right up to here with your threats!
Is it *you* that's the cringing coward after all?"
"Whoo!" said the man in green, "he's wrathful, too!

7. **reproof:** rebuke; scolding.

A LITERARY FOCUS

According to the Green Knight, what do Gawain's actions prove about his real character? Why is this contrary to a hero's character in a typical **romance**?

B LANGUAGE COACH

Shied is the past tense form of the verb *shy*. For verbs that end in *y*, change the *y* to an *i* and add *–ed* to make the word past tense. Name another verb that can be changed to past tense using the same method.

C READING FOCUS

What **causes** the Green Knight to say the words in lines 137–140?

No pauses, then; I'll pay up my pledge at once,
I vow!"
He takes his stride to strike
And lifts his lip and brow;
It's not a thing Gawain can like,
For nothing can save him now!

He raises that ax up lightly and flashes it down,
And that blinding bit bites in at the knight's bare neck—
But hard as he hammered it down, it hurt him no more
Than to nick the nape of his neck, so it split the skin;
The sharp blade slit to the flesh through the shiny hide,
And red blood shot to his shoulders and spattered the ground.
And when Gawain saw his blood where it blinked in the snow
He sprang from the man with a leap to the length of a spear;
He snatched up his helmet swiftly and slapped it on, D
Shifted his shield into place with a jerk of his shoulders,
And snapped his sword out faster than sight; said boldly—
And, mortal born of his mother that he was,

© Clive Barda/The Arena Pal Picture Library

D QUICK CHECK

Describe what happens in lines 150–158.

A READING FOCUS

According to Gawain, what will be the **effect** of the Green Knight trying to cut him again?

B LITERARY FOCUS

Does the Green Knight have any characteristics of a **romance** hero? Explain your answer.

C READING FOCUS

What **caused** the Green Knight to stop from striking Gawain the first two times?

There was never on earth a man so happy by half—
"No more strokes, my friend; you've had your swing!
I've stood one swipe of your ax without resistance;
If you offer me any more, I'll repay you at once
With all the force and fire I've got—as you
will see.
I take one stroke, that's all,
For that was the compact we
Arranged in Arthur's hall;
But now, no more for me!" **A**

The Green Knight remained where he stood, relaxing on his ax—
Settled the shaft on the rocks and leaned on the sharp end—
And studied the young man standing there, shoulders hunched,
And considered that staunch[8] and doughty[9] stance he took,
Undaunted yet, and in his heart he liked it;
And then he said merrily, with a mighty voice—
With a roar like rushing wind he reproved the knight—
"Here, don't be such an ogre on your ground!
Nobody here has behaved with bad manners toward you
Or done a thing except as the contract said.
I owed you a stroke, and I've struck; consider yourself
Well paid. And now I release you from all further duties. **B**
If I'd cared to hustle, it may be, perchance, that I might
Have hit somewhat harder, and then you might well be cross!
The first time I lifted my ax it was lighthearted sport,
I merely feinted and made no mark, as was right,
For you kept our pact of the first night with honor
And abided by your word and held yourself true to me,
Giving me all you owed as a good man should.
I feinted a second time, friend, for the morning
You kissed my pretty wife twice and returned me the kisses;
And so for the first two days, mere feints, nothing more
severe. **C**
A man who's true to his word,

8. **staunch:** steadfast; stubborn.
9. **doughty** (DOW TEE): courageous.

There's nothing he needs to fear;
You failed me, though, on the third
Exchange, so I've tapped you here.

"That sash you wear by your scabbard[10] belongs to me;
My own wife gave it to you, as I ought to know.
I know, too, of your kisses and all your words
And my wife's advances, for I myself arranged them.
It was I who sent her to test you. **D** I'm convinced
You're the finest man that ever walked this earth.
As a pearl is of greater price than dry white peas,
So Gawain indeed stands out above all other knights.
But you lacked a little, sir; you were less than loyal;
But since it was not for the sash itself or for lust
But because you loved your life, I blame you less."
Sir Gawain stood in a study[11] a long, long while,
So miserable with disgrace that he wept within,
And all the blood of his chest went up to his face
And he shrank away in shame from the man's gentle words.
The first words Gawain could find to say were these:
"Cursed be cowardice and covetousness both, **E**
Villainy and vice that destroy all virtue!"
He caught at the knots of the girdle[12] and loosened them
And fiercely flung the sash at the Green Knight.
"There, there's my fault! The foul fiend vex it! **F**
Foolish cowardice taught me, from fear of your stroke,
To bargain, covetous, and abandon my kind,
The selflessness and loyalty suitable in knights;
Here I stand, faulty and false, much as I've feared them,
Both of them, untruth and treachery; may they see sorrow
and care!
I can't deny my guilt;
My works shine none too fair!
Give me your good will

10. **scabbard:** carrying case that covers the blade of a sword; sheath.
11. **stood in a study:** stood thinking deeply.
12. **girdle:** a sash worn as a belt.

D VOCABULARY

Academic Vocabulary

Why does the Green Knight put so much *emphasis*, or importance, on keeping one's word?

E VOCABULARY

Selection Vocabulary

Covet means "to desire something that belongs to someone else". *Covetousness* was a serious flaw for medieval knights. Write a sentence of your own using a form of the word *covet*.

F LITERARY FOCUS

Adventures in medieval **romances** often involve magic. How did the Green Knight use magic to trick Gawain?

A READING FOCUS

What is the **effect** of Gawain's choice to take the blow, confess his wrongdoing, and apologize?

B LITERARY ANALYSIS

What lesson might Sir Gawain have learned from his experience with the Green Knight?

And henceforth I'll beware."

At that, the Green Knight laughed, saying graciously,
"Whatever harm I've had, I hold it amended
Since now you're confessed so clean, acknowledging sins
And bearing the plain penance of my point;
I consider you polished as white and as perfectly clean
As if you had never fallen since first you were born.
And I give you, sir, this gold-embroidered girdle,
For the cloth is as green as my gown. Sir Gawain, think
On this when you go forth among great princes;
Remember our struggle here; recall to your mind
This rich token. Remember the Green Chapel.
And now, come on, let's both go back to my castle
And finish the New Year's revels[13] with feasting and joy,
not strife,
I beg you," said the lord,
And said, "As for my wife,
She'll be your friend, no more
A threat against your life." A B

13. **revels:** festivities, often as part of a celebration.

from Sir Gawain and the Green Knight

USE A VENN DIAGRAM

DIRECTIONS: Use the Venn diagram below to compare and contrast the personalities of Sir Gawain and the Green Knight. Write differences in the outer sections of the circles. Write similarities in the section where the two circles overlap. Be sure to include personality traits of a **romance** hero for one or both characters.

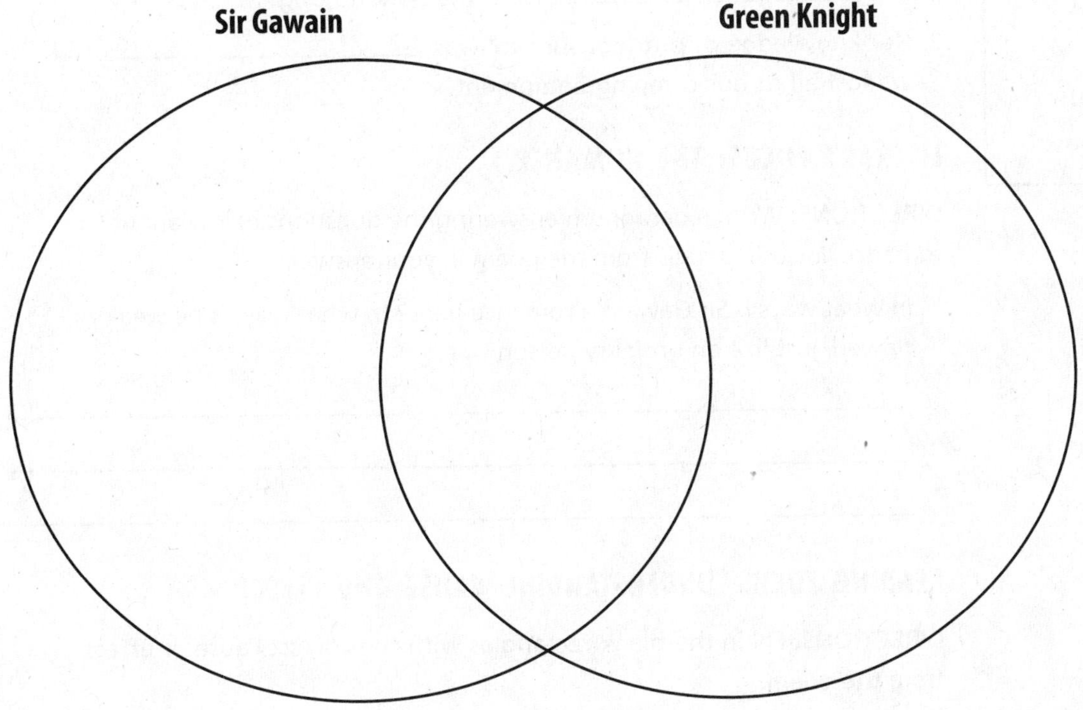

Applying Your Skills

from Sir Gawain and the Green Knight

VOCABULARY DEVELOPMENT

DIRECTIONS: Complete the sentences by filling in each blank with the correct vocabulary word from the Word Box. Some words will not be used.

Word Box

- whetting
- daunted
- shied
- efficacious
- covetousness

1. The criminal's ____________________ for the bank money led to his downfall.
2. She ____________________ from the barking dog.
3. Her knowledge of outdoor survival was ____________________ after we lost all of our camping equipment.

LITERARY FOCUS: THE ROMANCE

DIRECTIONS: Write a paragraph answering the questions below about the **romance.** Include details from the poem in your answer.

In what ways is Sir Gawain a romance hero? In what ways is he weak or flawed, just like an ordinary person?

____

____

____

READING FOCUS: UNDERSTANDING CAUSE AND EFFECT

DIRECTIONS: Fill in the blank rectangles with the correct **cause** or **effect** from the poem.

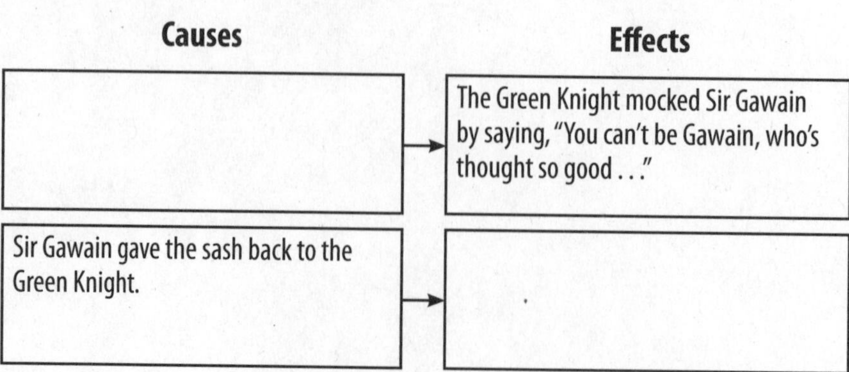

Literary Skills Analyze a medieval romance story.

Reading Skills Understand cause and effect.

Skills Review

Collection 2

LANGUAGE COACH

It can be easy to confuse words that have similar sounds or spellings. For example, *eminent* is an adjective that describes someone or something of high standing. *Imminent* is an adjective that means "about to happen."

DIRECTIONS: Look at the pairs of commonly confused words below. Look up the definition of each word in a dictionary. Then, write a sentence of your own that correctly uses that word.

1. accept: ______________________

   except: ______________________

2. affect: ______________________

   effect: ______________________

3. principal: ______________________

   principle: ______________________

4. whetting: ______________________

   wetting: ______________________

5. capital: ______________________

   capitol: ______________________

6. precede: ______________________

   proceed: ______________________

ORAL LANGUAGE ACTIVITY

DIRECTIONS: Literature that contains words with Anglo-Saxon spellings can be difficult to read. Look back at the poem "Lord Randall." Practice reciting the poem aloud in front of a partner. Ask your partner for any advice on how to recite the poem more clearly. Then switch roles.

Vocabulary Review

Unit 1

DIRECTIONS: The Word Box below includes vocabulary words from Unit 1. Read the sentences and write the correct vocabulary word on each blank line. One word will not be used.

Word Box

attribute
benign
concept
covetousness
daunted
diverse
efficacious
emphasis
extolled
guile
infallible
obstinate
shied
status
vehemently
whetting

1. I came up with the ____________ of acting out the story for our group's literature project.
2. The ____________ girl gave her last piece of candy to the other child.
3. Her ____________ in the company increased as a result of her job promotion.
4. After dipping my toe in, I ____________ from the ocean water because it was much too cold.
5. The tornado ____________ tore through the small town.
6. The parents ____________ their daughter's bad attitude to a lack of sleep.
7. The ointment on my wound was ____________ at preventing infection.
8. The mayor ____________ the rescue workers for heroically saving several skiers trapped on the mountain.
9. He was not ____________ by all of the homework he had to do, even though he knew it would take several hours.
10. During our lesson on the American Revolution, our teacher put a lot of ____________ on the causes of the war.
11. The ____________ dog pulled at its leash and refused to walk into the veterinarian's office with its owner.
12. He is a superb writer, but he is not ____________, and I even found a mistake in his book.
13. The man had no ____________ during the bargaining process and ended up paying too much for the used car.
14. Her ____________ was obvious by the way she looked longingly at her friend's new stereo.
15. Our city has a very ____________ population and includes people from many different areas of the world.

Applying the Key Concepts

Unit 1

DIRECTIONS: Review the Key Concepts at the beginning of this unit. Then answer the following questions:

THE ANGLO-SAXON LEGACY

- *Beowulf* describes a society in which violence seems to have played a major role. Why do you think fighting was such an important part of Anglo-Saxon society? Back up your answer with an example from the poem.

THE NORMANS INVADE BRITAIN

- Both *Beowulf* and *Sir Gawain and the Green Knight* are long poems about heroes who fight against terrible foes. How do they differ in what they tell us about the values of the people who created the poems?

LIFE IN MEDIEVAL SOCIETY

- Medieval British society was organized into distinct classes. Some members of those classes are characters in *The Canterbury Tales*. Do Chaucer's tales maintain the divisions between the classes, or do they actually tend to break them down? Explain your answer.

- What are some clues that "Lord Randall" was a ballad that the common people told to each other?

Unit 2

The Renaissance: A Flourish of Genius 1485–1660

National Gallery, London/Erich Lessing/Art Resource, NY

Key Concepts

THE BEGINNINGS OF TUDOR RULE

History of the Times Henry Tudor defeated King Richard III and established the Tudor dynasty, or bloodline. Under Henry Tudor, called King Henry VII, the middle class gained more power, trade developed, and England prospered. The Tudors ruled for 118 years.

Literature of the Times The printing press was invented in Germany. Its use spread throughout Europe. Literacy increased, and Europe experienced a rebirth of the arts.

THE PROTESTANT REFORMATION

History of the Times King Henry VIII wanted a divorce so he could marry a woman who might give birth to a male heir. The pope refused to grant the divorce. In turn, Henry declared himself head of the church in England. Great social and religious changes swept across the country.

Literature of the Times The Renaissance encouraged individual curiosity and creativity. During this time, bold new thoughts, beautiful poetry, and powerful plays emerged.

ENGLAND'S GREATEST MONARCH

History of the Times Henry VIII was succeeded by his sickly son Edward. His two daughters, Mary and Elizabeth, would change English history. To this day, Elizabeth I is generally considered England's greatest ruler.

Literature of the Times The Renaissance was a wonderful age for literature. Poetry and drama flourished alongside religious and philosophical works.

ACADEMIC VOCABULARY

established (EHS TAB LIHSHT) *v.:* set up; caused to happen. *Henry VII established the Tudor bloodline.*

ensure (EHN SHOOR) *v.:* to make certain. *During his reign, Henry VII acted to ensure that the Tudor line would continue.*

widespread (WYD SPREHD) *adj.:* occurring over a wide area. *Henry had widespread support for his decision.*

controversies (KAHN TRUH VUHR SEEZ) *n. pl.:* lengthy disagreements. *In spite of its controversies, the Tudor period was a time of great achievements.*

contradiction (KAHN TRUH DIHK SHUHN) *n.:* statement in opposition to another; inconsistency. *The Catholic Church felt that ending Henry VIII's marriage would be a contradiction with an earlier decision.*

Collection 3

Love, Time, and Death

© Louvre, Paris, Inv. 2156/Erich Lessing/ Art Resource, NY

Preparing to Read

The Passionate Shepherd to His Love

by Christopher Marlowe

The Nymph's Reply to the Shepherd

by Sir Walter Raleigh

LITERARY FOCUS: PASTORAL POEMS

Christopher Marlowe's "The Passionate Shepherd to His Love" is a pastoral. **Pastorals** are poems that portray country life in a positive way. In pastoral poems, handsome shepherds and beautiful maidens, called nymphs, live in perfect peace with nature. Such poems ignore the harsh realities of farm life. Sir Walter Raleigh's "The Nymph's Reply to the Shepherd" is called an **antipastoral** because it makes fun of this ideal version of country life.

READING FOCUS: UNDERSTANDING INVERTED WORD ORDER

Inverted word order, or inversion, is the rearranging of standard word order in a phrase or sentence. The normal word order in English is subject, then verb, and then object or complement. Inverted word order reverses the normal order. For example:

- Normal word order: *We will read poetry.*
- Inverted word order: *Poetry we will read.*

Poets use inversion to create a certain **tone** or to point out a particular word or idea. They might also invert words to fit the poem's meter or rhyme scheme.

Use the Skill Use a chart like this one to record examples of inverted word order in the two poems. Then rewrite the phrases in normal word order.

Inverted word order	Normal word order
And we will all the pleasures prove.	And we will prove all the pleasures.
wool/Which from our pretty lambs we pull	

Literary Skills Understand pastoral and antipastoral poems.

Reading Skills Understand inverted word order.

The Passionate Shepherd to His Love *and* The Nymph's Reply to the Shepherd

SELECTION VOCABULARY

melodious (MUH LOH DEE UHS) *adj.:* producing pleasant sounds.
The shepherd awoke to the melodious sounds of birds.

fragrant (FRAY GRUHNT) *adj.:* sweet-smelling.
We walked with the lambs through a meadow of fragrant grass and flowers.

embroidered (EHM BROY DUHRD) *adj.:* ornamented with needlework or as if with needlework.
She wore a beautiful dress embroidered with flowers.

folly (FAHL EE) *n.:* foolishness.
It would be folly for a shepherd to play all the time and never work.

WORD STUDY

DIRECTIONS: Write "Yes" after each sentence if the vocabulary word is being used correctly. Write "No" if it is being used incorrectly, and rewrite the sentence so that it uses the word correctly.

1. The *embroidered* quilt had pictures of trees on it. ____________________

____

____

2. The blaring car horn was *melodious* and annoying. ____________________

____

____

3. I loved the *fragrant* perfume that I received as a gift and used it all the time. ____________________

____

____

4. It was very wise and *folly* of her to study hard for the test. ____________________

____

____

The Passionate Shepherd to His Love

by Christopher Marlowe

BACKGROUND

In the 1500s and 1600s, London was a fast-growing city facing problems of overcrowding and pollution. Many city residents began to view the countryside as a peaceful place free of urban problems. For this reason, pastorals became very popular. Marlowe's poem is probably the most famous of the English pastoral poems. It has often been set to music, and several poets have written answers or sequels to it. Sir Walter Raleigh's reply is perhaps the most famous of these answers.

Come live with me, and be my love,
And we will all the pleasures prove[1] (A)
That valleys, groves, hills, and fields,
Woods, or steepy mountain yields.

And we will sit upon the rocks,
Seeing the shepherds feed their flocks
By shallow rivers, to whose falls
Melodious birds sing madrigals.[2] (B)

And I will make thee beds of roses,
And a thousand fragrant posies,
A cap of flowers, and a kirtle,[3]
Embroidered all with leaves of myrtle.

1. **prove:** experience.
2. **madrigals:** complicated songs for several voices.
3. **kirtle:** old word meaning "dress," "gown," or "skirt."

A READING FOCUS

Line 2 is written in **inverted word order**. Rewrite the line in normal word order.

B LANGUAGE COACH

The **suffix** *-ous* means "having" or "full of." What is the root word in *melodious*, and what does it mean?

A LITERARY FOCUS

Circle words in this **pastoral** that describe plants or animals common in the country. How does the shepherd claim he will use these natural things for his love?

B LITERARY ANALYSIS

The shepherd says he will make slippers with pure gold buckles for his love. Why is this an exaggerated claim?

C VOCABULARY

Word Study

Thy is an archaic word that means "your." Archaic words are words that are no longer commonly used. Circle another word on this page that you think is archaic. What does the word mean?

© Victoria and Albert Museum, London

A gown made of the finest wool
Which from our pretty lambs we pull, **A**
Fair lined slippers for the cold,
With buckles of the purest gold. **B**

A belt of straw and ivy buds,
With coral clasps and amber studs,
And if these pleasures may thee move,
Come live with me, and be my love.

The shepherd swains[4] shall dance and sing
For thy delight each May morning. **C**
If these delights thy mind may move,
Then live with me, and be my love.

4. **swains:** young boys.

THE NYMPH'S REPLY TO THE SHEPHERD

by Sir Walter Raleigh

© Manchester Art Gallery, UK/The Bridgeman Art Library

If all the world and love were young,
And truth in every shepherd's tongue,
These pretty pleasures might me move **A**
To live with thee and be thy love.

But Time drives flocks from field to fold,[1]
When rivers rage and rocks grow cold,
And Philomel[2] becometh dumb;
The rest complains of cares to come.

The flowers do fade, and wanton[3] fields
To wayward winter reckoning yields;
A honey tongue, a heart of gall[4]
Is fancy's spring, but sorrow's fall. **B**

1. **fold:** pen where sheep are kept in winter.
2. **Philomel:** the nightingale.
3. **wanton:** luxuriant, or richly abundant.
4. **gall:** bitter substance.

A READING FOCUS

Line 3 uses **inverted word order**. Rewrite this line in normal word order.

B LITERARY FOCUS

Remember that an **antipastoral** points out harsh realities of country life. What is the nymph's general view of nature in the countryside?

 VOCABULARY

Selection Vocabulary

Folly means "foolishness." Think of an antonym (word with the opposite meaning) for *folly* and write it below.

B QUICK CHECK

Under what conditions would the nymph go to live with the shepherd? Does that mean she will or will not go?

 VOCABULARY

Academic Vocabulary

How has the author *established*, or set up, a tone (attitude) of sarcasm and insincerity throughout the poem?

Thy gowns, thy shoes, thy beds of roses,
Thy cap, thy kirtle, and thy posies.
Soon break, soon wither, soon forgotten,
In folly ripe, in reason rotten. A

Thy belt of straw and ivy buds,
Thy coral clasps and amber studs,
All these in me no means can move
To come to thee and be thy love.

But could youth last and love still breed,
Had joys no date, nor age no need,
Then these delights my mind might move
To live with thee and be thy love. B C

The Passionate Shepherd to His Love *and* The Nymph's Reply to the Shepherd

USE AN IMAGERY CHART

DIRECTIONS: Fill in the left column with words or phrases from either the **pastoral** or the **antipastoral** you just read that conjure up strong images in your imagination. Describe the images you picture in the column on the right.

Word or phrase	Images I picture

Applying Your Skills

The Passionate Shepherd to His Love *and* The Nymph's Reply to the Shepherd

VOCABULARY DEVELOPMENT

DIRECTIONS: Write the vocabulary word that is the best antonym for each word below. Remember that an antonym is a word that has the opposite meaning of another word. One word will not be used.

Word Box

melodious
fragrant
embroidered
folly

1. earsplitting ________________
2. stinky ________________
3. wisdom ________________

LITERARY FOCUS: PASTORAL POEMS

DIRECTIONS: On a separate sheet of paper, make a Venn diagram like the one below and compare and contrast the shepherd's and nymph's views of life in the country from "The Passionate Shepherd to His Love" and "The Nymph's Reply to the Shepherd."

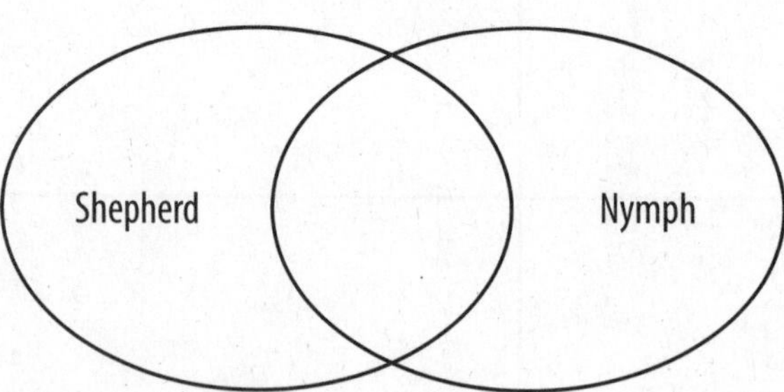

Literary Skills Understand pastoral and antipastoral poems.

Reading Skills Understand inverted word order.

READING FOCUS: UNDERSTANDING INVERTED WORD ORDER

DIRECTIONS: Review the **inverted word order** chart you made in the Preparing to Read section. On a separate sheet of paper, write a short poem that uses inverted word order. Not every line has to be inverted.

Preparing to Read

A Valediction: Forbidding Mourning

by John Donne

LITERARY FOCUS: METAPHYSICAL CONCEITS

Poets sometimes use surprising comparisons to get you to think about their subjects in a different way. John Donne uses complex and clever **figures of speech** called **metaphysical conceits** to compare things that you ordinarily wouldn't think of as being similar.

Here are some examples of unusual metaphysical conceits that writers have created:

- A lover's tears *are compared to* newly minted coins.
- A king's court *is compared to* a bowling alley.
- A man *is compared to* a world.

"A Valediction: Forbidding Mourning" contains one of the most famous metaphysical conceits of all time. Donne compares lovers to the two pointed legs of a compass, a tool used in geometry to draw circles.

Literary Skills
Understand metaphysical conceits.

Reading Skills
Recognize comparisons and contrasts.

READING FOCUS: RECOGNIZING COMPARISONS AND CONTRASTS

A **comparison** of two objects shows the ways in which they are alike. A **contrast** of two objects focuses on their differences. As you read "A Valediction: Forbidding Mourning," make a list of the comparisons and contrasts in the poem.

A Valediction: Forbidding Mourning

SELECTION VOCABULARY

virtuous (VUHR CHOO UHS) *adj.:* moral; righteous.

Her virtuous life was an example for everyone.

reckon (REHK UHN) *v.:* estimate; consider.

I can only reckon why he dropped out of school.

endure (EHN DUR) *v.:* undergo; bear.

We will endure the hardships of the winter months.

WORD STUDY

DIRECTIONS: Match each vocabulary word in the first column with its synonym (word that means the same) in the second column.

_____ **1.** reckon — **a.** judge

_____ **2.** virtuous — **b.** withstand

_____ **3.** endure — **c.** ethical

A Valediction: Forbidding Mourning

by John Donne

BACKGROUND

In this poem, the speaker is about to take a long journey, and he says a farewell ("a valediction") to the woman he loves. He tells her not to cry or feel sad (he is "forbidding mourning").

© Victoria and Albert Museum, London/Art Resource, NY

As virtuous men pass mildly away, (A)
And whisper to their souls, to go,
Whilst some of their sad friends do say,
The breath goes now, and some say, no:

So let us melt, and make no noise,
No tear-floods, nor sigh-tempests move,
'Twere profanation[1] of our joys
To tell the laity[2] our love.

Moving of th' earth[3] brings harms and fears,
Men reckon what it did and meant,[4]
But trepidation of the spheres,[5]
Though greater far, is innocent.[6] (B)

---

1. **profanation:** lack of reverence or respect.
2. **laity:** laypersons; here, those unable to understand the "religion" of true love.
3. **moving of th' earth:** earthquake.
4. **meant:** "What does it mean?" was a question ordinarily asked of any unusual phenomenon.
5. **trepidation of the spheres:** irregularities in the movements of remote heavenly bodies.
6. **innocent:** unobserved and harmless compared with earthquakes.

(A) VOCABULARY

Selection Vocabulary

Virtuous means "moral" or "righteous." What might be some qualities of virtuous men?

(B) READING FOCUS

What **comparison** is being made in this stanza?

Dull sublunary[7] lovers' love
(Whose soul[8] is sense[9]) cannot admit
Absence, because it doth remove **A**
Those things which elemented[10] it.

But we by a love, so much refined,
That ourselves know not what it is,
Interassurèd of the mind,
Care less eyes, lips, and hands to miss. **B**

Our two souls therefore, which are one,
Though I must go, endure not yet
A breach,[11] but an expansion,
Like gold to airy thinness beat.

If they be two, they are two so
As stiff twin compasses are two,
Thy soul the fixed foot, makes no show
To move, but doth, if th' other do.

And though it in the center sit,
Yet when the other far doth roam,
It leans, and hearkens after it,
And grows erect, as that comes home.

Such wilt thou be to me, who must
Like th' other foot, obliquely[12] run;
Thy firmness[13] makes my circle just,[14]
And makes me end, where I begun. **C**

A VOCABULARY

Word Study

Doth is an archaic word that means "do." Circle another word on this page that you think might be archaic, or no longer commonly used. Look up its definition and write it below.

B LANGUAGE COACH

Endure comes from the Latin root word that means "to harden." How does the meaning of the root help you understand the meaning of *endure*?

C LITERARY FOCUS

In lines 25–36, Donne uses a **metaphysical conceit** to compare two lovers to the two pointed legs of a compass. Underline words that describe what the "fixed foot" of the compass does when the other foot moves.

7. **sublunary:** under the moon, therefore subject to change.
8. **soul:** essence.
9. **sense:** the body with its five senses; that is, purely physical rather than spiritual.
10. **elemented:** comprised; composed.
11. **breach:** break; split.
12. **obliquely:** off course.
13. **firmness:** fidelity; loyalty.
14. **just:** perfect. A circle symbolizes perfection, hence wedding rings.

A Valediction: Forbidding Mourning

USE A COMPARISON AND CONTRAST CHART

DIRECTIONS: Review the details in the poem that describe the lovers and the love they share. The first column below lists three **comparisons** or **contrasts** that Donne makes in the poem. Complete the chart by explaining the point Donne makes in each comparison. Then, briefly describe any comparisons you find unusual.

Comparison or contrast	What point the comparison makes	Is the comparison unusual? Explain.
The effects of an earthquake are contrasted with the movements of the spheres. (lines 9–12)		
The speaker and his lover are contrasted with "sublunary lovers." (lines 13–20)		
The speaker and his lover are compared to the two legs of a compass. (lines 25–36)		

Applying Your Skills

A Valediction: Forbidding Mourning

VOCABULARY DEVELOPMENT

DIRECTIONS: Complete the sentences with vocabulary words from the Word Box. Some words will not be used.

Word Box

virtuous
reckon
endure

1. My mother is a very ________________ person, and she is always doing what she can to help others.
2. How did you ________________ a camping trip with almost no supplies?
3. I ________________ we won't have a test today since the teacher is out sick.

LITERARY FOCUS: METAPHYSICAL CONCEITS

DIRECTIONS: On a separate sheet of a paper, answer the following questions: What is a **metaphysical** conceit? Name one metaphysical conceit that Donne uses in "A Valediction: Forbidding Mourning." What makes this a metaphysical conceit?

READING FOCUS: RECOGNIZING COMPARISONS AND CONTRASTS

DIRECTIONS: Use the chart below to give examples of two **comparisons** and two **contrasts** from the poem.

Comparisons	Contrasts
1.	3.
2.	4.

SKILLS FOCUS

Literary Skills Understand metaphysical conceits.

Reading Skills Recognize comparisons and contrasts.

Preparing to Read

The Fall of Satan *from* Paradise Lost

by John Milton

LITERARY FOCUS: STYLE

The special way in which writers use language to express their ideas is called **style**. An author's style is closely connected to **diction**, or word choice, and **syntax**, which is the way sentences are put together. John Milton writes in **blank verse**, a style of unrhymed poetry in which each line is made up of five beats, each containing an unstressed and a stressed syllable. Blank verse reflects the natural rhythm of English speech. Milton also uses **epic similes**, long comparisons involving two very different things.

READING FOCUS: ANALYZING MILTON'S STYLE

John Milton's writings include many references to the Bible and stories from ancient Greek and Roman literature. The footnotes will help you understand unfamiliar names and terms. Use **context clues** (hints from surrounding words) to help you understand the meanings of other unfamiliar words. Milton's syntax does not always follow the usual subject-verb-object order. Analyze long sentences by **paraphrasing** them in your own words.

Use the Skill As you read, use a chart like the one below to note some specific phrases or lines that you find challenging, and paraphrase them in your own words.

Difficult lines	My paraphrase

Literary Skills Understand elements of style.

Reading Skills Analyze an author's style.

The Fall of Satan *from* Paradise Lost

SELECTION VOCABULARY

transgress (TRANS GREHS) *v.:* sin against; violate a limit.

He told the court that he did not transgress the law in any way.

infernal (IHN FUR NUHL) *adj.:* hellish; fiendish.

The infernal heat of summer was hard to bear.

contention (KUHN TEHN SHUHN) *n.:* struggle.

The team was in contention for the title.

impetuous (IHM PEHCH YOO UHS) *adj.:* forceful; violent.

Her impetuous act hurt many people.

desolation (DEHS UH LAY SHUHN) *n.:* utter misery; extreme loneliness.

They were stranded in desolation on the island.

WORD STUDY

DIRECTIONS: Write sentences of your own that correctly use each of the vocabulary words listed above.

1. ______________________________
____

2. ______________________________
____

3. ______________________________
____

4. ______________________________
____

5. ______________________________
____

THE FALL OF SATAN *from* PARADISE LOST

by John Milton

BACKGROUND

John Milton's epic poem "Paradise Lost" is about the struggle between good (represented by God in Heaven) and evil (represented by the fallen angel Satan in Hell). This theme of choosing good or evil runs throughout the poem. The following section describes what happens after Satan tries to lead a rebellion in Heaven and fails. The rebellious angels are defeated and thrown into Hell. Milton vividly describes Satan and the horrors of Hell that await those who choose evil over good.

Of man's first disobedience, and the fruit
Of that forbidden tree, whose mortal taste
Brought death into the world, and all our woe,
With loss of Eden, till one greater Man[1]
Restore us, and regain the blissful seat, (A)
Sing, Heavenly Muse,[2] that on the secret top
Of Oreb, or of Sinai,[3] didst inspire
That shepherd,[4] who first taught the chosen seed[5]
In the beginning how the Heavens and Earth
Rose out of Chaos; or if Sion hill[6]
Delight thee more, and Siloa's brook[7] that flowed

(A) LITERARY ANALYSIS

According to the Bible, Adam and Eve were the first people to live on Earth. They lived in the perfect world of Eden, but were tricked by a snake into eating fruit forbidden by God. This act separated humans from God. Most Christians believe that Jesus Christ died to reunite people with God. Knowing this, what do you think "the blissful seat" is?

1. **one greater Man:** Jesus Christ.
2. **Heavenly Muse:** Urania, muse of astronomy and sacred poetry. Milton hopes to be inspired by Urania, just as the Bible says that Moses was inspired to receive God's word for the Hebrews.
3. **Oreb . . . Sinai:** names for the mountain where Moses was said to have received God's inspiration.
4. **shepherd:** Moses.
5. **chosen seed:** the Hebrews.
6. **Sion hill:** Zion, a hill near Jerusalem.
7. **Siloa's brook:** stream that flowed past the Temple, "the oracle of God," on Mount Zion.

A READING FOCUS

Paraphrase this long sentence, which starts on line 1.

B VOCABULARY

Selection Vocabulary

Infernal is used to describe the Serpent, or Satan. Knowing this, and using other clues from the text, write a definition for *infernal*.

Fast by the oracle of God, I thence
Invoke thy aid to my adventurous song,
That with no middle flight intends to soar
Above the Aonian mount,[8] while it pursues
Things unattempted yet in prose or rhyme. **A**
And chiefly thou, O Spirit,[9] that dost prefer
Before all temples the upright heart and pure,
Instruct me, for thou know'st; thou from the first
Wast present, and with mighty wings outspread
Dove-like sat'st brooding on the vast abyss
And mad'st it pregnant: what in me is dark
Illumine, what is low raise and support;
That to the height of this great argument
I may assert Eternal Providence,
And justify the ways of God to men.
Say first, for Heaven hides nothing from thy view,
Nor the deep tract of Hell, say first what cause
Moved our grand parents[10] in that happy state,
Favored of Heaven so highly, to fall off
From their Creator, and transgress his will
For one restraint,[11] lords of the world besides?[12]
Who first seduced them to that foul revolt?
The infernal Serpent;[13] he it was, whose guile, **B**
Stirred up with envy and revenge, deceived
The mother of mankind, what time his pride
Had cast him out from Heaven, with all his host
Of rebel angels, by whose aid aspiring
To set himself in glory above his peers,[14]
He trusted to have equaled the Most High,
If he opposed; and with ambitious aim

8. **Aonian mount:** in Greek mythology, Mount Helicon, the home of the Muses.
9. **Spirit:** Holy Spirit; divine inspiration.
10. **grand parents:** Adam and Eve.
11. **one restraint:** the command not to eat fruit of the tree of knowledge.
12. **besides:** in every other way.
13. **Serpent:** Milton is referring to Satan's final form.
14. **peers:** equals; the other archangels.

© Harvard University Art Museums, Fogg Art Museum Gift of W.A. White, 1915.8./ Rick Stafford © President and Fellows of Harvard College

Against the throne and monarchy of God,
Raised impious war in Heaven and battle proud
With vain attempt. **C** Him the Almighty Power
Hurled headlong flaming from the ethereal[15] sky
With hideous ruin and combustion down
To bottomless perdition,[16] there to dwell
In adamantine[17] chains and penal[18] fire,
Who durst[19] defy the Omnipotent to arms.
Nine times the space that measures day and night
To mortal men, he with his horrid crew
Lay vanquished, rolling in the fiery gulf,
Confounded though immortal. But his doom

15. **ethereal:** heavenly.
16. **perdition:** damnation.
17. **adamantine** (AD UH MAN TEEN): unbreakable.
18. **penal:** punishing.
19. **durst:** dared.

C READING FOCUS

Use **context clues** to determine the meaning of *impious*. Write your definition below.

A QUICK CHECK

What most torments Satan in Hell?

B LITERARY FOCUS

How does Milton's **diction** in lines 61–69 help you to imagine Hell?

Reserved him to more wrath; for now the thought
Both of lost happiness and lasting pain
Torments him; round he throws his baleful eyes,
That witnessed huge affliction and dismay
Mixed with obdurate[20] pride and steadfast hate. **A**
At once as far as angels ken[21] he views
The dismal situation waste and wild:
A dungeon horrible on all sides round
As one great furnace flamed, yet from those flames
No light, but rather darkness visible
Served only to discover sights of woe,
Regions of sorrow, doleful shades, where peace
And rest can never dwell, hope never comes
That comes to all; but torture without end
Still urges,[22] and a fiery deluge, fed
With ever-burning sulfur unconsumed: **B**
Such place Eternal Justice had prepared
For those rebellious, here their prison ordained
In utter darkness, and their portion set
As far removed from God and light of Heaven
As from the center thrice to the utmost pole.[23]
O how unlike the place from whence they fell!
There the companions of his fall, o'erwhelmed
With floods and whirlwinds of tempestuous fire,
He soon discerns, and weltering[24] by his side
One next himself in power, and next in crime,
Long after known in Palestine, and named
Beelzebub.[25] To whom the Arch-Enemy,

20. **obdurate:** stubborn; unrepentant.
21. **ken:** range of view.
22. **still urges:** always afflicts.
23. **center . . . pole:** three times the distance from Earth, or "center," to the outermost point in the universe. In Milton's cosmos, Earth is the center of ten spheres.
24. **weltering:** rolling about.
25. **Beelzebub** (BEE EHL ZUH BUHB): next in power to Satan; described as prince of the devils in the Bible in Matthew 12:24.

And then in Heaven called Satan,[26] with bold words
Breaking the horrid silence thus began:
"If thou beest he—but O how fallen! how changed
From him, who in the happy realms of light
Clothed with transcendent brightness didst outshine
Myriads though bright—if he whom mutual league,
United thoughts and counsels, equal hope
And hazard in the glorious enterprise,
Joined with me once, now misery hath joined
In equal ruin: into what pit thou seest
From what height fallen! so much the stronger proved
He with his thunder;[27] and till then who knew
The force of those dire arms? Yet not for those,
Nor what the potent Victor in his rage
Can else inflict, do I repent or change,
Though changed in outward luster, that fixed mind
And high disdain, from sense of injured merit, **C**
That with the Mightiest raised me to contend,
And to the fierce contention brought along **D**
Innumerable force of spirits armed
That durst dislike his reign, and, me preferring,
His utmost power with adverse power opposed
In dubious battle on the plains of Heaven,
And shook his throne. What though the field be lost?
All is not lost; the unconquerable will,
And study[28] of revenge, immortal hate,
And courage never to submit or yield:
And what is else not to be overcome?
That glory never shall his wrath or might
Extort from me. To bow and sue for grace
With suppliant[29] knee, and deify his power
Who from the terror of this arm so late

C LITERARY FOCUS

Lines 94–98 use nonstandard **syntax**. Why do you think Milton used this **style**?

D VOCABULARY

Selection Vocabulary

The word *contention* here means "struggle." What is the cause of this contention?

---

26. **Satan:** the devil; Hebrew for "adversary; opponent."
27. **He . . . thunder:** God.
28. **study:** pursuit.
29. **suppliant:** humble.

A LITERARY ANALYSIS

What is Satan's attitude toward his defeat?

B LITERARY FOCUS

Why is the **blank verse** style of writing especially powerful for speeches, such as Satan's and Beelzebub's speeches?

C LANGUAGE COACH

Event is a word with **multiple meanings**, although its meaning here is no longer commonly used. Circle another word on this page with multiple meanings that also uses a meaning that is not common today.

Doubted[30] his empire, that were low indeed,
That were an ignominy and shame beneath
This downfall; since by fate the strength of gods
And this empyreal substance[31] cannot fail,
Since through experience of this great event,
In arms not worse, in foresight much advanced,
We may with more successful hope resolve
To wage by force or guile eternal war
Irreconcilable to our grand Foe,
Who now triumphs, and in the excess of joy
Sole reigning holds the tyranny of Heaven." A
So spake the apostate[32] Angel, though in pain,
Vaunting[33] aloud, but racked with deep despair;
And him thus answered soon his bold compeer:[34]
"O Prince, O Chief of many thronèd Powers,
That led the embattled Seraphim[35] to war
Under thy conduct, and in dreadful deeds
Fearless, endangered Heaven's perpetual King,
And put to proof his high supremacy,
Whether upheld by strength, or chance, or fate; B
Too well I see and rue the dire event,[36] C
That with sad overthrow and foul defeat
Hath lost us Heaven, and all this mighty host
In horrible destruction laid thus low,
As far as gods and heavenly essences
Can perish: for the mind and spirit remains
Invincible, and vigor soon returns,
Though all our glory extinct, and happy state
Here swallowed up in endless misery.

30. **doubted:** archaic usage meaning "feared for."
31. **empyreal** (EHM PIHR EE UHL) **substance:** heavenly—and therefore indestructible—substance of which all angels (including Satan) are made.
32. **apostate:** guilty of abandoning one's beliefs. Satan is apostate.
33. **vaunting:** boasting.
34. **compeer:** companion; equal. Now Beelzebub speaks.
35. **Seraphim:** highest order of angels.
36. **event:** archaic word meaning "outcome."

© Private Collection/Christopher Wood Gallery, London/The Bridgeman Art Library

But what if he our Conqueror (whom I now
Of force[37] believe almighty, since no less
Than such could have o'erpowered such force as ours)
Have left us this our spirit and strength entire
Strongly to suffer and support our pains,
That we may so suffice[38] his vengeful ire,
Or do him mightier service as his thralls[39] **D**
By right of war, whate'er his business be,
Here in the heart of Hell to work in fire,
Or do his errands in the gloomy deep?
What can it then avail,[40] though yet we feel
Strength undiminished, or eternal being
To undergo eternal punishment?" **E**
Whereto with speedy words the Arch-Fiend replied:
"Fallen Cherub, to be weak is miserable,
Doing or suffering:[41] But of this be sure,
To do aught[42] good never will be our task,
But ever to do ill our sole delight,
As being the contrary to his high will

37. of force: of necessity.
38. suffice: archaic for "satisfy."
39. thralls: slaves.
40. avail: be of help or advantage.
41. doing or suffering: whether active or passive.
42. aught: anything; whatever.

D QUICK CHECK

What does Beezlebub admit about God?

E LITERARY ANALYSIS

Beelzebub notes that, although the fallen angels have been banished to Hell forever, they still have their strength and understanding. What do you think Milton is trying to say about their punishment?

A READING FOCUS

Paraphrase the vow Satan makes in lines 162–168.

B VOCABULARY

Selection Vocabulary
Satan describes the fall from Heaven as ending in "the seat of *desolation*," a place of misery. Underline the words in this sentence that provide clues about the meaning of *desolation*.

Whom we resist. If then his providence
Out of our evil seek to bring forth good,
Our labor must be to pervert that end,
And out of good still[43] to find means of evil;
Which oftimes may succeed, so as perhaps
Shall grieve him, if I fail not, and disturb
His inmost counsels from their destined aim. **A**
But see the angry Victor[44] hath recalled
His ministers of vengeance and pursuit
Back to the gates of Heaven; the sulfurous hail
Shot after us in storm, o'erblown hath laid
The fiery surge, that from the precipice
Of Heaven received us falling, and the thunder,
Winged with red lightning and impetuous rage,
Perhaps hath spent his shafts, and ceases now
To bellow through the vast and boundless deep.
Let us not slip[45] the occasion, whether scorn
Or satiate[46] fury yield it from our Foe.
Seest thou yon dreary plain, forlorn and wild,
The seat of desolation, void of light,
Save what the glimmering of these livid flames
Casts pale and dreadful? **B** Thither let us tend
From off the tossing of these fiery waves,
There rest, if any rest can harbor there,
And reassembling our afflicted powers,
Consult how we may henceforth most offend
Our Enemy, our own loss how repair,
How overcome this dire calamity,
What reinforcement we may gain from hope,
If not, what resolution from despair."
    Thus Satan talking to his nearest mate
With head uplift above the wave, and eyes

43. still: always.
44. angry Victor: God.
45. slip: lose.
46. satiate: satisfied

That sparkling blazed; his other parts besides,
Prone on the flood, extended long and large,
Lay floating many a rood,[47] in bulk as huge
As whom the fables name of monstrous size,
Titanian or Earth-born, that warred on Jove,
Briareos or Typhon,[48] whom the den
By ancient Tarsus held, or that sea-beast **C**
Leviathan,[49] which God of all his works

C LITERARY FOCUS

Lines 196–208 make up one example of an **epic simile**. In lines 196–200, Milton compares Satan to the evil Titans of Greek mythology. Typhon attacked heaven and was imprisoned by Zeus (Jove). How is this similar to what happened to Satan?

---

47. **rood:** old unit of measure varying locally from about six to eight yards.
48. **Titanian . . . Typhon:** Titanians, Titans or evil giants from ancient Greek mythology; Typhon, a hundred-headed serpent-monster from Cilicia (near Tarsus).
49. **Leviathan:** biblical sea monster defeated by God.

© Charles Walker/Topfoto, UK

A LITERARY FOCUS

In this **epic simile**, Milton compares Satan to Leviathan, a sea beast defeated by God three times in biblical stories. Why do you think Milton uses this example?

B VOCABULARY

Academic Vocabulary

What *contradiction*, or inconsistency, is present in God's plan for leaving Satan "to his own dark designs"?

Created hugest that swim the ocean stream:
Him haply slumbering on the Norway foam,
The pilot of some small night-foundered[50] skiff,
Deeming some island, oft, as seamen tell,
With fixèd anchor in his scaly rind
Moors by his side under the lee, while night
Invests[51] the sea, and wishèd morn delays: **A**
So stretched out huge in length the Arch-Fiend lay
Chained on the burning lake; nor ever thence
Had risen or heaved his head, but that the will
And high permission of all-ruling Heaven
Left him at large to his own dark designs,
That with reiterated crimes he might
Heap on himself damnation, while he sought
Evil to others, and enraged might see
How all his malice served but to bring forth
Infinite goodness, grace, and mercy shown
On man by him seduced, but on himself
Treble confusion, wrath, and vengeance poured. **B**
    Forthwith upright he rears from off the pool
His mighty stature; on each hand the flames
Driven backward slope their pointing spires, and rolled
In billows, leave in the midst a horrid vale.
Then with expanded wings he steers his flight
Aloft, incumbent[52] on the dusky air
That felt unusual weight, till on dry land
He lights, if it were land that ever burned
With solid, as the lake with liquid fire;
And such appeared in hue, as when the force
Of subterranean wind transports a hill
Torn from Pelorus,[53] or the shattered side

50. **night-foundered:** overtaken by night.
51. **invests:** covers.
52. **incumbent:** lying.
53. **Pelorus:** headland in Sicily, Italy; now called Cape Faro.

Of thundering Etna,[54] whose combustible
And fueled entrails thence conceiving fire,
Sublimed[55] with mineral fury, aid the winds,
And leave a singèd bottom all involved[56]
With stench and smoke: such resting found the sole
Of unblest feet. **C** Him followed his next mate,
Both glorying to have scaped the Stygian[57] flood
As gods, and by their own recovered strength,
Not by the sufferance[58] of supernal[59] power.
"Is this the region, this the soil, the clime,"
Said then the lost Archangel, "this the seat
That we must change for Heaven, this mournful gloom
For that celestial light? **D** Be it so, since he
Who now is sovereign can dispose and bid
What shall be right: farthest from him is best,
Whom reason hath equaled, force hath made supreme
Above his equals. Farewell, happy fields,
Where joy forever dwells! Hail, horrors! hail,
Infernal world! and thou, profoundest[60] Hell,
Receive thy new possessor; one who brings
A mind not to be changed by place or time.
The mind is its own place, and in itself
Can make a Heaven of Hell, a Hell of Heaven.
What matter where, if I be still the same,
And what I should be, all but less than he
Whom thunder hath made greater? Here at least
We shall be free; the Almighty hath not built
Here for his envy, will not drive us hence:
Here we may reign secure, and in my choice
To reign is worth ambition, though in Hell:

54. Etna: volcano in Sicily, Italy.
55. sublimed: vaporized.
56. involved: enveloped.
57. Stygian (STIHJ EE UHN): of or like the river Styx; infernal, hellish. In Greek mythology the river Styx encircles the underworld.
58. sufferance: permission.
59. supernal (SOO PUR NUHL): heavenly.
60. profoundest: lowest; deepest.

C LITERARY ANALYSIS

In lines 221–238, Milton uses vivid language to depict Satan. What images do the comparisons create in your mind? How does Milton's vivid language help you to better understand the poem?

D VOCABULARY

Word Study

Mournful means "sorrowful" and *celestial* means "pertaining to Heaven." Think of a synonym, or a word with a similar meaning, for *mournful* and a synonym for *celestial*. Do these synonyms have the same powerful impact as the original words? Why or why not?

A READING FOCUS

At times Satan seems almost satisfied with his punishment in Hell. Paraphrase why Satan prefers to live in Hell rather than return to Heaven.

B LITERARY FOCUS

How would you describe Milton's **style** to someone who had never read this poem? What effect does this style have on the poem?

Better to reign in Hell than serve in Heaven. **A**
But wherefore let we then our faithful friends,
The associates and copartners of our loss,
Lie thus astonished[61] on the oblivious[62] pool,
And call them not to share with us their part
In this unhappy mansion, or once more
With rallied arms to try what may be yet
Regained in Heaven, or what more lost in Hell?" **B**

61. **astonished:** dazed.
62. **oblivious:** causing forgetfulness.

The Fall of Satan *from* Paradise Lost

USE A CONCEPT MAP

DIRECTIONS: In the graphic organizer below, list four **epic similes** that Milton uses in "The Fall of Satan."

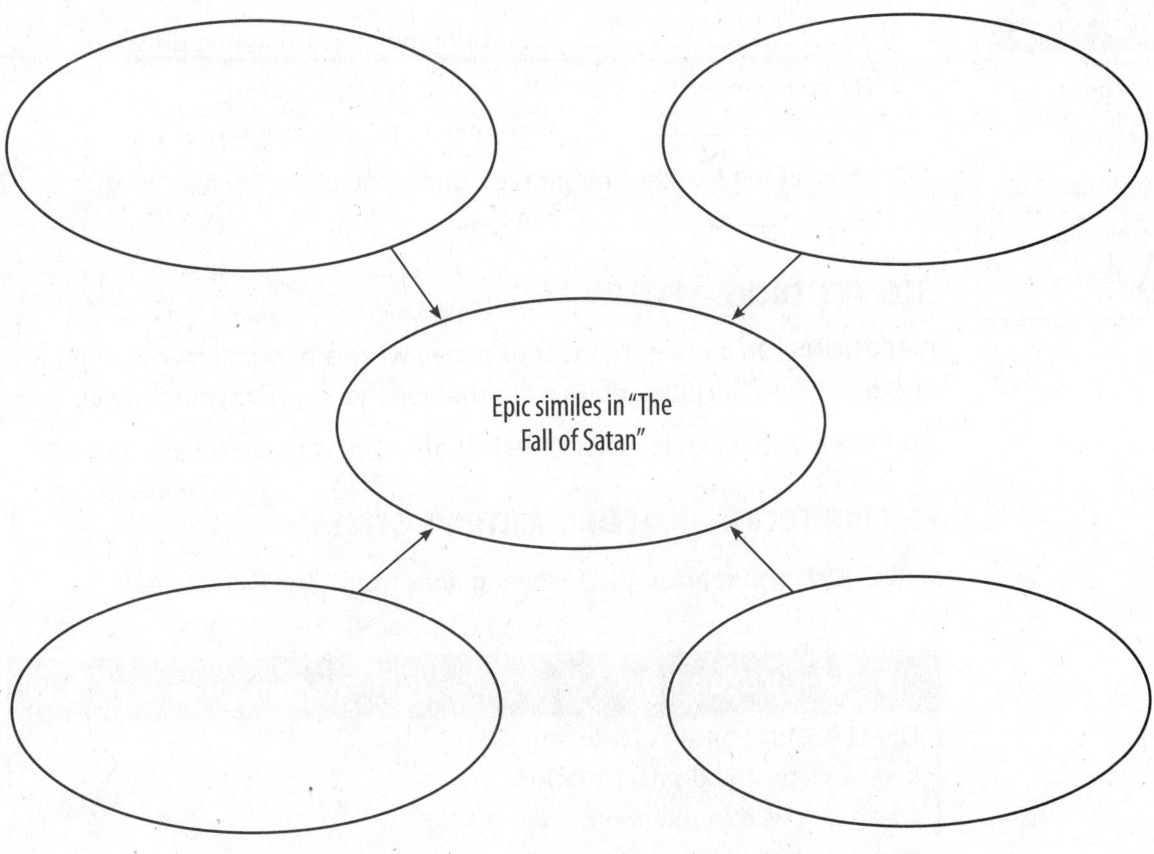

The Fall of Satan *from* Paradise Lost

VOCABULARY DEVELOPMENT

DIRECTIONS: Complete each sentence with a vocabulary word from the Word Box. Some words will not be used.

Word Box

transgress
infernal
contention
impetuous
desolation

1. The ______________ young boy ran screaming down the hall.
2. His commander had made the rules very clear, and to ______________ them would be a serious mistake.
3. They all felt like they might melt under the blistering heat of that ______________ summer.

LITERARY FOCUS: STYLE

DIRECTIONS: On a separate sheet of paper, write a paragraph answering the question below. Include details from the poem to support your answer.

How does Milton's **style** make "The Fall of Satan" a powerful epic poem?

READING FOCUS: ANALYZING MILTON'S STYLE

DIRECTIONS: **Paraphrase** the following lines from "The Fall of Satan":

Difficult lines	My paraphrase
Lines 59–61: At once as far as angels ken he views/The dismal situation waste and wild:/A dungeon horrible on all sides round	
Lines 258–260: Here at least/We shall be free; the Almighty hath not built/Here for his envy, will not drive us hence:	

Literary Skills Understand elements of style.

Reading Skills Analyze an author's style.

Collection 3

LANGUAGE COACH

DIRECTIONS: Each of the italicized words in the sentences below has **multiple meanings**. Circle the letter of the meaning for each word as it is being used in the sentence.

1. I didn't have enough money with me to pay for dinner, so my sister had to *foot* the bill.

   a. body part **b.** pay **c.** bottom; base

2. If I keep working hard, maybe one day I'll become the *head* of the company!

   a. body part **b.** leader **c.** proceed; go

3. The military had to *arm* the soldiers quickly to prepare for the battle.

   a. body part **b.** branch of an organization
   c. equip with weapons

4. We became hopelessly lost after our compass broke during the last *leg* of our hiking trip.

   a. body part **b.** part of a compass **c.** part; section

5. Father was so worried about me that when I returned, he gave me a great big hug and held me against his *chest*.

   a. body part **b.** box **c.** public fund

WRITING ACTIVITY

DIRECTIONS: Reread the poems "The Passionate Shepherd to His Love" and "The Nymph's Reply to the Shepherd." How would "The Nymph's Reply to the Shepherd" have been different if, instead of sarcastic, the tone was positive and sincere? Write two stanzas of this poem in which the speaker (the nymph) expresses fondness for the countryside. Use the same writing style that Sir Walter Raleigh used (rhyme scheme, etc.).

Collection 4

William Shakespeare

Private Collection/Ken Welsh/The Bridgeman Art Library

Sonnet 29

by William Shakespeare

LITERARY FOCUS: SHAKESPEAREAN SONNET

A **Shakespearean sonnet** is a fourteen-line poem. The sonnet's rhymes are arranged in three **quatrains**, or rhyming groups of four lines each, followed by a final two-line **couplet**. The **rhyme scheme** of a Shakespearean sonnet looks like this: *abab* (first quatrain), *cdcd* (second quatrain), *efef* (third quatrain), and *gg* (couplet). The **meter,** or rhythmic pattern, of the Shakespearean sonnet is called **iambic pentameter**. An **iamb** is an unstressed syllable followed by a stressed syllable. Each line of the sonnet has five unstressed syllables that alternate with five stressed syllables. The line below shows which syllables are stressed (´) and unstressed (˘).

Ĭ áll ălóne bĕwéep my̆ óutcăst státe,

READING FOCUS: USING TEXT STRUCTURE TO UNDERSTAND MEANING

The message of a Shakespearean sonnet is shaped by the poem's rhyming pattern and structure. The three quatrains of a Shakespearean sonnet often express related ideas. A **turn**, or a shift in the thought or mood, occurs within the quatrains. The couplet sums up the point of the poem.

Use the Skill As you read "Sonnet 29," locate the poem's turn. Then, explain why you think this section is the turn. Fill in the information in the chart below.

Turn	Explanation

Literary Skills
Understand the characteristics of a Shakespearean sonnet.

Reading Skills
Use text structure to understand meaning.

Vocabulary Development

Sonnet 29

SELECTION VOCABULARY

scorn (SKAWRN) *v.:* refuse; reject by showing contempt.

The young knights scorn the idea of having to make peace with their enemy.

WORD STUDY

DIRECTIONS: All of the words listed below are formed from the root word *scorn*. Look up these words in the dictionary and write their meanings below. Then, write sentences of your own using each word correctly.

1. scornful, *adj.:* ______________________________

____

____

2. scornfulness, *n.:* ______________________________

____

____

3. scornfully, *adv.:* ______________________________

____

____

4. scorner, *n.:* ______________________________

____

____

SONNET 29

by William Shakespeare

Summer, 1895, by Walter Crane/Private Collection/
© Christopher Wood Gallery, London, UK/
The Bridgeman Art Library

When, in disgrace[1] with Fortune and men's eyes, A
I all alone beweep my outcast state,
And trouble deaf heaven with my bootless[2] cries,
And look upon myself and curse my fate,
Wishing me like to one more rich in hope,
Featured like him, like him[3] with friends possessed,
Desiring this man's art,[4] and that man's scope,[5]
With what I most enjoy contented least;
Yet in these thoughts myself almost despising,
Haply[6] I think on thee, and then my state,
Like to the lark[7] at break of day arising
From sullen[8] earth, sings hymns at heaven's gate; B
    For thy sweet love remembered such wealth brings
    That then I scorn to change my state with kings. C

1. **disgrace:** loss of favor.
2. **bootless:** useless; futile.
3. **one . . . him . . . him:** three men whom the speaker envies.
4. **art:** literary ability.
5. **scope:** power.
6. **haply:** by chance.
7. **lark:** English skylark, a bird whose song seems to pour down from the sky.
8. **sullen:** gloomy.

A LITERARY FOCUS

Scan the poem. How can you tell, even before you read the entire poem closely, that this is a **Shakespearean sonnet**?

B READING FOCUS

Underline the **turn**. How does the idea in the first two quatrains differ from what is being said in the turn?

C VOCABULARY

Selection Vocabulary

Scorn means to "refuse" or "reject." What does the speaker scorn? Why?

Sonnet 29

VOCABULARY DEVELOPMENT

DIRECTIONS: Write "Yes" if the word *scorn* is being used correctly in the sentences below. Write "No" if it is being used incorrectly.

1. She plans to *scorn* him by accepting his marriage proposal. ________
2. The position paid much too little, so I had to *scorn* her job offer. ________
3. They cooked hamburgers and *scorn* on the grill outside. ________

LITERARY FOCUS: SHAKESPEAREAN SONNET

DIRECTIONS: Look back at "Sonnet 29." First, circle each **quatrain**. Next, draw a rectangle around the **couplet**. Then, write a letter after each line to show the poem's **rhyme scheme** (*a*, *b*, *c*, *d*. . .). Finally, draw symbols above each line to show which lines are stressed (´) and which are unstressed (˘).

READING FOCUS: USING TEXT STRUCTURE TO UNDERSTAND MEANING

Literary Skills Understand the characteristics of a Shakespearean sonnet.

Reading Skills Use text structure to understand meaning.

DIRECTIONS: Look at your notes from the Preparing to Read page. Then, on a separate sheet of paper, answer the questions below.

1. What is the main idea of "Sonnet 29" before the **turn**?
2. In what lines can this main idea be found?
3. What is the main idea of the turn in the poem?
4. What is the main idea in the couplet?
5. How does this three-part structure help you to better understand the poem?

Preparing to Read

from The Tragedy of Macbeth

by William Shakespeare

LITERARY FOCUS: TRAGEDY

A **tragedy** is a story in which a heroic character dies or comes to another unfortunate end. In many tragedies, the main character is dignified, brave, and high ranking. His or her downfall happens because of a **tragic flaw**—a weakness or error in judgment—or because of circumstances beyond his or her control. By the end of the story, the tragic hero has usually gained some wisdom or insight. In the play you are about to read, the main character, Macbeth, is a tragic hero.

Use the Skill As you read, fill in the chart below. Record characteristics of Macbeth's tragic flaw in the first column. Write the effects of his tragic flaw in the second column.

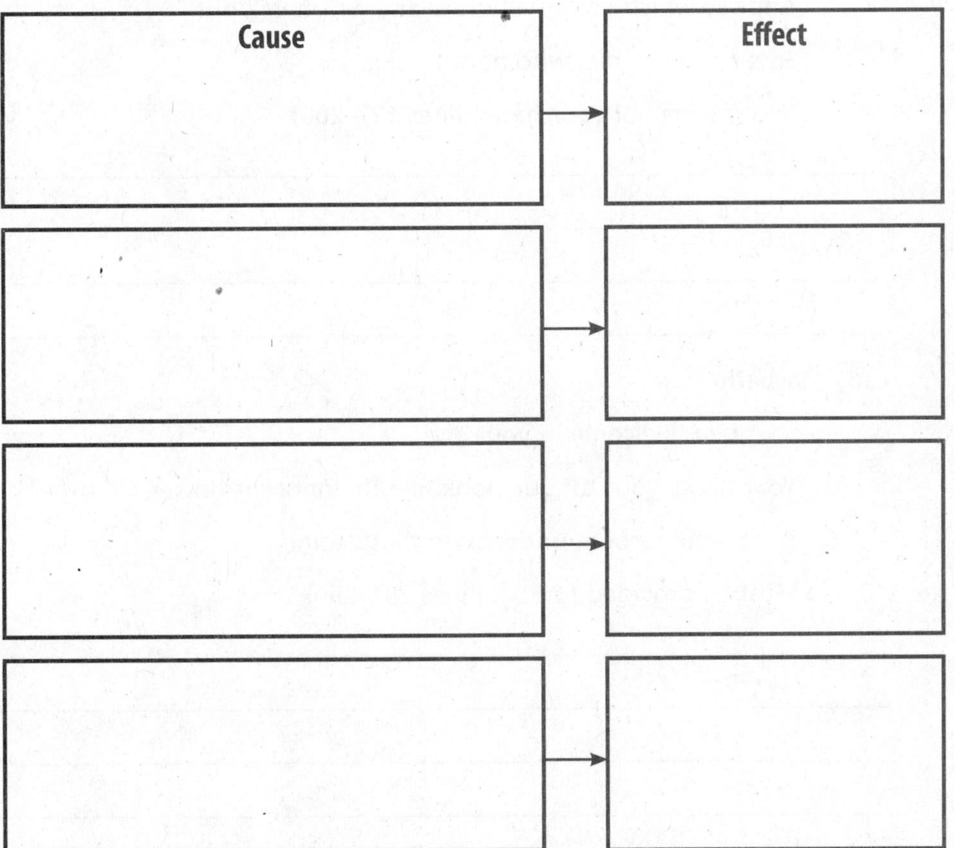

Literary Skills Understand characteristics of a tragedy.

Preparing to Read

from The Tragedy of Macbeth

READING FOCUS: USING QUESTIONING TO MONITOR READING

Because it was written around four hundred years ago, *The Tragedy of Macbeth* contains language and ideas that might be unfamiliar to you. Read the footnotes in the text to help you understand the meaning of unfamiliar words.

Another way to increase your understanding of the play is **to ask yourself questions to monitor your reading**.

Use the Skill Read these passages from the play. In the space provided, write a question about each passage. As you read *The Tragedy of Macbeth,* write answers to your questions.

Banquo:

If you can look into the seeds of time,
And say which grain will grow and which will not,
Speak then to me, who neither beg nor fear
Your favors nor your hate. (lines 197–200)

____

____

____

____

Lady Macbeth:

. . . . bear welcome in your eye,
Your hand, your tongue: look like th' innocent flower,
But be the serpent under't. He that's coming
Must be provided for. . . . (lines 257–260)

____

____

____

____

Reading Skills
Use questioning to monitor reading.

from THE TRAGEDY OF MACBETH

by William Shakespeare

BACKGROUND

"Macbeth" is one of William Shakespeare's best-known plays. Shakespeare (1564–1616) may have written this play as a tribute to King James I, both as a reference to the King's Scottish ancestry and as a way of discussing the Gunpowder Plot. This plot was an assassination attempt against the king and his Parliament in 1605. The plot was discovered and prevented.

Act I Scene 1. *An open place.*

Thunder and lightning. Enter three WITCHES.

First Witch.

When shall we three meet again?
In thunder, lightning, or in rain?

Second Witch.

When the hurlyburly's done,
When the battle's lost and won.

Third Witch.

That will be ere the set of sun.

First Witch.

Where the place?

Second Witch. Upon the heath.

Third Witch.

There to meet with Macbeth. 

First Witch.

I come, Graymalkin.[1]

A READING FOCUS

After reading these first lines of the play, what **questions** can you ask about the play?

---

1. **Graymalkin:** the first witch's attendant or familiar, a gray cat.

A LITERARY FOCUS

What in this first scene sets the stage for the **tragedy** to come?

© David Robertson/Alamy

Second Witch.

Paddock[2] calls.

Third Witch. Anon![3]

All.

Fair is foul, and foul is fair.
Hover through the fog and filthy air.

[Exeunt.] **A**

Scene 2. *A camp.*

Alarum within. Enter KING DUNCAN, MALCOLM, DONALBAIN, LENNOX, *with* ATTENDANTS, *meeting a bleeding* CAPTAIN.

King.

What bloody man is that? He can report,
As seemeth by his plight, of the revolt
The newest state.

---

2. **Paddock:** a toad, the second witch's familiar.
3. **anon:** soon.

Malcolm. This is the sergeant
Who like a good and hardy soldier fought
'Gainst my captivity. Hail, brave friend!
Say to the king the knowledge of the broil[4]
As thou didst leave it. B

Captain. Doubtful it stood,
As two spent swimmers, that do cling together
And choke their art.[5] The merciless Macdonwald—
Worthy to be a rebel for to that
The multiplying villainies of nature
Do swarm upon him—from the Western Isles[6]
Of kerns and gallowglasses[7] is supplied;
And Fortune, on his damnèd quarrel smiling,
Showed like a rebel's whore: but all's too weak:
For brave Macbeth—well he deserves that name—
Disdaining Fortune, with his brandished steel,
Which smoked with bloody execution,
Like valor's minion[8] carved out his passage
Till he faced the slave;
Which nev'r shook hands, nor bade farewell to him,
Till he unseamed him from the nave to th' chops,[9] C
And fixed his head upon our battlements. D

King.
O valiant cousin! Worthy gentleman!

Captain.
As whence the sun 'gins his reflection[10]
Shipwracking storms and direful thunders break,
So from that spring whence comfort seemed to come
Discomfort swells. Mark, King of Scotland, mark:

---

4. **broil:** quarrel.
5. **choke their art:** hinder each other's ability to swim.
6. **Western Isles:** a region of western Scotland comprising the Outer Hebrides.
7. **kerns and gallowglasses:** lightly armed Irish soldiers and heavily armed soldiers.
8. **minion:** favorite.
9. **unseamed . . . chops:** split him from navel to jaws.
10. **'gins his reflection:** rises.

B LITERARY ANALYSIS

Based on the information in beginning of Scene 2, what do you think is happening off-stage?

C VOCABULARY

Word Study

A *seam* is "the line formed by sewing together pieces of cloth." Based on your knowledge of the prefix *un-*, what do you think *unseamed* might mean?

D LITERARY FOCUS

Underline any words in this speech that might foreshadow, or hint at, the **tragedy** to come.

A READING FOCUS

This line closely links Macbeth and Banquo, but the title of the play contains just *Macbeth*. What **question** does this raise for you about the relationship between the two characters?

B QUICK CHECK

What do you know about Macbeth's character so far?

C LANGUAGE COACH

Strange has multiple meanings. It can mean that something is odd, hard to explain, out of place, alien, or not previously experienced. Which definition do you think is used here? Explain your answer.

No sooner justice had, with valor armed,
Compelled these skipping kerns to trust their heels
But the Norweyan[11] lord, surveying vantage,[12]
With furbished arms and new supplies of men,
Began a fresh assault.

King. Dismayed not this
Our captains, Macbeth and Banquo? **A**

Captain. Yes;
As[13] sparrows eagles, or the hare the lion.
If I say sooth,[14] I must report they were
As cannons overcharged with double cracks;
So they doubly redoubled strokes upon the foe.
Except[15] they meant to bathe in reeking wounds,
Or memorize another Golgotha,[16]
I cannot tell—
But I am faint; my gashes cry for help.

King.
So well thy words become thee as thy wounds;
They smack of honor both. Go get him surgeons. **B**

[*Exit* CAPTAIN *attended.*]

[*Enter* ROSS *and* ANGUS.]

Who comes here?

Malcolm. The worthy Thane[17] of Ross.

Lennox.
What a haste looks through his eyes! So should he look
That seems to[18] speak things strange. **C**

Ross. God save the king!

---

11. **Norweyan:** Norwegian.
12. **surveying vantage:** seeing an opportunity.
13. **as:** No more than.
14. **sooth:** truth.
15. **Except:** unless.
16. **memorize another Golgotha:** make the place as memorable as Golgotha, where Jesus Christ was crucified.
17. **Thane:** Scottish title of nobility.
18. **seems to:** seems about to.

© Donald Cooper/Photostage

King.
Whence cam'st thou, worthy thane?
Ross. From Fife, great king;
Where the Norweyan banners flout the sky
And fan our people cold.
Norway himself,[19] with terrible numbers,
Assisted by that most disloyal traitor
The Thane of Cawdor, began a dismal conflict; **D**
Till that Bellona's bridegroom,[20] lapped in proof,[21]
Confronted him with self-comparisons,[22]
Point against point, rebellious arm 'gainst arm,
Curbing his lavish[23] spirit: and, to conclude,
The victory fell on us.
King. Great happiness!
Ross. That now
Sweno, the Norways' king, craves composition;[24]

---

19. **Norway himself:** that is, the king of Norway.
20. **Bellona's bridegroom:** Bellona is the goddess of war. Macbeth, who is a great soldier, is called her mate.
21. **lapped in proof:** clad in armor.
22. **self-comparisons:** countermovements.
23. **lavish:** insolent; rude.
24. **composition:** peace terms.

D **LITERARY ANALYSIS**

Based on this passage, we can tell that the Norwegian King fought alongside his army. Why do you think King Duncan of Scotland did not fight in the battle as well?

A QUICK CHECK

What does King Duncan receive from the Norwegians after his army's victory?

B LITERARY FOCUS

Based on what you have read so far, predict one **tragic flaw** that Macbeth might have.

Nor would we deign him burial of his men
Till he disbursèd, at Saint Colme's Inch,[25]
Ten thousand dollars to our general use. **A**

King.

No more that Thane of Cawdor shall deceive
Our bosom interest:[26] go pronounce his present[27] death,
And with his former title greet Macbeth.

Ross.

I'll see it done.

King.

What he hath lost, noble Macbeth hath won. **B**

[*Exeunt.*]

Scene 3. *A heath.*

Thunder. Enter the three WITCHES.

First Witch.

Where hast thou been, sister?

Second Witch.

Killing swine.

Third Witch.

Sister, where thou?

First Witch.

A sailor's wife had chestnuts in her lap,
And mounched, and mounched, and mounched. "Give me," quoth I.
"Aroint thee,[28] witch!" the rump-fed ronyon[29] cries.
Her husband's to Aleppo gone, master o' th' *Tiger*:
But in a sieve[30] I'll thither sail,
And, like a rat without a tail,
I'll do, I'll do, and I'll do.

25. **Saint Colme's Inch:** island off the coast of Scotland.
26. **bosom interest:** heart's trust.
27. **present:** immediate.
28. **Aroint thee:** begone.
29. **rump-fed ronyon:** fat-rumped, scabby creature.
30. **But in a sieve:** Witches were believed to have the power to sail in sieves.

Second Witch.

I'll give thee a wind.

First Witch.

Th' art kind.

Third Witch.

And I another.

First Witch.

I myself have all the other;
And the very ports they blow,[31] C
All the quarters that they know D
I' th' shipman's card.[32]
I'll drain him dry as hay:
Sleep shall neither night nor day
Hang upon his penthouse lid;[33]
He shall live a man forbid:[34]
Weary sev'nights nine times nine
Shall he dwindle, peak,[35] and pine:
Though his bark cannot be lost,
Yet it shall be tempest-tossed.
Look what I have. E

Second Witch.

Show me, show me.

First Witch.

Here I have a pilot's thumb,
Wracked as homeward he did come.

[*Drum within.*]

Third Witch.

A drum, a drum!
Macbeth doth come.

All.

The weird sisters, hand in hand,

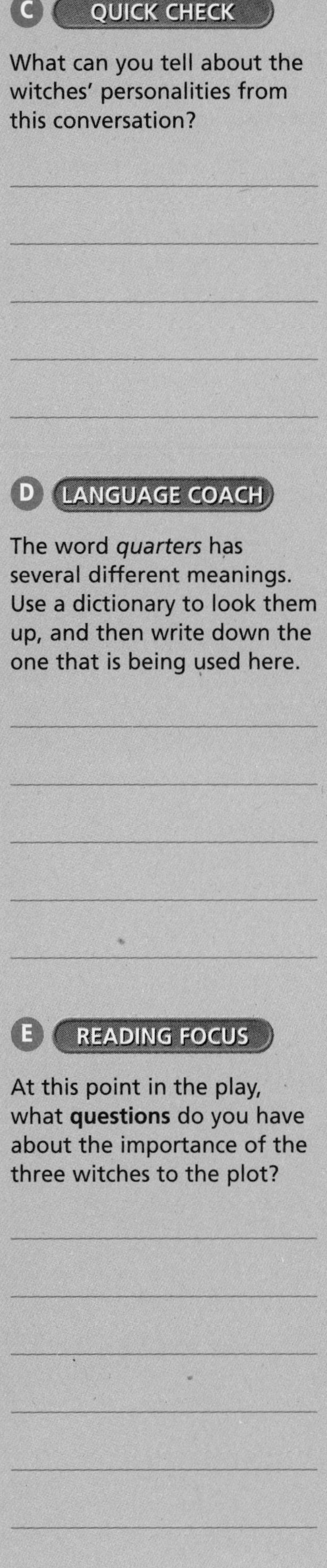

C QUICK CHECK

What can you tell about the witches' personalities from this conversation?

D LANGUAGE COACH

The word *quarters* has several different meanings. Use a dictionary to look them up, and then write down the one that is being used here.

E READING FOCUS

At this point in the play, what **questions** do you have about the importance of the three witches to the plot?

31. **ports they blow:** harbors they blow into.
32. **card:** compass.
33. **penthouse lid:** eyelid.
34. **forbid:** curse.
35. **peak:** grow pale.

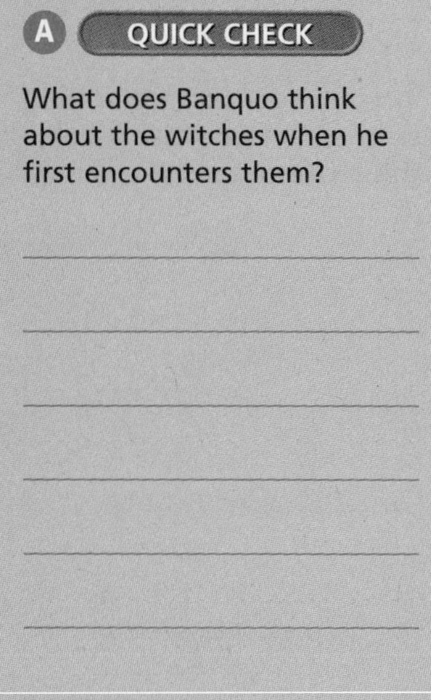

Posters[36] of the sea and land,
Thus do go about, about:
Thrice to thine, and thrice to mine,
And thrice again, to make up nine.
Peace! The charm's wound up.

[*Enter* MACBETH *and* BANQUO.]

Macbeth.
So foul and fair a day I have not seen.

Banquo.
How far is't called to Forres?[37] What are these
So withered, and so wild in their attire,
That look not like th' inhabitants o' th' earth,
And yet are on't? Live you, or are you aught
That man may question? You seem to understand me,
By each at once her choppy[38] finger laying
Upon her skinny lips. You should[39] be women,
And yet your beards forbid me to interpret
That you are so. (A)

Macbeth. Speak, if you can: what are you?

First Witch.
All hail, Macbeth! Hail to thee, Thane of Glamis!

Second Witch.
All hail, Macbeth! Hail to thee, Thane of Cawdor!

Third Witch.
All hail, Macbeth, that shalt be king hereafter!

Banquo.
Good sir, why do you start, and seem to fear
Things that do sound so fair? I' th' name of truth,
Are ye fantastical, or that indeed
Which outwardly ye show? My noble partner
You greet with present grace and great prediction
Of noble having and of royal hope,

---

36. posters: travelers.
37. Forres: town in northeast Scotland and site of King Duncan's castle.
38. choppy: chapped; sore.
39. should: must.

That he seems rapt withal:[40] to me you speak not.
If you can look into the seeds of time,
And say which grain will grow and which will not,
Speak then to me, who neither beg nor fear
Your favors nor your hate. (B)

First Witch. Hail!

Second Witch. Hail!

Third Witch. Hail!

First Witch.
Lesser than Macbeth, and greater.

Second Witch.
Not so happy,[41] yet much happier.

Third Witch.
Thou shalt get[42] kings, though thou be none.
So all hail, Macbeth and Banquo!

First Witch.
Banquo and Macbeth, all hail!

Macbeth.
Stay, you imperfect[43] speakers, tell me more:
By Sinel's death I know I am Thane of Glamis;
But how of Cawdor? The Thane of Cawdor lives,
A prosperous gentleman; and to be king
Stands not within the prospect of belief,
No more than to be Cawdor. Say from whence (C)
You owe this strange intelligence?[44] Or why
Upon this blasted heath you stop our way
With such prophetic greeting? Speak, I charge you. (D)

[WITCHES *vanish.*]

WHAT HAPPENS NEXT Banquo and Macbeth consider the Witches' prophecies that Banquo's children will be kings and Macbeth will be made Thane, or lord, of Cawdor. The king's

40. rapt withal: entranced by it.
41. happy: lucky.
42. get: beget; give birth to.
43. imperfect: unfinished.
44. Say from whence . . . intelligence?: How do you have this information?

B LITERARY ANALYSIS

Based on Banquo's speech, what can you tell about Macbeth's reaction to the witches' greeting?

C LITERARY ANALYSIS

At this point in the play, what does the audience know that Macbeth does not?

D VOCABULARY

Word Study

Prophetic means "predictive" or "ominous." Use a thesaurus to find a synonym, or word with the same meaning, for *prophetic*. Use the synonym in a sentence of your own.

A LITERARY ANALYSIS

Based on this speech, what can you tell about Lady Macbeth's personality?

B READING FOCUS

What **questions** can you ask about Lady Macbeth's role in her husband's downfall?

messengers arrive to tell Macbeth that the Thane of Cawdor has been sentenced to death for treason and that Macbeth will replace him. Macbeth feels danger may be ahead, but he doesn't know why. Macbeth and Banquo meet with the king and Macbeth receives the title of thane. Lady Macbeth reads a letter from her husband telling her his news. A messenger tells Lady Macbeth that the king and Macbeth are on their way.

Scene 5. *Inverness. Macbeth's castle.*

Lady Macbeth.

The raven himself is hoarse
That croaks the fatal entrance of Duncan
Under my battlements. Come, you spirits
That tend on mortal[45] thoughts, unsex me here,
And fill me, from the crown to the toe, top-full
Of direst cruelty! Make thick my blood,
Stop up th' access and passage to remorse,
That no compunctious visitings of nature[46]
Shake my fell[47] purpose, nor keep peace between
Th' effect and it! Come to my woman's breasts,
And take my milk for gall,[48] you murd'ring ministers,[49]
Wherever in your sightless[50] substances
You wait on nature's mischief! Come, thick night,
And pall[51] thee in the dunnest[52] smoke of hell,
That my keen knife see not the wound it makes,
Nor heaven peep through the blanket of the dark,
To cry "Hold, hold!" **A** **B**

[*Enter* MACBETH.]

Great Glamis! Worthy Cawdor!

45. **mortal:** deadly.
46. **compunctious . . . nature:** natural feelings of compassion.
47. **fell:** savage.
48. **gall:** a bitter substance; bile.
49. **murd'ring ministers:** agents of murder.
50. **sightless:** invisible.
51. **pall:** cover with a shroud, a burial cloth.
52. **dunnest:** darkest.

© Ben Graville/PhotoNews Service LTD.

Greater than both, by the all-hail hereafter!
Thy letters have transported me beyond
This ignorant present, and I feel now **C**
The future in the instant.

Macbeth. My dearest love,
Duncan comes here tonight.

Lady Macbeth. And when goes hence?

Macbeth.
Tomorrow, as he purposes.

Lady Macbeth. O, never
Shall sun that morrow see!
Your face, my thane, is as a book where men
May read strange matters. To beguile the time,[53]
Look like the time; bear welcome in your eye,
Your hand, your tongue: look like th' innocent flower,
But be the serpent under't. He that's coming
Must be provided for: and you shall put
This night's great business into my dispatch;[54]
Which shall to all our nights and days to come

---

53. beguile the time: deceive those around you.
54. dispatch: management.

C VOCABULARY

Word Study

Present can be pronounced PREHZ uhnt or pree ZEHNT. Which pronunciation is used here? Is the word used as a verb or a noun? What does it mean in this sentence?

A QUICK CHECK

What is Lady Macbeth telling her husband here?

B QUICK CHECK

What consequences of the assassination does Macbeth fear?

Give solely sovereign sway and masterdom. A

Macbeth.

We will speak further.

Lady Macbeth. Only look up clear.[55]

To alter favor ever is to fear.[56]

Leave all the rest to me.

[*Exeunt.*]

WHAT HAPPENS NEXT King Duncan arrives, and is greeted by Lady Macbeth. He asks to be taken to Macbeth.

Scene 7. *Macbeth's castle.*

Hautboys.[57] *Torches. Enter a* SEWER,[58] and diverse SERVANTS *with dishes and service, and pass over the stage. Then enter* MACBETH.

Macbeth.

If it were done when 'tis done, then 'twere well
It were done quickly. If th' assassination
Could trammel up the consequence, and catch,
With his surcease,[59] success; that but this blow
Might be the be-all and the end-all—here,
But here, upon this bank and shoal of time,
We'd jump[60] the life to come. B But in these cases
We still have judgment here; that we but teach
Bloody instructions, which, being taught, return
To plague th' inventor: this even-handed[61] justice
Commends[62] th' ingredients of our poisoned chalice
To our own lips. He's here in double trust:
First, as I am his kinsman and his subject,

55. **clear:** undisturbed.
56. **To alter . . . fear:** To show an altered face is dangerous.
57. **hautboys:** oboes.
58. **Sewer:** butler.
59. **his surcease:** Duncan's death.
60. **jump:** risk (Macbeth knows he will be condemned to hell for the sin of murder).
61. **even-handed:** impartial.
62. **commends:** offers.

Strong both against the deed; then, as his host,
Who should against his murderer shut the door,
Not bear the knife myself. Besides, this Duncan
Hath borne his faculties[63] so meek, hath been
So clear[64] in his great office, that his virtues
Will plead like angels trumpet-tongued against
The deep damnation of his taking-off;[65]
And pity, like a naked newborn babe,
Striding the blast, or heaven's cherubin horsed
Upon the sightless couriers[66] of the air,
Shall blow the horrid deed in every eye,
That[67] tears shall drown the wind. I have no spur
To prick the sides of my intent, but only
Vaulting ambition, which o'erleaps itself
And falls on th' other— C D

[*Enter* LADY MACBETH.]

How now! What news?

Lady Macbeth.
He has almost supped. Why have you left the chamber?

Macbeth.
Hath he asked for me?

Lady Macbeth. Know you not he has?

Macbeth.
We will proceed no further in this business:
He hath honored me of late, and I have bought
Golden opinions from all sorts of people,
Which would be worn now in their newest gloss,
Not cast aside so soon.

WHAT HAPPENS NEXT As Macbeth expresses hesitation about killing the king, Lady Macbeth tells her husband not

63. faculties: powers.
64. clear: clean.
65. taking-off: murder.
66. sightless couriers: winds.
67. that: so that.

C QUICK CHECK

Does the rest of the speech confirm your guess about Macbeth's fears? Now what consequences do you think he fears most?

D LITERARY FOCUS

What **tragic flaw** is Macbeth demonstrating in this speech?

A LITERARY FOCUS

How do Banquo's words foreshadow the **tragedy** to come?

to be a coward. She claims she could kill her own infant if she wanted to do so as much as Macbeth has wanted to kill Duncan. Lady Macbeth says she will make sure the king's chamberlains, or attendants, are drunk so they cannot protect the king. Macbeth and Lady Macbeth decide to use the chamberlains' own daggers to commit the murder. They agree to smear the chamberlains with blood as they sleep so it will look like the king was killed by his own men. Macbeth says he will commit the murder.

Act II Scene 1. *Inverness. Court of Macbeth's castle.*

Enter BANQUO, *and* FLEANCE, *with a torch before him (on the way to bed).*

Banquo.

How goes the night, boy?

Fleance.

The moon is down; I have not heard the clock.

Banquo.

And she goes down at twelve

Fleance. I take't, 'tis later, sir.

Banquo.

Hold, take my sword. There's husbandry[68] in heaven.
Their candles are all out. Take thee that too.
A heavy summons[69] lies like lead upon me,
And yet I would not sleep. Merciful powers,
Restrain in me the cursèd thoughts that nature
Gives way to in repose! **A**

[*Enter* MACBETH, *and a* SERVANT *with a torch.*]

Give me my sword!
Who's there?

68. **husbandry:** economizing (that is, putting out the lights to save money on candles).
69. **summons:** call to sleep.

Macbeth.
A friend.

Banquo.
What, sir, not yet at rest? The king's a-bed:
He hath been in unusual pleasure, and
Sent forth great largess to your offices:[70]
This diamond he greets your wife withal,
By the name of most kind hostess; and shut up[71]
In measureless content. **B**

Macbeth. Being unprepared,
Our will became the servant to defect,[72]
Which else should free have wrought.

Banquo. All's well.
I dreamt last night of the three weird sisters:
To you they have showed some truth.

Macbeth. I think not of them.
Yet, when we can entreat an hour to serve,
We would spend it in some words upon that business,
If you would grant the time.

Banquo. At your kind'st leisure.

Macbeth.
If you shall cleave to my consent, when 'tis,[73]
It shall make honor for you. **C**

Banquo. So[74] I lose none
In seeking to augment it, but still keep
My bosom franchised and allegiance clear,[75]
I shall be counseled. **D**

Macbeth. Good repose the while!

Banquo.
Thanks, sir. The like to you!

[*Exit* BANQUO, *with* FLEANCE.]

---

70. **largess to your offices:** gifts to your servants' quarters.
71. **shut up:** concluded.
72. **to defect:** to insufficient preparations.
73. **cleave . . . 'tis:** join my cause, when the time comes.
74. **so:** provided that.
75. **franchised:** free (from guilt). **clear:** clean.

B READING FOCUS

Duncan's generous gifts show that he doesn't know about Macbeth's plans. What **questions** do you have about how this ignorance might affect Macbeth's actions?

C LITERARY ANALYSIS

In these lines Macbeth seems to be hinting to Banquo about his plans. Why might he want to tell Banquo what he is about to do?

D QUICK CHECK

Do you think Banquo understands what Macbeth is planning? Explain.

A VOCABULARY

Word Study

The word *instrument* has multiple meanings. What meaning do you think is intended here? Use a dictionary if you need help.

____

____

____

____

Macbeth.

Go bid thy mistress, when my drink is ready,
She strike upon the bell. Get thee to bed.

[*Exit* SERVANT.]

Is this a dagger which I see before me,
The handle toward my hand? Come, let me clutch thee.
I have thee not, and yet I see thee still.
Art thou not, fatal vision, sensible[76]
To feeling as to sight, or art thou but
A dagger of the mind, a false creation,
Proceeding from the heat-oppressèd brain?
I see thee yet, in form as palpable[77]
As this which now I draw.
Thou marshal'st me the way that I was going;
And such an instrument I was to use. A
Mine eyes are made the fools o' th' other senses,
Or else worth all the rest. I see thee still;
And on thy blade and dudgeon[78] gouts[79] of blood,
Which was not so before. There's no such thing.
It is the bloody business which informs[80]
Thus to mine eyes. Now o'er the one half-world
Nature seems dead, and wicked dreams abuse[81]
The curtained sleep; witchcraft celebrates
Pale Hecate's[82] offerings; and withered murder,
Alarumed[83] by his sentinel, the wolf,
Whose howl's his watch, thus with his stealthy pace,
With Tarquin's[84] ravishing strides, towards his design

76. **sensible:** perceptible to the senses.
77. **palpable:** obvious.
78. **dudgeon:** hilt.
79. **gouts:** large drops.
80. **informs:** gives shape.
81. **abuse:** deceive.
82. **Hecate's:** Hecate (HEHK IHT), the goddess of sorcery.
83. **Alarumed:** called to action.
84. **Tarquin's:** Tarquin was a Roman tyrant who raped a woman named Lucrece.

Moves like a ghost. Thou sure and firm-set earth,
Hear not my steps, which way they walk, for fear
Thy very stones prate of my whereabout,
And take the present horror from the time,
Which now suits with it.[85] Whiles I threat, he lives:
Words to the heat of deeds too cold breath gives. **B**

[*A bell rings.*]

I go, and it is done: the bell invites me.
Hear it not, Duncan, for it is a knell
That summons thee to heaven, or to hell.

[*Exit.*]

Scene 2. *Macbeth's castle.*

Enter LADY MACBETH.

Lady Macbeth.
That which hath made them drunk hath made me bold;
What hath quenched them hath given me fire. Hark!
Peace!
It was the owl that shrieked, the fatal bellman,
Which gives the stern'st good-night.[86] He is about it.
The doors are open, and the surfeited grooms
Do mock their charge with snores. I have drugged their possets,[87]
That death and nature do contend about them,
Whether they live or die. **C**

Macbeth (*within*). Who's there? What, ho?

Lady Macbeth.
Alack, I am afraid they have awaked.
And 'tis not done! Th' attempt and not the deed

85. now suits with it: now seems suitable to it.

86. It was the owl . . . stern'st good-night: The owl's call is supposed to portend death. The bellman was a person who rang a bell outside a condemned person's cell the night before his execution, to warn him to confess his sins.

87. possets: bedtime drinks.

B READING FOCUS

This speech is a combination of hallucination, imagery, and fact. What **questions** could you ask to help yourself figure out what is happening?

C QUICK CHECK

What has Lady Macbeth done to help her husband's assassination attempt?

A LITERARY FOCUS

How does the conversation between Macbeth and Lady Macbeth after the murder reflect the characteristics of a **tragedy**?

B READING FOCUS

What **questions** can you ask to help you understand lines 442–453?

Confounds[88] us. Hark! I laid their daggers ready;
He could not miss 'em. Had he not resembled
My father as he slept, I had done't.

[*Enter* MACBETH.]

My husband!

Macbeth.
I have done the deed. Didst thou not hear a noise?

Lady Macbeth.
I heard the owl scream and the crickets cry.
Did not you speak?

Macbeth. When?

Lady Macbeth. Now.

Macbeth. As I descended?

Lady Macbeth. Ay.

Macbeth. Hark!
Who lies i' th' second chamber?

Lady Macbeth. Donalbain.

Macbeth. This is a sorry sight.

Lady Macbeth.
A foolish thought, to say a sorry sight. **A**

Macbeth.
There's one did laugh in 's sleep, and one cried "Murder!"
That they did wake each other. I stood and heard them.
But they did say their prayers, and addressed them
Again to sleep.

Lady Macbeth. There are two lodged together.

Macbeth.
One cried "God bless us!" and "Amen" the other,
As they had seen me with these hangman's hands:
List'ning their fear, I could not say "Amen,"
When they did say "God bless us!"

Lady Macbeth. Consider it not so deeply. **B**

88. **confounds:** ruins.

Macbeth.
But wherefore could not I pronounce "Amen"?
I had most need of blessing, and "Amen"
Stuck in my throat.

Lady Macbeth. These deeds must not be thought
After these ways; so, it will make us mad. (C)

Macbeth.
Methought I heard a voice cry "Sleep no more! (D)
Macbeth does murder sleep"—the innocent sleep,
Sleep that knits up the raveled sleave[89] of care,
The death of each day's life, sore labor's bath,
Balm of hurt minds, great nature's second course,[90]
Chief nourisher in life's feast—

Lady Macbeth. What do you mean?

Macbeth.
Still it cried "Sleep no more!" to all the house:
"Glamis hath murdered sleep, and therefore Cawdor
Shall sleep no more: Macbeth shall sleep no more."

Lady Macbeth.
Who was it that thus cried? Why, worthy thane,
You do unbend your noble strength, to think
So brainsickly of things. Go get some water,
And wash this filthy witness from your hand. (E)
Why did you bring these daggers from the place?
They must lie there: go carry them, and smear
The sleepy grooms with blood.

Macbeth. I'll go no more.
I am afraid to think what I have done;
Look on 't again I dare not.

Lady Macbeth. Infirm of purpose!
Give me the daggers. The sleeping and the dead
Are but as pictures. 'Tis the eye of childhood
That fears a painted devil. If he do bleed,
I'll gild the faces of the grooms withal,

---

89. raveled sleave: tangled thread.
90. second course: sleep (the less substantial first course is food).

(C) LITERARY ANALYSIS

How would you describe Macbeth's state of mind now?

(D) VOCABULARY

Word Study

Use your knowledge of modern English to guess the meaning of the archaic (no longer commonly used) word *methought*. What unusual prefix does the word contain?

(E) LITERARY ANALYSIS

What do you think Lady Macbeth means by the phrase "filthy witness"?

A VOCABULARY

Academic Vocabulary
What does Lady Macbeth plan to do to *ensure*, or make certain, that neither she nor her husband are blamed for King Duncan's death?

B LITERARY ANALYSIS

Based on the context clues, what do you think Lady Macbeth means when she accuses her husband of wearing "a heart so white"?

© Cromwell/Lamancha/Grampian TV/The Kobal Collection

For it must seem their guilt. **A**

[*Exit. Knock within.*]

Macbeth. Whence is that knocking?
How is't with me, when every noise appalls me?
What hands are here? Ha! They pluck out mine eyes!
Will all great Neptune's ocean wash this blood
Clean from my hand? No; this my hand will rather
The multitudinous seas incarnadine,[91]
Making the green one red.

[*Enter* LADY MACBETH.]

Lady Macbeth.
My hands are of your color, but I shame
To wear a heart so white. (*Knock.*) I hear a knocking **B**
At the south entry. Retire we to our chamber.
A little water clears us of this deed:
How easy is it then! Your constancy
Hath left you unattended.[92] (*Knock.*) Hark! more knocking.

---

91. **incarnadine:** make red.
92. **Your . . . unattended:** Your firmness has deserted you.

Get on your nightgown, lest occasion call us
And show us to be watchers.[93] Be not lost
So poorly in your thoughts.

Macbeth.
To know my deed, 'twere best not know myself.

[*Knock.*]

Wake Duncan with thy knocking! I would thou
couldst! (C)

[*Exeunt.*]

WHAT HAPPENS NEXT In the remaining scenes of Act Two, Macduff and Lennox arrive at Macbeth's castle. Macduff discovers the king has been killed. Macbeth claims that the king's chamberlains murdered him. Macbeth explains that in a fit of rage he, Macbeth, killed the chamberlains for their crime.

In Act Three, Banquo tells Macbeth the Witches' prophecies have come true for Macbeth. Banquo wonders if he will become the father of many kings as the Witches have claimed. Unable to bear the thought of Banquo's descendants becoming kings, Macbeth hires two murderers to kill Banquo and his son Fleance. The murderers kill Banquo, but Fleance escapes, which troubles Macbeth. Banquo's ghost appears at a feast the Macbeths hold for the thanes, causing Macbeth further distress.

Lennox reveals to a rebel lord that he suspects Macbeth killed Duncan. The other lord tells Lennox that Macduff has left Scotland to join forces in England with Malcolm, one of the murdered king's sons. Both Lennox and the rebel lord pray that Macbeth will receive God's vengeance and that peace will return to Scotland.

In Act Four, Macbeth pays another visit to the Weird Sisters. He asks to be shown visions of what his future holds. In the first vision, the disembodied head of a warrior warns Macbeth that he is in danger from Duncan's son Malcolm. In

---

93. **watchers:** that is, up late.

(C) **READING FOCUS**

Now that Macbeth has murdered Duncan, what **questions** can you ask about how he feels?

A **LITERARY ANALYSIS**

How do the doctor's comments on sleep compare to Macbeth's words on sleep and guilt in lines 461–471?

the second, a blood-covered child tells Macbeth he cannot be killed by any man "of woman born." In the third, a child wearing a crown and holding a tree promises Macbeth that he cannot lose in a battle until Birnam Wood physically moves toward Macbeth's fort at Dunsinane. Happy that these visions show such impossibilities, Macbeth asks whether Banquo's descendants will reign in the land. The Witches show a procession of kings all descended from Banquo. Furious, Macbeth decides to have the family of Macduff killed. His hired murderers kill Lady Macduff and her son.

In England, Macduff learns of the slaughter of his family. He agrees to join the rebel army and declares he will take personal revenge upon Macbeth.

Act V Scene 1. *Dunsinane. In the castle.*

Enter a DOCTOR *of physic and a waiting* GENTLEWOMAN.

Doctor. I have two nights watched with you, but can perceive no truth in your report. When was it she last walked?

Gentlewoman. Since his majesty went into the field, I have seen her rise from her bed, throw her nightgown upon her, unlock her closet,[94] take forth paper, fold it, write upon't, read it, afterwards seal it, and again return to bed; yet all this while in a most fast sleep.

Doctor. A great perturbation in nature, to receive at once the benefit of sleep and do the effects of watching![95] In this slumb'ry agitation, besides her walking and other actual performances,[96] what, at any time, have you heard her say? **A**

Gentlewoman. That, sir, which I will not report after her.

Doctor. You may to me, and 'tis most meet[97] you should.

94. **closet:** chest.
95. **effects of watching:** deeds of one awake.
96. **actual performances:** deeds.
97. **meet:** suitable.

© Matti Kolho/Lebrecht Music & Arts

Gentlewoman. Neither to you nor anyone, having no witness to confirm my speech. **B**

[*Enter* LADY MACBETH, *with a taper.*]

Lo you, here she comes! This is her very guise,[98] and, upon my life, fast asleep! Observe her; stand close.[99]

Doctor. How came she by that light?

Gentlewoman. Why, it stood by her. She has light by her continually. 'Tis her command.

Doctor. You see, her eyes are open.

Gentlewoman. Ay, but their sense[100] are shut.

Doctor. What is it she does now? Look, how she rubs her hands.

---

98. guise: custom.
99. close: hidden.
100. sense: powers of sight

B READING FOCUS

What **questions** do you have about this exchange between the Doctor and the Gentlewoman?

A VOCABULARY

Word Study

List a synonym, or word with a similar meaning, for *remembrance*. Use the synonym in a sentence of your own.

B LITERARY FOCUS

Lady Macbeth's sleepwalking is a result of her actions. Do you think this fits in with the plot structure of a **tragedy**? Why or why not?

Gentlewoman. It is an accustomed action with her, to seem thus washing her hands: I have known her continue in this a quarter of an hour.

Lady Macbeth. Yet here's a spot.

Doctor. Hark! she speaks. I will set down what comes from her, to satisfy[101] my remembrance the more strongly. **A**

Lady Macbeth. Out, damned spot! Out, I say! One: two: why, then 'tis time to do't. Hell is murky. Fie, my lord, fie! A soldier, and afeard? What need we fear who knows it, when none can call our pow'r to accompt?[102] Yet who would have thought the old man to have had so much blood in him?

Doctor. Do you mark that?

Lady Macbeth. The Thane of Fife had a wife. Where is she now? What, will these hands ne'er be clean? No more o' that, my lord, no more o' that! You mar all with this starting.

Doctor. Go to, go to![103] You have known what you should not.

Gentlewoman. She has spoke what she should not, I am sure of that. Heaven knows what she has known.

Lady Macbeth. Here's the smell of the blood still. All the perfumes of Arabia will not sweeten this little hand. Oh, oh, oh! **B**

Doctor. What a sigh is there! The heart is sorely charged.[104]

Gentlewoman. I would not have such a heart in my bosom for the dignity[105] of the whole body.

Doctor. Well, well, well—

Gentlewoman. Pray God it be, sir.

Doctor. This disease is beyond my practice.[106] Yet I have known those which have walked in their sleep who have died holily in their beds.

---

101. satisfy: confirm.
102. to accompt: to account.
103. Go to, go to!: an exclamation.
104. charged: burdened.
105. dignity: worth; rank.
106. practice: professional skill.

Lady Macbeth. Wash your hands; put on your nightgown; look not so pale! I tell you yet again, Banquo's buried. He cannot come out on 's[107] grave. (C)

Doctor. Even so?

Lady Macbeth. To bed, to bed! There's knocking at the gate. Come, come, come, come, give me your hand! What's done cannot be undone. To bed, to bed, to bed!

[*Exit* LADY MACBETH.]

Doctor. Will she go now to bed?

Gentlewoman. Directly.

Doctor.

Foul whisp'rings are abroad. Unnatural deeds
Do breed unnatural troubles. Infected minds
To their deaf pillows will discharge their secrets. (D)
More needs she the divine[108] than the physician.
God, God forgive us all! Look after her;
Remove from her the means of all annoyance,[109]
And still[110] keep eyes upon her. So good night.
My mind she has mated[111] and amazed my sight:
I think, but dare not speak. (E)

Gentlewoman. Good night, good doctor.

[*Exeunt.*]

WHAT HAPPENS NEXT Four lords of Scotland—Lennox, Menteth, Angus, and Caithness—agree to help Malcolm and the English forces. The rebel army has marched into Scotland and is encamped at Birnam Wood not far from Dunsinane.

Macbeth is confident when faced with the threat of invasion. He trusts the prophecies of the visions which seemed to promise him victory in battle. He dons his armor to prepare for battle.

---

107. on's: of his.
108. divine: priest.
109. annoyance: injury.
110. still: continuously.
111. mated: baffled.

(C) **QUICK CHECK**

To whom does Lady Macbeth think she is speaking?

(D) **QUICK CHECK**

What does the doctor think is wrong with Lady Macbeth?

(E) **LITERARY ANALYSIS**

What suggestions does the doctor offer for Lady Macbeth's care? Based on these suggestions, do you think the doctor knows that Lady Macbeth has committed murder? why or why not?

A LITERARY ANALYSIS

What larger lesson does Macbeth take from the death of his wife?

The English and rebel Scottish armies, led by Malcolm, meet at Birnam Wood. Malcolm orders each soldier to cut a branch and carry it front of him as camouflage so that they can hide the size of their army.

Suddenly, Macbeth and his soldiers hear women crying from within the castle.

Scene 5. *Dunsinane. Within the castle.*

Seyton.
The queen, my lord, is dead.

Macbeth.
She should[112] have died hereafter;
There would have been a time for such a word.[113]
Tomorrow, and tomorrow, and tomorrow
Creeps in this petty pace from day to day,
To the last syllable of recorded time;
And all our yesterdays have lighted fools
The way to dusty death. Out, out, brief candle!
Life's but a walking shadow, a poor player
That struts and frets his hour upon the stage
And then is heard no more. It is a tale
Told by an idiot, full of sound and fury,
Signifying nothing. A

WHAT HAPPENS NEXT A messenger tells Macbeth that he saw Birnam Wood move. In fact, Malcolm and his troops have reached Dunsinane holding branches in front of them. Birnam Wood has come to Dunsinane as the Witches predicted.

Macbeth is challenged by and then kills the bold son of Siward, claiming that no man "of woman born" can overcome him. As the alarms sound, Macduff looks for Macbeth. Malcolm and Siward enter Macbeth's castle.

---

112. should: inevitably would.
113. word: message.

© Columbia Pictures/Photofest, NY

Scene 8. *Another part of the field.*

Enter MACBETH.

Macbeth.
Why should I play the Roman fool, and die
On mine own sword? Whiles I see lives,[114] the gashes
Do better upon them.

[*Enter* MACDUFF.]

Macduff. Turn, hell-hound, turn!

Macbeth.
Of all men else I have avoided thee.
But get thee back! My soul is too much charged[115]
With blood of thine already. **B**

Macduff. I have no words:
My voice is in my sword, thou bloodier villain
Than terms can give thee out![116]

[*Fight. Alarum.*]

B QUICK CHECK

Why doesn't Macbeth want to fight Macduff?

---

114. Whiles . . . lives: so long as I see living men.
115. charged: burdened.
116. terms . . . out: words can describe you.

A LITERARY ANALYSIS

How do Macduff's words relate to the witches' prophesies (predictions) for Macbeth?

____

____

____

____

____

____

____

Macbeth. Thou losest labor:
As easy mayst thou the intrenchant[117] air
With thy keen sword impress[118] as make me bleed:
Let fall thy blade on vulnerable crests;[119]
I bear a charmèd life, which must not yield
To one of woman born.

Macduff. Despair[120] thy charm,
And let the angel[121] whom thou still hast served
Tell thee, Macduff was from his mother's womb
Untimely ripped. **A**

Macbeth.
Accursèd be that tongue that tells me so,
For it hath cowed my better part of man![122]
And be these juggling fiends no more believed,
That palter[123] with us in a double sense;
That keep the word of promise to our ear,
And break it to our hope. I'll not fight with thee.

Macduff.
Then yield thee, coward,
And live to be the show and gaze o' th' time:[124]
We'll have thee, as our rarer monsters[125] are,
Painted upon a pole,[126] and underwrit,
"Here may you see the tyrant."

Macbeth. I will not yield,
To kiss the ground before young Malcolm's feet,
And to be baited[127] with the rabble's curse.
Though Birnam Wood be come to Dunsinane,
And thou opposed, being of no woman born,

---

117. intrenchant: incapable of being cut.
118. impress: make an impression on.
119. vulnerable crests: heads that can be wounded.
120. Despair: despair of.
121. angel: that is, fallen angel; fiend.
122. better . . . man: manly spirit.
123. palter: equivocate.
124. gaze . . . time: spectacle of the age.
125. monsters: freaks.
126. Painted . . . pole: pictured on a banner set by a showman's booth.
127. baited: assailed (like a bear by dogs).

Yet I will try the last. Before my body
I throw my warlike shield. Lay on, Macduff;
And damned be him that first cries "Hold, enough!" **B**

[*Exeunt, fighting. Alarums.*]

[*Reenter fighting, and* MACBETH *slain. Exit* MACDUFF, *with* MACBETH. *Retreat and flourish.*[128] *Enter, with drum and colors,* MALCOLM, SIWARD, ROSS, THANES, *and* SOLDIERS.]

Malcolm.
I would the friends we miss were safe arrived.

Siward.
Some must go off;[129] and yet, by these I see,
So great a day as this is cheaply bought.

Malcolm.
Macduff is missing, and your noble son.

Ross.
Your son, my lord, has paid a soldier's debt:
He only lived but till he was a man;
The which no sooner had his prowess confirmed
In the unshrinking station[130] where he fought,
But like a man he died.

Siward. Then he is dead?

Ross.
Ay, and brought off the field. Your cause of sorrow
Must not be measured by his worth, for then
It hath no end. **C**

Siward. Had he his hurts before?

Ross. Ay, on the front.

Siward. Why then, God's soldier be he!
Had I as many sons as I have hairs,
I would not wish them to a fairer death:
And so his knell is knolled.

---

128. Retreat and flourish: trumpet call to withdraw, and fanfare.
129. go off: die (theatrical metaphor).
130. unshrinking station: that is, place at which he stood firmly.

B LITERARY FOCUS

In a **tragedy**, a writer often reminds the audience of the hero's better qualities before his or her unfortunate end. How does this speech show Macbeth's positive qualities?

C QUICK CHECK

What is Ross saying about Siward's son in these lines?

A READING FOCUS

What **questions** can you ask to better understand Siward's attitude toward his son's death?

B LITERARY FOCUS

What **tragic flaw** in Macbeth's character do you think contributed to his downfall? What circumstances beyond his control do you think contributed?

Malcolm. He's worth more sorrow,
And that I'll spend for him.

Siward. He's worth no more:
They say he parted well and paid his score:[131]
And so God be with him! Here comes newer comfort. **A**

[*Enter* MACDUFF, *with Macbeth's head.*] **B**

Macduff.
Hail, king! for so thou art: behold, where stands
Th' usurper's cursèd head. The time is free.[132]
I see thee compassed[133] with thy kingdom's pearl,
That speak my salutation in their minds,
Whose voices I desire aloud with mine:
Hail, King of Scotland!

All. Hail, King of Scotland!

[*Flourish.*]

Malcolm.
We shall not spend a large expense of time
Before we reckon with your several loves,[134]
And make us even with you. My thanes and kinsmen,
Henceforth be earls, the first that ever Scotland
In such an honor named. What's more to do,
Which would be planted newly with the time[135]—
As calling home our exiled friends abroad
That fled the snares of watchful tyranny,
Producing forth the cruel ministers[136]
Of this dead butcher and his fiendlike queen,
Who, as 'tis thought, by self and violent hands[137]

131. **parted . . . score:** departed well and settled his account.
132. **The time is free:** The world is liberated.
133. **compassed:** surrounded.
134. **reckon . . . loves:** reward the devotion of each of you.
135. **What's more . . . time:** what else must be done that should be newly established in this age.
136. **ministers:** agents.
137. **self . . . hands:** her own violent hands.

Took off her life—this, and what needful else
That calls upon us,[138] by the grace of Grace
We will perform in measure, time, and place:[139]
So thanks to all at once and to each one,
Whom we invite to see us crowned at Scone. (A)

[*Flourish. Exeunt omnes.*]

(A) LITERARY FOCUS

The end of the play promises a return of peace and stability to Scotland. Yet, the story is undoubtedly still a **tragedy**. Why do you think Shakespeare chose to end the tragedy on this positive note?

138. calls upon us: demands my attention.
139. in measure . . . place: fittingly, at the appropriate time and place.

Applying Your Skills

from The Tragedy of Macbeth

LITERARY FOCUS: TRAGEDY

DIRECTIONS: In the space provided, write a brief paragraph that describes Macbeth's **tragic flaw**. How does it cause his downfall?

____

____

____

____

____

____

READING FOCUS: USING QUESTIONING TO MONITOR READING

DIRECTIONS: For each passage from *The Tragedy of Macbeth* shown below, write a **question** that can help you better understand the play. Then, look back at the play and answer your question.

Lines from play	Difference	Answers
Lady Macbeth: The Thane of Fife had a wife. Where is she now? What, will these hands ne'er be clean? No more o' that, my lord, no more o' that! You mar all with this starting. (lines 555–559)	**1.**	
Macbeth: Life's but a walking shadow, a poor player/ That struts and frets his hour upon the stage/ And then is heard no more. (lines 608–610)	**2.**	

Literary Skills Understand characteristics of a tragedy.

Reading Skills Use questioning to monitor reading.

Collection 4

LANGUAGE COACH

DIRECTIONS: Many words have **multiple meanings**. You can usually figure out which meaning is intended for a word by looking at how the word is used in a sentence. Each sentence below contains an underlined word that has multiple meanings. Figure out which meaning is intended for the word in each sentence and write that definition below the sentence. Try to write a definition before looking the word up in a dictionary.

1. Peter was in an awful state after he found out that his home had been burglarized.

2. I need to season the chicken before I cook it.

3. Do you mind if I turn the volume up on the television?

4. After looking at the problem from every angle, the detective was finally able to solve the mystery.

5. Hopefully the reconstructed dam will stem the flow of the river.

6. I can't bear the thought that I may have failed my final exam.

7. She ran a few laps around the track to warm up before the competition.

8. The couple hopes to get married in the spring of next year.

9. After saving enough money, Cara opened up her own law practice.

10. Buying insurance for the house was a sound decision.

ORAL LANGUAGE ACTIVITY

DIRECTIONS: With a partner, take turns reading William Shakespeare's "Sonnet 29" aloud. Try to capture the different moods of the poem with your voice. How does your voice change as the speaker's mood changes? Ask your partner for pointers on how to better express what the speaker is feeling.

Vocabulary Review

Unit 2

DIRECTIONS: Match each vocabulary word in the first column with its correct definition in the second column. Write the letter of each definition next to the correct vocabulary word.

______	**1.** widespread	**a.** foolishness
______	**2.** transgress	**b.** undergo; bear
______	**3.** virtuous	**c.** set up; caused to happen
______	**4.** contention	**d.** forceful; violent
______	**5.** endure	**e.** sweet-smelling
______	**6.** scorn	**f.** occurring over a wide area
______	**7.** fragrant	**g.** lengthy disagreements
______	**8.** established	**h.** estimate; consider
______	**9.** folly	**i.** to make certain
______	**10.** infernal	**j.** struggle
______	**11.** embroidered	**k.** hellish; fiendish
______	**12.** controversies	**l.** producing pleasant sounds
______	**13.** impetuous	**m.** moral; righteous
______	**14.** ensure	**n.** sin against; violate a limit
______	**15.** desolation	**o.** refuse; reject by showing contempt
______	**16.** reckon	**p.** utter misery
______	**17.** melodious	**q.** ornamented with needlework or as if with needlework

Applying the Key Concepts

Unit 2

DIRECTIONS: Review the Key Concepts at the beginning of this unit. Then answer the following questions:

THE BEGINNINGS OF TUDOR RULE

- How do you think the invention of the printing press affected connections between poets, such as Christopher Marlowe ("The Passionate Shepherd to His Love") and Sir Walter Raleigh ("The Nymph's Reply to the Shepherd")?

THE PROTESTANT REFORMATION

- A nation's history can affect how people respond to literature. How might England's history have affected how people reacted to *Macbeth*?

ENGLAND'S GREATEST MONARCH

- During the Renaissance, many forms of literature flourished—poetry, drama, and religious works. Name an example of each of these forms from the selections in Unit 2. Of these selections, which did you enjoy the most? The least? Explain your answers.

Unit 3

The Restoration and the Eighteenth Century 1660–1800

© Skyscan Photolibrary/Alamy

Key Concepts

ORDER AND REASON

History of the Times England had endured civil war and the rule of Oliver Cromwell, a dictator. When England invited a new king to rule, stability returned. Fire and disease almost destroyed London in the 1660s. By the mid-1700s, the city was calm again. A new age based on science and reason, called the Enlightenment, was born.

Literature of the Times Theater reflected the life of the upper classes. Writers poked fun at the immorality and bad taste of the age. The first newspapers were published. Writers tried to mimic the order and balance found in the literature of ancient Rome.

SOCIAL CLASSES

History of the Times England had a class system, with the hereditary nobility at the top and the large mass of the poor at the bottom. Toward the end of the period, the Industrial Revolution was creating overcrowded slums and miserable working conditions.

Literature of the Times On the stage, comedies appealed to men and women of fashion. Writers still needed rich supporters, but eventually large numbers of professional writers created works for the middle classes.

VALUES AND BELIEFS

History of the Times The labels *Age of Enlightenment* and *Age of Reason* reveal how people viewed themselves. Religious views were influenced by the philosophy of rationalism.

Literature of the Times Writers used humor to expose wickedness and the love of money. Journalists also wrote about problems to bring about improvements. At the end of the period, writing became more emotional.

ACADEMIC VOCABULARY

approach (UH PROHCH) *v.:* way of addressing something. *The writer tried to approach the ridicule of society with a satirical style.*

convince (KUHN VIHNS) *v.:* persuade; cause to believe. *Writers of the 1700s tried to convince readers to correct social problems.*

dominate (DAHM UH NAYT) *v.:* hold a commanding position. *What ideas dominate the study of Enlightenment literature?*

enhance (EHN HANS) *v.:* improve the quality of. *Enhance your writing by using colorful language.*

participate (PAHR TIHS US PAYT) *v.:* take part in. *The rulers limited the rights of Catholics to participate in government.*

Collection 5

The Rise of the Novel

© Hans Georg Roth/Corbis

Preparing to Read

A Modest Proposal

by Jonathan Swift

LITERARY FOCUS: VERBAL IRONY

You use **verbal irony** whenever you say one thing but mean the opposite. Saying "thanks a lot" to someone who refuses to help you is an example of verbal irony. Your tone of voice signals to listeners that you don't really mean what you are saying. Writers use details and word choice to reveal their "tone of voice." The following essay by Jonathan Swift is a classic example of verbal irony.

READING FOCUS: RECOGNIZING PERSUASIVE TECHNIQUES

In "A Modest Proposal," Swift uses the three types of persuasive techniques listed below to convince the reader that England's treatment of the Irish is heartless and immoral.

- **Logical appeal**: the use of facts or statistics to support a position.
- **Emotional appeal**: the use of words that stir up strong feelings.
- **Ethical appeal**: the use of details that will convince readers that the writer is fair and trustworthy.

Use the Skill Use a chart like the one below to keep track of some of the persuasive techniques used in this essay. Summarize each persuasive appeal. Then, check off whether it is an example of a logical, emotional, or ethical appeal.

Example	Logical	Emotional	Ethical
In the first paragraph, the speaker describes the sad sight of crowds of beggars asking for help for themselves and their children.		√	

Literary Skills Understand verbal irony.

Reading Skills Understand persuasive techniques (logical, emotional, and ethical appeals).

Vocabulary Development

A Modest Proposal

SELECTION VOCABULARY

sustenance (SUHS TUH NUHNS) *n.:* food or provisions needed to support life.
Poor mothers beg for sustenance for their children.

prodigious (PROH DIHJ UHS) *adj.:* huge; very great.
A prodigious number of children grow up in poverty.

scrupulous (SKROO PYOO LUHS) *adj.:* extremely careful in deciding what is right or wrong.
Some scrupulous people might think that these proposals are too cruel.

censure (SEHN SHUHR) *v.:* express disapproval of.
People who censure these proposals should suggest an alternate.

expedient (EHK SPEE DEE UHNT) *n.:* way of getting something; a means for achieving an end.
An expedient has been proposed, but there is no hope of putting it into practice.

digressed (DY GREHSD) *v.:* wandered away from the subject.
I have digressed and will now return to discussing the main points of my proposal.

animosities (AN IH MAHS UH TEEZ) *n. pl.:* hostilities; violent hatreds or resentments.
If political animosities are allowed to continue, we will not find a useful solution.

WORD STUDY

DIRECTIONS: For each sentence, write "Yes" if the vocabulary word is being used correctly. Write "No" if it is being used incorrectly, and rewrite the sentence so that it is used correctly.

1. The mayor intends to *censure* the firefighters for their heroic deeds.

   ____

   ____

2. The *animosities* between the rival teams grew worse every year.

   ____

   ____

3. The *prodigious* bacteria could not be seen without a microscope.

   ____

   ____

ARY ANALYSIS

words in this h that Swift uses be a young, healthy sed on these details, n do you think out to propose to ch Ireland's starving ption?

handicraft,[12] or agriculture; we neither build houses (I mean in the country) nor cultivate land: They can very seldom pick up a livelihood by stealing until they arrive at six years old, except where they are of towardly parts,[13] although, I confess they learn the rudiments much earlier, during which time, they can however be properly looked upon only as probationers,[14] as I have been informed by a principal gentleman in the county of Cavan,[15] who protested to me, that he never knew above one or two instances under the age of six, even in a part of the kingdom so renowned for the quickest proficiency in that art.[16]

I am assured by our merchants, that a boy or girl, before twelve years old, is no saleable commodity, and even when they come to this age, they will not yield above three pounds, or three pounds and half a crown at most on the exchange, which cannot turn to account[17] either to the parents or the kingdom, the charge of nutriment and rags having been at least four times that value.

I shall now therefore humbly propose my own thoughts, which I hope will not be liable to the least objection.

I have been assured by a very knowing American[18] of my acquaintance in London, that a young healthy child well nursed is at a year old a most delicious, nourishing, and wholesome food, whether stewed, roasted, baked, or boiled, and I make no doubt that it will equally serve in a fricassee,[19] or ragout.[20] (A)

I do therefore humbly offer it to public consideration, that of the hundred and twenty thousand children, already computed, twenty thousand may be reserved for breed, whereof only one-fourth part to be males, which is more than we allow to sheep, black cattle, or swine, and my reason is that these children are

12. **handicraft:** manufacturing.
13. **of towardly parts:** exceptionally advanced or mature for their age.
14. **probationers:** apprentices.
15. **Cavan:** inland county in Ireland that is remote from Dublin.
16. **that art:** stealing.
17. **turn to account:** be profitable.
18. **American:** To Swift's readers this label would suggest a barbaric person.
19. **fricassee** (FRIHK UH SEE): stew with a light gravy.
20. **ragout** (RA GOO): highly flavored stew.

A MODEST PROPOSAL

by Jonathan Swift

For preventing the children of poor people in Ireland from being a burden to their parents or country, and for making them beneficial to the public

BACKGROUND

In the late 1720s, Ireland suffered from several years of poor harvests. Farmers had trouble paying the rents demanded by their English landlords. Many children and adults were forced to beg or starve. Most of the money collected by the landlords was sent to England; very little was spent in Ireland on locally produced goods.

Here, Swift pretends to be an economic planner who suggests a shocking solution to the problem. Watch for the sharp contrast between Swift's direct, logical style and the outrageous proposal he describes.

It is a melancholy object to those, who walk through this great town,[1] or travel in the country, when they see the streets, the roads, and cabin doors, crowded with beggars of the female sex, followed by three, four, or six children, all in rags, and importuning every passenger for an alms.[2] (A) These mothers, instead of being able to work for their honest livelihood, are forced to employ all their time in strolling, to beg sustenance for their helpless infants, who, as they grow up either turn thieves for want[3] of work, or leave their dear native country to fight for the Pretender[4] in Spain, or sell themselves to the Barbadoes.[5]

(A) QUICK CHECK

Melancholy, in line 1, means "sad." Using that knowledge, paraphrase the first sentence.

1. **this great town:** Dublin.
2. **importuning . . . alms:** asking passersby for a handout.
3. **want:** lack; need.
4. **the Pretender:** James Edward (1688–1766), son of England's last Catholic king, the deposed James II (1633–1701); James Edward kept trying to gain the English throne.
5. **sell . . . Barbadoes:** go to the West Indies and work as indentured servants.

seldom the fruits of marriage, a circumstance not much regarded by our savages; therefore one male will be sufficient to serve four females. That the remaining hundred thousand may at a year old be offered in sale to the persons of quality, and fortune, through the kingdom, always advising the mother to let them suck plentifully in the last month, so as to render them plump, and fat for a good table. A child will make two dishes at an entertainment for friends, and when the family dines alone, the fore or hind quarter will make a reasonable dish, and seasoned with a little pepper or salt will be very good boiled on the fourth day, especially in winter. **B**

I have reckoned upon a medium, that a child just born will weigh twelve pounds, and in a solar year if tolerably nursed increaseth to twenty-eight pounds.

I grant this food will be somewhat dear,[21] and therefore very proper for landlords, who, as they have already devoured[22] most of the parents, seem to have the best title to the children. **C**

Infant's flesh will be in season throughout the year, but more plentiful in March, and a little before and after, for we are told by a grave author,[23] an eminent French physician, that fish being a prolific diet, there are more children born in Roman Catholic countries about nine months after Lent, than at any other season, therefore reckoning a year after Lent, the markets will be more glutted than usual, because the number of popish[24] infants, is at least three to one in this kingdom, and therefore it will have one other collateral advantage by lessening the number of papists among us. **D**

I have already computed the charge of nursing a beggar's child (in which list I reckon all cottagers,[25] laborers, and four-fifths of the farmers) to be about two shillings per annum,[26] rags included, and I believe no gentleman would repine to give ten

---

21. **dear:** expensive.
22. **devoured:** made poor by charging high rents.
23. **grave author:** The French satirist François Rabelais. His work is comic, not "grave."
24. **popish:** derogatory term meaning "Roman Catholic."
25. **cottagers:** tenant farmers.
26. **per annum:** Latin for "by the year"; annually.

B QUICK CHECK

The speaker provides details in support of his outrageous plan. What are these details?

C LITERARY FOCUS

In this sentence, Swift uses **verbal irony** to expose a major cause of the poverty in Ireland. Re-write the sentence in your own words.

D QUICK CHECK

According to the speaker, what is a desirable effect of having a glut, or large supply, of infants on the market?

A READING FOCUS

What type of **appeal** is the speaker making in this paragraph?

B READING FOCUS

Swift is making an **emotional appeal** in this paragraph. What effect do you think he expects his word choice to have on readers?

shillings for the carcass of a good fat child, which, as I have said will make four dishes of excellent nutritive meat, when he hath only some particular friend, or his own family to dine with him. Thus the squire will learn to be a good landlord, and grow popular among his tenants, the mother will have eight shillings net profit, and be fit for work until she produceth another child. **A**

Those who are more thrifty (as I must confess the times require) may flay[27] the carcass; the skin of which, artificially[28] dressed, will make admirable gloves for ladies, and summer boots for fine gentlemen.

As to our city of Dublin, shambles[29] may be appointed for this purpose, in the most convenient parts of it, and butchers we may be assured will not be wanting, although I rather recommend buying the children alive, and dressing them hot from the knife[30], as we do roasting pigs. **B**

A very worthy person, a true lover of his country, and whose virtues I highly esteem, was lately pleased, in discoursing on this matter, to offer a refinement upon my scheme. He said, that many gentlemen of this kingdom, having of late destroyed their deer, he conceived that the want of venison might be well supplied by the bodies of young lads and maidens, not exceeding fourteen years of age, nor under twelve, so great a number of both sexes in every country being now ready to starve, for want of work and service:[31] and these to be disposed of by their parents if alive, or otherwise by their nearest relations. But with due deference to so excellent a friend, and so deserving a patriot, I cannot be altogether in his sentiments, for as to the males, my American acquaintance assured me from frequent experience, that their flesh was generally tough and lean, like that of our schoolboys, by continual exercise, and their taste disagreeable, and to fatten them would not answer the charge. Then as to the

27. **flay:** remove the skin of.
28. **artificially:** with great artifice; skillfully.
29. **shambles:** slaughterhouse.
30. **dressing them hot from the knife:** Killing the infant only moments before cooking it.
31. **service:** employment as servants.

females, it would, I think with humble submission,[32] be a loss to the public, because they soon would become breeders themselves: And besides it is not improbable that some scrupulous people might be apt to censure such a practice (although indeed very unjustly) as a little bordering upon cruelty, which, I confess, hath always been with me the strongest objection against any project, how well soever intended.

But in order to justify my friend, he confessed that this expedient was put into his head by the famous Sallmanaazor,[33] a native of the island Formosa, who came from thence to London, above twenty years ago, and in conversation told my friend, that in his country when any young person happened to be put to death, the executioner sold the carcass to persons of quality, as a prime dainty, and that, in his time, the body of a plump girl of fifteen, who was crucified for an attempt to poison the emperor, was sold to his imperial majesty's prime minister of state, and other great mandarins[34] of the court, in joints[35] from the gibbet,[36] at four hundred crowns. **C** **D** Neither indeed can I deny, that if the same use were made of several plump young girls in this town, who, without one single groat to their fortunes, cannot stir abroad without a chair,[37] and appear at the playhouse, and assemblies in foreign fineries, which they never will pay for; the kingdom would not be the worse.

Some persons of a desponding spirit are in great concern about that vast number of poor people, who are aged, diseased, or maimed, and I have been desired to employ my thoughts what course may be taken, to ease the nation of so grievous an encumbrance. But I am not in the least pain upon that matter,

---

32. **with humble submission:** with all due respect to those who hold such opinions.
33. **Sallmanaazor:** George Psalmanazar (c. 1679–1763), a Frenchman who pretended to be from Formosa, an old Portuguese name for Taiwan. His writings were fraudulent.
34. **mandarins** (MAN DAH RIHNZ): officials. The term comes from *mandarim*, the Portuguese word describing high-ranking officials in the Chinese Empire, with which the Portuguese traded.
35. **joints:** large cuts of meat, including the bone.
36. **gibbet** (JIHB IHT): gallows.
37. **chair:** sedan chair; a covered seat carried by servants.

C LITERARY FOCUS

Read footnote 33. Is Sallmanaazor a trustworthy source? Do you think Swift's inclusion of Sallmanaazor is another example of **irony**? Why or why not?

D LANGUAGE COACH

Practice saying the selection vocabulary words on this page aloud: *scrupulous*, *censure*, and *expedient*. Circle the stressed syllable in each word.

VOCABULARY

Selection Vocabulary

The Latin word origin of *digress* is *digressus*, which means "to go apart." How does the word origin of *digress* relate to the word's meaning?

because it is very well known, that they are every day dying, and rotting, by cold, and famine, and filth, and vermin,[38] as fast as can be reasonably expected. And as to the younger laborers they are now in almost as hopeful[39] a condition. They cannot get work, and consequently pine away for want of nourishment, to a degree, that if at any time they are accidentally hired to common labor, they have not strength to perform it, and thus the country and themselves are in a fair way[40] of being soon delivered from the evils to come.

I have too long digressed, and therefore shall return to my subject. (A) I think the advantages by the proposal which I have made are obvious and many as well as of the highest importance.

For first, as I have already observed, it would greatly lessen the number of papists, with whom we are yearly overrun, being the principal breeders of the nation, as well as our most dangerous enemies, and who stay at home on purpose with a design to deliver the kingdom to the Pretender, hoping to take their advantage by the absence of so many good Protestants,[41] who have chosen rather to leave their country, than stay at home, and pay tithes[42] against their conscience, to an idolatrous Episcopal curate.

Secondly, the poorer tenants will have something valuable of their own, which by law may be made liable to distress,[43] and help to pay their landlord's rent, their corn and cattle being already seized, and money a thing unknown.

Thirdly, whereas the maintenance of an hundred thousand children, from two years old, and upwards, cannot be computed at less than ten shillings apiece per annum, the nation's stock will be thereby increased fifty thousand pounds per annum, besides

38. **vermin:** pests such as lice, fleas, and bedbugs.
39. **hopeful:** actually, hopeless. Swift is using the word with intentional irony.
40. **are in a fair way:** have a good chance.
41. **good Protestants:** that is, in Swift's view, bad Protestants, because they object to the Church of Ireland's bishops and regard them as "idolatrous."
42. **tithes** (TY THZ): monetary gifts to the church equivalent to one tenth of each donor's income.
43. **liable to distress:** that is, the money from the sale of their children may be seized by their landlords.

the profit of a new dish, introduced to the tables of all gentlemen of fortune in the kingdom, who have any refinement in taste, and the money will circulate among ourselves, the goods being entirely of our own growth and manufacture.[44]

Fourthly, the constant breeders, besides the gain of eight shillings sterling per annum, by the sale of their children, will be rid of the charge of maintaining them after the first year.

Fifthly, this food would likewise bring great custom to taverns, where the vintners[45] will certainly be so prudent as to procure the best receipts[46] for dressing it to perfection, and consequently have their houses frequented by all the fine gentlemen, who justly value themselves upon their knowledge in good eating, and a skillful cook, who understands how to oblige his guests will contrive to make it as expensive as they please. **B**

Sixthly, this would be a great inducement to marriage, which all wise nations have either encouraged by rewards, or enforced by laws and penalties. It would increase the care and tenderness of mothers toward their children, when they were sure of a settlement for life to the poor babes, provided in some sort by the public to their annual profit instead of expense, we should soon see an honest emulation[47] among the married women, which of them could bring the fattest child to the market, men would become as fond of their wives, during the time of their pregnancy, as they are now of their mares in foal, their cows in calf, or sows when they are ready to farrow,[48] nor offer to beat or kick them (as is too frequent a practice) for fear of a miscarriage. **C**

Many other advantages might be enumerated. For instance, the addition of some thousand carcasses in our exportation of barreled beef. The propagation of swine's flesh, and improvement in the art of making good bacon, so much wanted among us by the great destruction of pigs, too frequent at our tables, which

44. **own growth and manufacture:** homegrown, edible children, not imported ones.
45. **vintners** (VIHNT NUHRZ): wine merchants.
46. **receipts:** archaic for "recipes."
47. **emulation** (EHM YOO LAY SHUHN): competition.
48. **farrow** (FA ROH): produce piglets.

B VOCABULARY

Word Study

Use context clues to help you write a definition for the word *procure*. Check your answer in a dictionary. Then, write a synonym for *procure*.

C VOCABULARY

Academic Vocabulary

Do any of the six "advantages" Swift lists *convince*, or persuade, you to agree with his proposal? Do you think he wants you to agree with the proposal? Explain.

A LITERARY FOCUS

Explain the **irony** in the speaker's claim to "brevity." If you do not know the meaning of *brevity*, look it up in a dictionary to help you answer the question.

B QUICK CHECK

What objection does the speaker anticipate? How does he answer the objection?

are no way comparable in taste, or magnificence to a well-grown, fat yearling child, which roasted whole will make a considerable figure at a Lord Mayor's feast, or any other public entertainment. But this, and many others I omit being studious of brevity. **A**

Supposing that one thousand families in this city, would be constant customers for infants' flesh, besides others who might have it at merry meetings, particularly weddings and christenings, I compute that Dublin would take off annually about twenty thousand carcasses, and the rest of the kingdom (where probably they will be sold somewhat cheaper) the remaining eighty thousand.

I can think of no one objection, that will possibly be raised against this proposal, unless it should be urged that the number of people will be thereby much lessened in the kingdom. This I freely own, and it was indeed one principal design in offering it to the world. I desire the reader will observe, that I calculate my remedy for this one individual kingdom of Ireland, and for no other that ever was, is, or, I think, ever can be upon earth. **B** Therefore let no man talk to me of other expedients:[49] *Of taxing our absentees*[50] *at five shillings a pound; of using neither clothes, nor household furniture, except what is of our own growth and manufacture; of utterly rejecting the materials and instruments that promote foreign luxury; of curing the expensiveness of pride, vanity, idleness, and gaming*[51] *in our women; of introducing a vein of parsimony,*[52] *prudence, and temperance; of learning to love our country, wherein we differ even from Laplanders, and the inhabitants of Topinamboo;*[53] *of quitting our animosities, and*

49. **other expedients:** At one time or another, Swift had advocated all these measures for the relief of Ireland, but they were all ignored by the government. The following section was italicized in all editions printed during Swift's lifetime to indicate that Swift made these proposals sincerely rather than ironically.
50. **absentees:** English landowners who refused to live on their Irish property.
51. **gaming:** gambling.
52. **parsimony** (PAHR SUH MOH NEE): thriftiness; economy.
53. **Topinamboo:** Swift is referring to a region of Brazil populated by native peoples collectively called the Tupinambá. Here, Swift suggests that if Brazilian peoples and Laplanders can love their seemingly inhospitable lands, the Irish should love Ireland.

factions,[54] nor act any longer like the Jews, who were murdering one another at the very moment their city[55] was taken; of being a little cautious not to sell our country and consciences for nothing; of teaching landlords to have at least one degree of mercy toward their tenants. Lastly of putting a spirit of honesty, industry, and skill into our shopkeepers, who, if a resolution could now be taken to buy only our native goods, would immediately unite to cheat and exact[56] upon us in the price, the measure, and the goodness, nor could ever yet be brought to make one fair proposal of just dealing, though often and earnestly invited to it. **C**

Therefore I repeat, let no man talk to me of these and the like expedients, till he hath at least a glimpse of hope, that there will ever be some hearty and sincere attempt to put them in practice.

But as to myself, having been wearied out for many years with offering vain, idle, visionary thoughts, and at length utterly despairing of success, I fortunately fell upon this proposal, which as it is wholly new, so it hath something solid and real, of no expense and little trouble, full in our own power, and whereby we can incur no danger in disobliging[57] England. For this kind of commodity will not bear exportation, the flesh being of too tender a consistence, to admit a long continuance in salt, although perhaps I could name a country,[58] which would be glad to eat up our whole nation without it. **D**

After all I am not so violently bent upon my own opinion, as to reject any offer, proposed by wise men, which shall be found equally innocent, cheap, easy, and effectual. But before something of that kind shall be advanced in contradiction to my scheme, and offering a better, I desire the author, or authors will be pleased maturely to consider two points. First, as things

C LITERARY FOCUS

Re-read footnote 49 on the previous page, which explains that Swift's essay is **ironic** except for this italicized passage. Why do you think Swift included this list of real solutions to the problems in Ireland?

D LITERARY ANALYSIS

What do you think Swift means when he says "I could name a country [England], which would be glad to eat up our whole nation. . ."?

---

54. factions: political groups that work against the interests of other such groups or against the main body of government.

55. their city: Jerusalem, which the Roman emperor Titus destroyed in A.D. 70 while Jewish factions fought one another.

56. exact: force payment.

57. disobliging: offending.

58. a country: England.

A QUICK CHECK

What is the first point that the speaker asks readers to consider before offering their own proposals?

© The Illustrated London News Picture Library

now stand, how they will be able to find food and raiment for a hundred thousand useless mouths and backs. **A** And secondly, there being a round million of creatures in human figure, throughout this kingdom, whose whole subsistence[59] put into a common stock would leave them in debt two millions of pounds sterling, adding those who are beggars by profession to the bulk of farmers, cottagers, and laborers, with their wives and children, who are beggars in effect; I desire those politicians, who dislike my overture, and may perhaps be so bold to attempt an answer,

59. **whole subsistence:** all their possessions.

that they will first ask the parents of these mortals, whether they would not at this day think it a great happiness to have been sold for food at a year old, in the manner I prescribe, and thereby have avoided such a perpetual scene of misfortunes, as they have since gone through, by the oppression of landlords, the impossibility of paying rent without money or trade, the want of common sustenance, with neither house nor clothes to cover them from inclemencies of weather, and the most inevitable prospect of entailing[60] the like, or great miseries, upon their breed forever. B

I profess in the sincerity of my heart that I have not the least personal interest in endeavoring to promote this necessary work, having no other motive than the public good of my country, by advancing our trade, providing for infants, relieving the poor, and giving some pleasure to the rich. I have no children, by which, I can propose to get a single penny; the youngest being nine years old, and my wife past childbearing. C

B QUICK CHECK

According to the speaker, what miseries will be eliminated for poor people if his proposal is adopted?

C READING FOCUS

Underline words and phrases in this paragraph that show how the speaker tries to win over the reader. What type of persuasive **appeal** is the speaker making here?

60. **entailing:** passing on to the next generation.

Applying Your Skills

A Modest Proposal

VOCABULARY DEVELOPMENT

DIRECTIONS: Complete the paragraph with vocabulary words from the Word Box. Some words will not be used.

Word Box

sustenance
prodigious
scrupulous
censure
expedient
digressed
animosities

Swift uses verbal irony to (1) ______________________ the way England ignores Irish poverty. He points out that Irish families are often forced to beg for their (2) ______________________. Swift pretends to offer a suitable answer to the problem, but the (3) ______________________ he suggests is shocking.

LITERARY FOCUS: VERBAL IRONY

DIRECTIONS: Swift uses **irony** to make a point about poverty in Ireland. On a separate sheet of paper, write a few sentences summarizing Swift's point.

READING FOCUS: RECOGNIZING PERSUASIVE TECHNIQUES

DIRECTIONS: The following passages from "A Modest Proposal" are examples of persuasive techniques. In the second column, write the type of **appeal** (**logical**, **emotional**, or **ethical**) that is used in each passage.

Passage	Type of persuasive technique
". . . although I rather recommend buying children alive, and dressing them hot from the knife, as we do roasting pigs." (lines 131–133)	**1.**
"I do therefore humbly offer it to public consideration, that of the hundred and twenty thousand children, already computed, twenty thousand may be reserved for breed. . . " (lines 83–85)	**2.**

Literary Skills Understand verbal irony.

Reading Skills Understand persuasive techniques (logical, emotional, and ethical appeals).

Preparing to Read

from Don Quixote

by Miguel de Cervantes

LITERARY FOCUS: PARODY

Don Quixote is a parody of the medieval tales of romantic love and heroic knights that were extremely popular in Cervantes's day. A literary **parody** imitates another work of literature for amusement or instruction. Parodies often contain exaggeration, verbal irony (saying one thing and meaning another thing), incongruity (purposefully pairing things that don't belong together, for example, a princess and a pig), and humorous imitation.

In *Don Quixote*, Cervantes makes fun of every aspect of medieval romances. Don Quixote is a poor, aging landowner who imagines himself to be a young, daring knight on a dangerous quest in honor of a lady. In reality, his armor is rusty, his horse is old, and the enemies he battles turn out to be windmills—all of which add to the story's comical effect.

READING FOCUS: DRAWING INFERENCES ABOUT CHARACTER

A **character** is an individual in a story or play. Sometimes writers tell us directly what a character is like. Other times, we must draw inferences (make educated guesses) about a character by paying attention to the character's words, appearance, actions, thoughts and feelings, and effect on other characters.

Use the Skill As you read, use a chart like the one below to note examples of the characters' words and behavior. In the second column, write down the inference you draw from each example.

Example	Inference about character
Don Quixote says, ". . . it is a great service to God to remove so accursed a breed from the face of the earth." (lines 9–10)	Quixote believes he is a servant of God on a divine mission.

Literary Skills Understand the characteristics of parody.

Reading Skills Draw inferences about characters.

Vocabulary Development

from Don Quixote

SELECTION VOCABULARY

vile (VYL) *adj.:* evil; disgusting.

Don Quixote vows to rid the world of the vile giants.

succor (SUHK UHR) *v.:* to help in time of distress.

Quixote prays that his beloved Dulcinea will succor him as he takes on the great giants.

enmity (EHN MUH TEE) *n.:* hostility.

Quixote believes that a powerful magician who bears enmity for him wants to deprive him of victory.

flaccid (FLAS IHD) *adj.:* limp; flabby.

Their water bag had gone flaccid—they would need to find water soon.

disposition (DIHS PUH ZIHSH UHN) *n.:* natural qualities of personality.

Sancho Panza claims that he has a gentle and peaceful disposition.

WORD STUDY

DIRECTIONS: Pair each vocabulary word in the first column with its synonym (word with a similar meaning) in the second column.

______ **1.** vile	**a.** hatred
______ **2.** enmity	**b.** temperament
______ **3.** flaccid	**c.** sickening
______ **4.** disposition	**d.** drooping

from DON QUIXOTE

by Miguel de Cervantes, translated by Samuel Putnam

BACKGROUND

Don Quixote is a middle-aged gentleman from the village of La Mancha. He spends all his time reading books about knights, unlike other gentlemen, who hunt and look after their property. Quixote's constant preoccupation with these tales of adventure and enchantment drive him mad, and he decides to become a knight-errant and go in search of adventure. He gets out the rusty family armor and names his old horse Rocinante. He knows that a knight-errant must have a fair lady to whom he can dedicate his dangerous battles and noble deeds, so he chooses a country girl he barely knows, Aldonza Lorenzo, and renames her Dulcinea del Toboso. Don Quixote sets out to right the world's injustices along with his squire, a poor farmer named Sancho Panza. The following excerpt from Chapter 8 of the novel tells what happens when Don Quixote and Sancho Panza catch sight of a group of windmills.

from Chapter 8

Of the good fortune which the valorous Don Quixote had in the terrifying and never-before-imagined adventure of the windmills, along with other events that deserve to be suitably recorded.

At this point they caught sight of thirty or forty windmills which were standing on the plain there, and no sooner had Don

Portrait of Miguel de Cervantes from Private Collection/Bridgeman Art Library

A QUICK CHECK

Circle the words that Don Quixote uses to describe the windmills. What does he plan to do?

B LITERARY FOCUS

Recall that a **parody** often contains verbal irony. What is ironic about what Quixote shouts at the windmills?

C LANGUAGE COACH

Vile and *vial* are **homonyms**—words with the same pronunciation but with different meanings and spellings. Write the definition of each word.

Quixote laid eyes upon them than he turned to his squire and said, "Fortune is guiding our affairs better than we could have wished; for you see there before you, friend Sancho Panza, some thirty or more lawless giants with whom I mean to do battle. **A** I shall deprive them of their lives, and with the spoils from this encounter we shall begin to enrich ourselves; for this is righteous warfare, and it is a great service to God to remove so accursed a breed from the face of the earth."

"What giants?" said Sancho Panza.

"Those that you see there," replied his master, "those with the long arms, some of which are as much as two leagues in length."

"But look, your Grace, those are not giants but windmills, and what appear to be arms are their wings which, when whirled in the breeze, cause the millstone to go."

"It is plain to be seen," said Don Quixote, "that you have had little experience in this matter of adventures. If you are afraid, go off to one side and say your prayers while I am engaging them in fierce, unequal combat."

Saying this, he gave spurs to his steed Rocinante, without paying any heed to Sancho's warning that these were truly windmills and not giants that he was riding forth to attack. Nor even when he was close upon them did he perceive what they really were, but shouted at the top of his lungs, "Do not seek to flee, cowards and vile creatures that you are, for it is but a single knight with whom you have to deal!" **B** **C**

At that moment a little wind came up and the big wings began turning.

"Though you flourish as many arms as did the giant Briareus,"[1] said Don Quixote when he perceived this, "you still shall have to answer to me."

He thereupon commended himself with all his heart to his lady Dulcinea, beseeching her to succor him in this peril; and, being well covered with his shield and with his lance at rest, he

1. **Briareus** (BRY AHR EE UHS): in Greek mythology, a giant with a hundred arms who helped Zeus overthrow the Titans.

bore down upon them at a full gallop and fell upon the first mill that stood in his way, giving a thrust at the wing, which was whirling at such a speed that his lance was broken into bits and both horse and horseman went rolling over the plain, very much battered indeed. Sancho upon his donkey came hurrying to his master's assistance as fast as he could, but when he reached the spot, the knight was unable to move, so great was the shock with which he and Rocinante had hit the ground. D

"God help us!" exclaimed Sancho, "did I not tell your Grace to look well, that those were nothing but windmills, a fact which no one could fail to see unless he had other mills of the same sort in his head?"

"Be quiet, friend Sancho," said Don Quixote. "Such are the fortunes of war, which more than any other are subject to constant change. What is more, when I come to think of it, I am sure that this must be the work of that magician Frestón, the one who robbed me of my study and my books, and who has thus changed the giants into windmills in order to deprive me of the glory of overcoming them, so great is the enmity that he bears me; but in the end his evil arts shall not prevail against this trusty sword of mine." E F

"May God's will be done," was Sancho Panza's response. And with the aid of his squire the knight was once more mounted on Rocinante, who stood there with one shoulder half out of joint. And so, speaking of the adventure that had just befallen them, they continued along the Puerto Lápice highway; for there, Don Quixote said, they could not fail to find many and varied adventures, this being a much-traveled thoroughfare. The only thing was, the knight was exceedingly downcast over the loss of his lance.

"I remember," he said to his squire, "having read of a Spanish knight by the name of Diego Pérez de Vargas, who, having broken his sword in battle, tore from an oak a heavy bough or branch and with it did such feats of valor that day, and pounded so many Moors, that he came to be known as

D LITERARY FOCUS

In this paragraph, underline details that describe Quixote's preparation for battle with the windmills. Circle details describing the outcome. What details are a **parody** of the typical medieval romance?

E READING FOCUS

What do you learn about Quixote's **character** from this explanation for his failure?

F VOCABULARY

Selection Vocabulary

Underline the context clues that can help you define *enmity*. Then write the definition below.

Machuca,[2] and he and his descendants from that day forth have been called Vargas y Machuca. I tell you this because I too, intend to provide myself with just such a bough as the one he wielded, and with it I propose to do such exploits that you shall deem yourself fortunate to have been found worthy to come with me and behold and witness things that are almost beyond belief." **A**

"God's will be done," said Sancho. "I believe everything that your Grace says; but straighten yourself up in the saddle a little, for you seem to be slipping down on one side, owing, no doubt, to the shaking up that you received in your fall." **B**

"Ah, that is the truth," replied Don Quixote, "and if I do not speak of my sufferings, it is for the reason that it is not permitted knights-errant to complain of any wound whatsoever, even though their bowels may be dropping out." **C**

"If that is the way it is," said Sancho, "I have nothing more to say; but, God knows, it would suit me better if your Grace did complain when something hurts him. I can assure you that I mean to do so, over the least little thing that ails me—that is, unless the same rule applies to squires as well."

Don Quixote laughed long and heartily over Sancho's simplicity, telling him that he might complain as much as he liked and where and when he liked, whether he had good cause or not; for he had read nothing to the contrary in the ordinances[3] of chivalry. Sancho then called his master's attention to the fact that it was time to eat. The knight replied that he himself had no need of food at the moment, but his squire might eat whenever he chose. Having been granted this permission, Sancho seated himself as best he could upon his beast, and, taking out from his saddlebags the provisions that he had stored there, he rode along leisurely behind his master, munching his victuals[4] and taking a good, hearty swig now and then at the leather flask in a manner that might well have caused the biggest-bellied tavern-

2. **Machuca** (MAH CHOO KUH): literally, "the pounder," the hero of an old ballad.
3. **ordinances** (OHRD IHN EHNS IHZ) *n. pl.:* authoritative commands.
4. **victuals:** provisions; food.

A LITERARY FOCUS

What does Quixote plan to replace his broken lance with? Circle that information. How does this detail demonstrate the use of incongruity?

B READING FOCUS

What can you infer about Sancho's **character** from what he has said so far?

C LITERARY FOCUS

Parodies often contain exaggeration. Underline the detail in this paragraph that is an example of exaggeration.

keeper of Málaga to envy him. Between drafts he gave not so much as a thought to any promise that his master might have made him, nor did he look upon it as any hardship, but rather as good sport, to go in quest of adventures however hazardous they might be. D

The short of the matter is, they spent the night under some trees, from one of which Don Quixote tore off a withered bough to serve him as a lance, placing it in the lance head from which he had removed the broken one. He did not sleep all night long for thinking of his lady Dulcinea; for this was in accordance with what he had read in his books, of men of arms in the forest or desert places who kept a wakeful vigil[5], sustained by the memory of their ladies fair. Not so with Sancho, whose stomach was full, and not with chicory water.[6] He fell into a dreamless slumber, and had not his master called him, he would not have been awakened either by the rays of the sun in his face or by the many birds who greeted the coming of the new day with their merry song.

Upon arising, he had another go at the flask, finding it somewhat more flaccid than it had been the night before, a circumstance which grieved his heart, for he could not see that they were on the way to remedying the deficiency within any very short space of time. Don Quixote did not wish any breakfast; for, as has been said, he was in the habit of nourishing himself on savorous memories. E F They then set out once more along the road to Puerto Lápice, and around three in the afternoon they came in sight of the pass that bears that name.

"There," said Don Quixote as his eyes fell upon it, "we may plunge our arms up to the elbow in what are known as adventures. But I must warn you that even though you see me in the greatest peril in the world, you are not to lay hand upon your sword to defend me, unless it be that those who attack me are rabble and men of low degree, in which case you may very well come to my aid; but if they be gentlemen, it is in no wise

5. **vigil:** staying watchfully awake.
6. **chicory water:** inexpensive coffee substitute.

D VOCABULARY

Academic Vocabulary

Underline words and phrases in this paragraph that reveal Sancho Panza's attitude toward the quest he is on with Don Quixote. Why do you think Sancho *participates*, or takes part, in Quixote's journey?

E READING FOCUS

Quixote does not eat breakfast. What can you infer about this **character's** state of mind from this detail?

 VOCABULARY

Word Study

In this sentence, *savorous* means "pleasing." Write a synonym for this word.

A **LITERARY ANALYSIS**

Do you predict Sancho will keep his promise? Explain.

permitted by the laws of chivalry that you should assist me until you yourself shall have been dubbed a knight."

"Most certainly, sir," replied Sancho, "your Grace shall be very well obeyed in this; all the more so for the reason that I myself am of a peaceful disposition and not fond of meddling in the quarrels and feuds of others. However, when it comes to protecting my own person, I shall not take account of those laws of which you speak, seeing that all laws, human and divine, permit each one to defend himself whenever he is attacked."

"I am willing to grant you that," assented Don Quixote, "but in this matter of defending me against gentlemen you must restrain your natural impulses."

"I promise you I shall do so," said Sancho. "I will observe this precept as I would the Sabbath day. . . ." **A**

Skills Practice

from Don Quixote

USE A PARODY CHART

DIRECTIONS: Re-read the **parody** to find details that poke fun at medieval romances. Then, complete this chart.

Techniques used in parodies	Details from *Don Quixote*
Exaggeration	**1.**
Incongruity (deliberately pairing things that don't belong together)	**2.**
Verbal irony (saying one thing but meaning another)	**3.**
Humorous imitation	**4.**

Applying Your Skills

from Don Quixote

VOCABULARY DEVELOPMENT

DIRECTIONS: Complete the paragraph with vocabulary words from the Word Box. Some words will not be used.

Word Box

vile
succor
enmity
flaccid
disposition

A medieval knight was expected to have a personality characterized by bravery, loyalty, and courtesy—in short, a nearly perfect (1) ____________________. When a knight saw people in danger or in need, he would offer (2) ____________________ and comfort without expecting anything in return. Though gentlemanly toward ladies, knights were capable of great (3) ____________________ toward their enemies in the heat of battle.

LITERARY FOCUS: PARODY

DIRECTIONS: Think of novels, plays, comic strips, magazines, movies, or songs that use **parody** to ridicule someone or something. Write two examples of these parodies and their targets in the chart below.

Examples of parody	Target of the parody
1.	
2.	

READING FOCUS: DRAWING INFERENCES ABOUT CHARACTER

DIRECTIONS: Draw inferences about the **characters** of Don Quixote and Sancho Panza. In the second column, describe their personalities. In the third column, give examples from the text that support your descriptions.

Literary Skills Understand the characteristics of parody.

Reading Skills Draw inferences about characters.

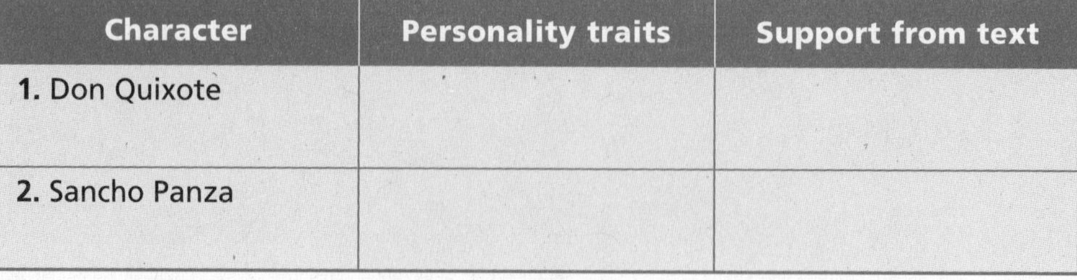

Character	Personality traits	Support from text
1. Don Quixote		
2. Sancho Panza		

Skills Review

Collection 5

LANGUAGE COACH

DIRECTIONS: Homonyms are words that sound the same but have different meanings and spellings. Look up the definitions of the following homonyms in a dictionary. Use each word correctly in a sentence of your own. For the last three exercises, list your own homonyms and write sentences for them.

1. err: ______________________________

heir: ______________________________

2. altar: ______________________________

alter: ______________________________

3. rapped: ______________________________

wrapped: ______________________________

4. cite: ______________________________

sight: ______________________________

5. wade: ______________________________

weighed: ______________________________

6. ______________________________

____

7. ______________________________

____

8. ______________________________

____

WRITING ACTIVITY

DIRECTIONS: Re-read "*from* Don Quixote." Write a few lines of dialogue between Don Quixote and Sancho Panza in which Sancho Panza refuses to go on further adventures because he believes Quixote is insane.

Collection 6

Examined Lives

Painting on the Terrace by Jules Frederic Ballavoine/Private Collection/Gemalde Mensing/The Bridgeman Art Library

from A Vindication of the Rights of Woman

by Mary Wollstonecraft

from The Education of Women

by Daniel Defoe

To the Ladies

by Mary, Lady Chudleigh

LITERARY FOCUS: TONE

Tone is the attitude a writer takes toward a topic. A tone can be angry, playful, cautious, polite, annoyed, excited, or any other attitude. One way that writers control tone is through the use of words with specific **connotations**— associations and emotions that are attached to a word. For example, *happy* and *joyous* have similar meanings, but *joyous* has a much more positive connotation.

READING FOCUS: ANALYZING RHETORICAL DEVICES

Rhetorical devices are methods writers or speakers use to make their language more persuasive. Rhetorical devices can include the following:

- **Rhetorical question:** The writer, to make a point, asks questions for which an answer is not expected. The writer assumes the audience agrees with his or her point.
- **Argument by analogy:** The writer points out a parallel between two subjects or situations in order to make a point.
- **Historical allusion:** The writer makes a reference to a person, place, or event from history that relates to the topic.
- **Repetition:** The writer emphasizes a point by restating it.
- **Appeals to authority:** The writer appeals to a higher authority, such as God or a government, to support an argument.

Literary Skills Understand how a word's connotations can affect tone.

Reading Skills Understand rhetorical devices.

Vocabulary Development

from A Vindication of the Rights of Woman, *from* The Education of Women, *and* To the Ladies

SELECTION VOCABULARY

fastidious (FAS TIHD EE UHS) *adj.:* picky; overly fussy.
The author says that men look at women with fastidious eyes.

specious (SPEE SHUHS) *adj.:* showy but false.
She says that men have fooled women with specious tributes to womanhood.

cursory (KUR SUH REE) *adj.:* hasty; superficial.
The introduction contains a cursory summary of the author's arguments.

propensity (PRUH PEHN SUH TEE) *n.:* natural inclination or tendency.
The author believes that women have developed a propensity to show their power in less-obvious ways.

manifest (MAN UH FEHST) *adj.:* evident; obvious.
To Defoe, it is manifest that the soul separates civilized people from barbarians.

vie (VY) *v.:* compete.
Men may fear that educated women will vie with them to achieve great things.

WORD STUDY

DIRECTIONS: Write "Yes" if the vocabulary word in each sentence is being used correctly. Write "No" if it is being used incorrectly, and rewrite the sentence so that the word is used correctly.

1. I *manifest* the horrible conditions in which they are forced to live. ________

____

2. The two athletes knew that they would have to *vie* with each other. ________

____

3. He spent a few minutes giving the essay a *propensity* first reading. ________

____

from A Vindication of the Rights of Woman

by Mary Wollstonecraft

BACKGROUND
Mary Wollstonecraft (1759–1797) demanded "JUSTICE for one half of the human race"—that is, women. When she wrote "A Vindication of the Rights of Woman," very few women received an education, and women didn't have the right to vote. Note that Wollstonecraft's use of the word *vindication* means "justification."

Introduction

After considering the historic page, and viewing the living world with anxious solicitude,[1] the most melancholy emotions of sorrowful indignation have depressed my spirits, and I have sighed when obliged to confess, that either nature has made a great difference between man and man, or that the civilization which has hitherto taken place in the world has been very partial.[2] **A** I have turned over various books written on the subject of education, and patiently observed the conduct of parents and the management of schools; but what has been the result?—a profound conviction that the neglected education of my fellow-creatures is the grand source of the misery I deplore; **B** and that women, in particular, are rendered weak and wretched by a variety of concurring causes, originating from one hasty conclusion. The conduct and manners of women, in fact, evidently prove that their minds are not in a healthy state; for, like the flowers which are planted in too rich a soil, strength and usefulness are sacrificed to beauty; and the flaunting leaves, after having pleased a fastidious eye, fade, disregarded on the

So far, what **tone** is Wollstonecraft using? Underline words in the text that support your answer.

B VOCABULARY

Word Study

To *deplore* is to regret or strongly disapprove of. Name a synonym, or word with similar meaning, for *deplore*.

1. **solicitude:** care; concern.
2. **partial:** biased.

A READING FOCUS

What **analogy** does Wollstonecraft use here? What point is she trying to make?

B VOCABULARY

Selection Vocabulary

Specious means "showy but false." Use the word in a sentence of your own.

Marriage á la Mode: I- The Marriage Settlement, c1743, by William Hogarth/ National Gallery, London/The Bridgeman Art Library

stalk, long before the season when they ought to have arrived at maturity. **A** —One cause of this barren blooming I attribute to a false system of education, gathered from the books written on this subject by men who, considering females rather as women than human creatures, have been more anxious to make them alluring mistresses than affectionate wives and rational mothers; and the understanding of the sex has been so bubbled[3] by this specious homage, that the civilized women of the present century, with a few exceptions, are only anxious to inspire love, when they ought to cherish a nobler ambition, and by their abilities and virtues exact[4] respect. **B**

In a treatise, therefore, on female rights and manners, the works which have been particularly written for their improvement must not be overlooked; especially when it is asserted, in direct terms, that the minds of women are enfeebled by false refinement; that the books of instruction, written by men of genius, have had the same tendency as more frivolous productions; and that, in the true style of Mahometanism,[5] they

3. **bubbled:** deluded with or distracted by flimsy evidence.
4. **exact:** demand; require.
5. **Mahometanism:** Islam, the religion of Muslims. Europeans mistakenly thought that the Koran teaches that women have no souls. In actuality, the Koran teaches that women are to be treated as equals to men.

are treated as a kind of subordinate beings, and not as a part of the human species, when improvable[6] reason is allowed to be the dignified distinction which raises men above the brute creation, and puts a natural scepter[7] in a feeble hand.

Yet, because I am a woman, I would not lead my readers to suppose that I mean violently to agitate the contested question respecting the equality or inferiority of the sex; but as the subject lies in my way, and I cannot pass it over without subjecting the main tendency of my reasoning to misconstruction,[8] I shall stop a moment to deliver, in a few words, my opinion. **C** —In the government of the physical world it is observable that the female in point of strength is, in general, inferior to the male. This is the law of nature; and it does not appear to be suspended or abrogated[9] in favor of woman. A degree of physical superiority cannot, therefore, be denied—and it is a noble prerogative![10] But not content with this natural pre-eminence, men endeavor to sink us still lower, merely to render us alluring objects for a moment; and women, intoxicated by the adoration which men, under the influence of their senses, pay them, do not seek to obtain a durable interest in their hearts, or to become the friends of the fellow creatures who find amusement in their society. **D**

I am aware of an obvious inference:—from every quarter have I heard exclamations against masculine women; but where are they to be found? **E** If by this appellation[11] men mean to inveigh[12] against their ardour in hunting, shooting, and gaming, I shall most cordially join in the cry; but if it be against the imitation of manly virtues, or, more properly speaking, the attainment of those talents and virtues, the exercise of which ennobles the human character, and which raise females in the scale of animal being, when they are comprehensively termed mankind;—all those who view them with a philosophic eye must,

6. **improvable:** capable of being improved.
7. **scepter** (SEHP TUHR): symbol of authority.
8. **misconstruction:** misunderstanding.
9. **abrogated:** abolished; repeated.
10. **prerogative:** privilege.
11. **appellation:** name.
12. **inveigh:** complain loudly.

C LITERARY FOCUS

Underline any words in this sentence that have strong **connotations** of violence or confrontation.

D LITERARY FOCUS

Do you think Wollstonecraft's **tone** is ironic when she says that she doesn't want to stir up controversy about women's equality? Why or why not?

E READING FOCUS

What **rhetorical device** is Wollstonecraft using here?

A VOCABULARY

Word Study

As it is used here, the word *faculties* means "natural abilities." The word has another common meaning. Look it up in a dictionary, and then use the word with this other meaning in a sentence.

B LITERARY FOCUS

In writings of this time period, *ladies* meant "upper-class women." How would you describe Wollstonecraft's **tone** toward these women?

C LANGUAGE COACH

Antonyms are words that mean the opposite of other words. List two antonyms of *cursory*.

I should think, wish with me, that they may every day grow more and more masculine.

This discussion naturally divides the subject. I shall first consider women in the grand light of human creatures, who, in common with men, are placed on this earth to unfold their faculties; **A** and afterwards I shall more particularly point out their peculiar designation.

I wish also to steer clear of an error which many respectable writers have fallen into; for the instruction which has hitherto been addressed to women, has rather been applicable to ladies, if the little indirect advice, that is scattered through Sandford and Merton,[13] be excepted; but, addressing my sex in a firmer tone, I pay particular attention to those in the middle class, because they appear to be in the most natural state. Perhaps the seeds of false refinement, immorality, and vanity, have ever been shed by the great. Weak, artificial beings, raised above the common wants and affections of their race, in a premature unnatural manner, undermine the very foundation of virtue, and spread corruption through the whole mass of society! As a class of mankind they have the strongest claim to pity; the education of the rich tends to render them vain and helpless, and the unfolding mind is not strengthened by the practice of those duties which dignify the human character.—They only live to amuse themselves, and by the same law which in nature invariably produces certain effects, they soon only afford barren amusement. **B**

But as I purpose[14] taking a separate view of the different ranks of society, and of the moral character of women in each, this hint is, for the present, sufficient; and I have only alluded to the subject, because it appears to me to be the very essence of an introduction to give a cursory account of the contents of the work it introduces. **C**

My own sex, I hope, will excuse me, if I treat them like rational creatures, instead of flattering their fascinating

13. **Sandford and Merton:** reference to *The History of Sandford and Merton*, a children's book. A character in the book often cites the moral superiority of a poor boy over a rich one.
14. **purpose:** intend.

graces, and viewing them as if they were in a state of perpetual childhood, unable to stand alone. I earnestly wish to point out in what true dignity and human happiness consists—I wish to persuade women to endeavor to acquire strength, both of mind and body, and to convince them that the soft phrases, susceptibility of heart, delicacy of sentiment, and refinement of taste, are almost synonymous with epithets[15] of weakness, and that those beings who are only the objects of pity and that kind of love, which has been termed its sister, will soon become objects of contempt. **D**

Dismissing then those pretty feminine phrases, which the men condescendingly use to soften our slavish dependence, and despising that weak elegancy of mind, exquisite sensibility, and sweet docility of manners, supposed to be the sexual characteristics of the weaker vessel, I wish to shew[16] that elegance is inferior to virtue, that the first object of laudable[17] ambition is to obtain a character as a human being, regardless of the distinction of sex; and that secondary views should be brought to this simple touchstone.[18] **E**

This is a rough sketch of my plan; and should I express my conviction with the energetic emotions that I feel whenever I think of the subject, the dictates of experience and reflection will be felt by some of my readers. Animated by this important object, I shall disdain to cull[19] my phrases or polish my style; —I aim at being useful, and sincerity will render me unaffected; for, wishing rather to persuade by the force of my arguments, than dazzle by the elegance of my language, I shall not waste my time in rounding periods, or in fabricating the turgid bombast[20] of artificial feelings, which, coming from the head, never reach the heart.—I shall be employed about things,

---

15. epithets (EHP UH THETS): names.
16. shew: archaic spelling of *show.*
17. laudable: praiseworthy.
18. touchstone: test or criterion; originally a stone used for testing the quality of gold and silver alloys by noting the color of the streak produced by rubbing the metals upon it.
19. cull: sort out.
20. turgid bombast: pompous rant or utterance.

D LITERARY FOCUS

How do the **connotations** of the words *soft, susceptibility,* and *delicacy* impact Wollstonecraft's **tone** in this paragraph?

E QUICK CHECK

In this paragraph, Wollstonecraft describes her goal in writing this piece. What does she hope to accomplish?

A VOCABULARY

Academic Vocabulary
How does the use of repetition *enhance*, or improve the quality of, Wollstonecraft's argument?

B READING FOCUS

What **rhetorical device** ends this paragraph? What point is Wollstonecraft making?

not words!—and, anxious to render my sex more respectable members of society, I shall try to avoid that flowery diction which has slided from essays into novels, and from novels into familiar letters and conversation.

These pretty superlatives,[21] dropping glibly from the tongue, vitiate[22] the taste, and create a kind of sickly delicacy that turns away from simple unadorned truth; and a deluge of false sentiments and overstretched feelings, stifling the natural emotions of the heart, render the domestic pleasures insipid,[23] that ought to sweeten the exercise of those severe duties, which educate a rational and immortal being for a nobler field of action. **A**

The education of women has, of late, been more attended to than formerly; yet they are still reckoned a frivolous sex, and ridiculed or pitied by the writers who endeavor by satire or instruction to improve them. It is acknowledged that they spend many of the first years of their lives in acquiring a smattering of accomplishments; meanwhile strength of body and mind are sacrificed to libertine[24] notions of beauty, to the desire of establishing themselves,—the only way women can rise in the world,—by marriage. And this desire making mere animals of them, when they marry they act as such children may be expected to act:—they dress; they paint, and nickname God's creatures. —Surely these weak beings are only fit for a seraglio![25] —Can they be expected to govern a family with judgment, or take care of the poor babes whom they bring into the world? **B**

If then it can be fairly deduced from the present conduct of the sex, from the prevalent fondness for pleasure which takes place of ambition and those nobler passions that open and enlarge the soul; that the instruction which women have hitherto

21. **superlatives:** exaggerations.
22. **vitiate:** impair; weaken; spoil.
23. **insipid:** dull; flat.
24. **libertine:** sensual.
25. **seraglio** (SUH RAL YOH, -RAHL-): a place in a Middle Eastern house where wives live; a harem.

received has only tended, with the constitution of civil society, to render them insignificant objects of desire—mere propagators[26] of fools!—if it can be proved that in aiming to accomplish them, without cultivating their understandings, they are taken out of their sphere of duties, and made ridiculous and useless when the short-lived bloom of beauty is over,* I presume that rational men will excuse me for endeavoring to persuade them to become more masculine and respectable. C

Indeed the word masculine is only a bugbear:[27] there is little reason to fear that women will acquire too much courage or fortitude; for their apparent inferiority with respect to bodily strength, must render them, in some degree, dependent on men in the various relations of life; but why should it be increased by prejudices that give a sex to virtue, and confound simple truths with sensual reveries?[28]

Women are, in fact, so much degraded by mistaken notions of female excellence, that I do not mean to add a paradox when I assert, that this artificial weakness produces a propensity to tyrannize, and gives birth to cunning, the natural opponent of strength, which leads them to play off those contemptible infantine airs that undermine esteem even whilst they excite desire. D Let men become more chaste and modest, and if women do not grow wiser in the same ratio, it will be clear that they have weaker understandings. It seems scarcely necessary to say, that I now speak of the sex in general. Many individuals have more sense than their male relatives; and, as nothing preponderates[29] where there is a constant struggle for equilibrium, without it has naturally more gravity, some women govern their husbands without degrading themselves, because intellect will always govern.

*A lively writer, I cannot recollect his name, asks what business women turned of forty have to do in the world? E

26. propagators: spreaders.
27. bugbear: anything causing needless fear.
28. reveries: musings.
29. preponderates: predominates.

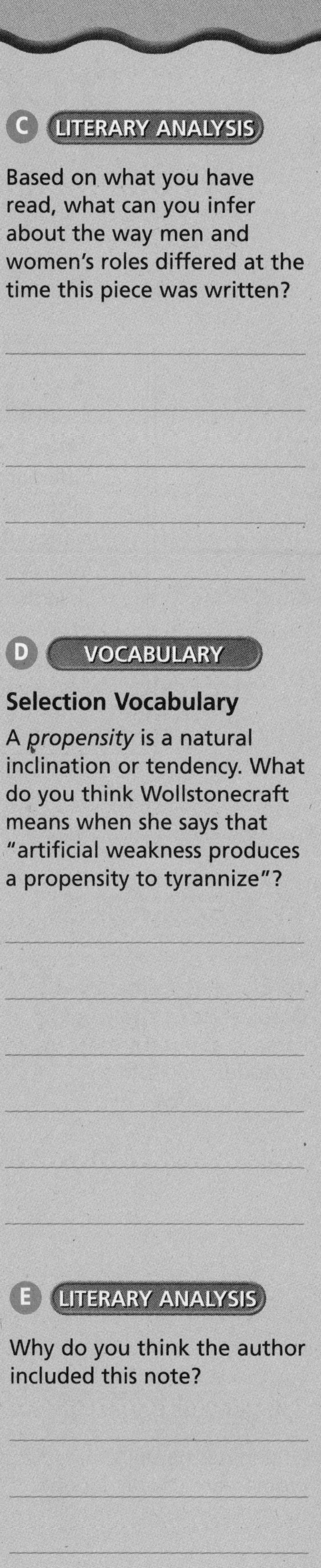

from THE EDUCATION OF WOMEN

by Daniel Defoe

BACKGROUND

Writer Daniel Defoe (1660–1731) was a businessman and a spy at different times in his life. He wrote on a variety of subjects, from how to choose a wife to the history of the devil. Despite writing on so many different topics, Defoe is mainly remembered today for his novel *Robinson Crusoe* (1719), the survival story of a shipwrecked sailor.

In the essay that follows, Defoe shares his thoughts on the education of women. In the eighteenth century, women in England were denied access to formal education. They were not allowed to own property, run a business, vote, or control their own lives or those of their children.

A LITERARY FOCUS

The word *barbarous* means "uncivilized." What does Defoe's use of this word suggest about his **tone**, or attitude, toward the education of women?

B QUICK CHECK

Underline the skills that women are usually taught.

I have often thought of it as one of the most barbarous customs in the world, considering us as a civilized and a Christian country, that we deny the advantages of learning to women. **A** We reproach the sex every day with folly and impertinence; while I am confident, had they the advantages of education equal to us, they would be guilty of less than ourselves.

One would wonder, indeed, how it should happen that women are conversible at all; since they are only beholden to natural parts, for all their knowledge. Their youth is spent to teach them to stitch and sew or make baubles. They are taught to read, indeed, and perhaps to write their names, or so; and that is the height of a woman's education. **B** And I would but ask any who slight the sex for their understanding, what is a man (a gentleman, I mean) good for, that is taught no more? I need not give instances, or examine the character of a gentleman, with a good estate, or a good family, and with tolerable parts; and examine what figure he makes for want of education.

The soul is placed in the body like a rough diamond; and must be polished, or the luster of it will never appear. And 'tis manifest, that as the rational soul distinguishes us from brutes; so education carries on the distinction, and makes some less brutish than others. **C** This is too evident to need any demonstration. But why then should women be denied the benefit of instruction? If knowledge and understanding had been useless additions to the sex, GOD Almighty would never have given them capacities; for he made nothing needless. Besides, I would ask such, What they can see in ignorance, that they should think it a necessary ornament to a woman? or how much worse is a wise woman than a fool? or what has the woman done to forfeit the privilege of being taught? Does she plague us with her pride and impertinence? Why did we not let her learn, that she might have had more wit? Shall we upbraid women with folly, when 'tis only the error of this inhuman custom, that hindered them from being made wiser? **D**

The capacities of women are supposed to be greater, and their senses quicker than those of the men; and what they might be capable of being bred to, is plain from some instances of female wit, which this age is not without. Which upbraids us with Injustice, and looks as if we denied women the advantages of education, for fear they should vie with the men in their improvements. . . . **E**

A Dame's School. 1845, by Thomas Webster/
Tate Gallery, London/Art Resource, NY

C READING FOCUS

To what does Defoe compare the human soul? What point about the value of education does Defoe make with this **analogy**?

D READING FOCUS

Underline the **rhetorical questions** in this paragraph. What answer does Defoe expect to each question?

E VOCABULARY

Selection Vocabulary

Vie means "compete." Why might men be afraid to compete with women?

A VOCABULARY

Word Study

Tongues has multiple meanings. What definition of *tongues* is used here?

B QUICK CHECK

According to this paragraph, what would be the positive effects of educating women?

C READING FOCUS

Defoe makes on **appleal to authority** in this paragraph. What is the appeal, and how does it support his argument?

[They] should be taught all sorts of breeding suitable both to their genius and quality. And in particular, Music and Dancing; which it would be cruelty to bar the sex of, because they are their darlings. But besides this, they should be taught languages, as particularly French and Italian: and I would venture the injury of giving a woman more tongues than one. **A** They should, as a particular study, be taught all the graces of speech, and all the necessary air of conversation; which our common education is so defective in, that I need not expose it. They should be brought to read books, and especially history; and so to read as to make them understand the world, and be able to know and judge of things when they hear of them.

To such whose genius would lead them to it, I would deny no sort of learning; but the chief thing, in general, is to cultivate the understandings of the sex, that they may be capable of all sorts of conversation; that their parts and judgments being improved, they may be as profitable in their conversation as they are pleasant. **B**

Women, in my observation, have little or no difference in them, but as they are or are not distinguished by education. Tempers, indeed, may in some degree influence them, but the main distinguishing part is their Breeding. . . .

The great distinguishing difference, which is seen in the world between men and women, is in their education; and this is manifested by comparing it with the difference between one man or woman, and another.

And herein it is that I take upon me to make such a bold assertion, That all the world are mistaken in their practice about women. For I cannot think that GOD Almighty ever made them so delicate, so glorious creatures; and furnished them with such charms, so agreeable and so delightful to mankind; with souls capable of the same accomplishments with men: and all, to be only Stewards of our Houses, Cooks, and Slaves. **C**

Not that I am for exalting the female government in the least: but, in short, *I would have men take women for companions, and educate them to be fit for it.* A woman of sense and breeding will scorn as much to encroach upon the prerogative of man, as a man of sense will scorn to oppress the weakness of the woman. **D** But if the women's souls were refined and improved by teaching, that word would be lost. To say, the *weakness* of the sex, as to judgment, would be nonsense; for ignorance and folly would be no more to be found among women than men.

I remember a passage, which I heard from a very fine woman. She had wit and capacity enough, an extraordinary shape and face, and a great fortune: but had been cloistered up all her time; and for fear of being stolen, had not had the liberty of being taught the common necessary knowledge of women's affairs. And when she came to converse in the world, her natural wit made her so sensible of the want of education, that she gave this short reflection on herself: "I am ashamed to talk with my very maids," says she, "for I don't know when they do right or wrong. I had more need go to school, than be married." . . . **E**

'Tis a thing will be more easily granted than remedied. . . . **F**

D QUICK CHECK

Defoe clearly states his opinion on the education of women in this paragraph. Restate his opinion in your own words.

E LITERARY ANALYSIS

What is the purpose of the anecdote (a short account of an interesting incident) told in this paragraph ?

F VOCABULARY

Academic Vocabulary

Do you think Defoe was able to *convince*, or persuade, many people of his time that women should be allowed to be formally educated? Why or why not?

The Betrothal, 1774, by Jacobus Buys/Tatton Park, Cheshire, UK/The Bridgeman Art Library

A READING FOCUS

What **rhetorical device** is being used here? What point is being made?

B QUICK CHECK

According to the speaker, how must a wife behave toward her husband?

C LITERARY FOCUS

What do you think is the **tone** of this poem? Explain.

TO THE LADIES

by Mary, Lady Chudleigh

BACKGROUND

Mary, Lady Chudleigh (1656–1710) strongly opposed the common idea of her time that wives should submit to the will of their husbands.

Wife and Servant are the same,
But only differ in the Name:
For when that fatal Knot is ty'd,
Which nothing, nothing can divide:
When she the word *obey* has said,
And Man by Law supreme has made,
Then all that's kind is laid aside,
And nothing left but State[1] and Pride:
Fierce as an Eastern Prince he grows,
And all his innate Rigor shows: **A**
Then but to look, to laugh, or speak,
Will the Nuptial Contract break.
Like Mutes she Signs alone must make,
And never any Freedom take:
But still be govern'd by a Nod,
And fear her Husband as her God:
Him still must serve, him still obey,
And nothing act, and nothing say,
But what her haughty Lord thinks fit,
Who with the Pow'r, has all the Wit. **B**
Then shun, oh! shun that wretched State,
And all the fawning Flatt'rers hate:
Value your selves, and Men despise,
You must be proud, if you'll be wise. **C**

1. **State:** ostentation; pretentiousness.

Skills Practice

from A Vindication of the Rights of Woman, *from* The Education of Women, and To the Ladies

USE A CONCEPT MAP

DIRECTIONS: Choose one of the three selections in this collection. Write its title on the line below. In the center oval, describe what you think is the **tone** of the selection you have chosen. In the surrounding ovals, give reasons why you think this is the tone of the selection. Provide examples from the text to support your answer.

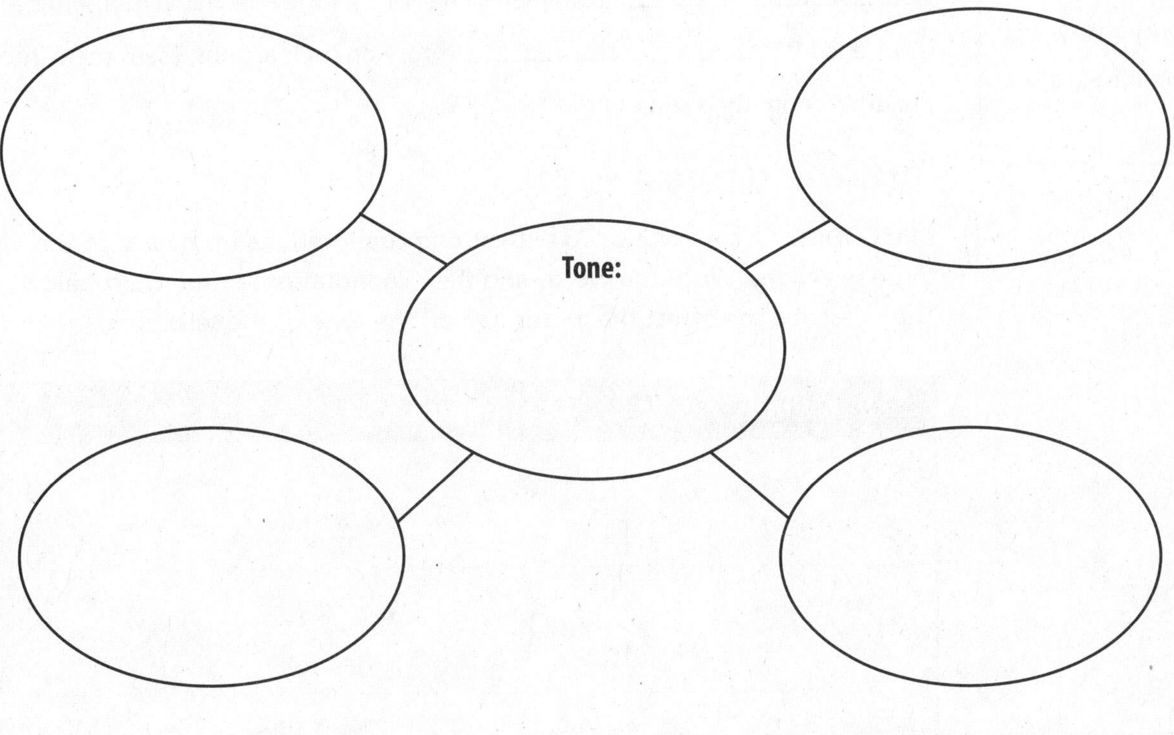

Title: ______________________________

from A Vindication of the Rights of Woman, *from* The Education of Women, *and* To the Ladies

VOCABULARY DEVELOPMENT

DIRECTIONS: Complete the paragraph with vocabulary words from the Word Box. Some of the words will be not used.

Word Box

fastidious
specious
cursory
propensity
manifest
vie

During playtime, I saw the two children (1) ______________ for the same toy. They are both normally well-behaved children, and I knew that neither has a (2) ______________ for violence. It was (3) ______________. from their behavior that they needed a nap. After a quick and (4) ______________ lecture on their actions, I sent them into the other room for a rest.

LITERARY FOCUS: TONE

DIRECTIONS: Choose one word with strong **connotations** from each of the three selections. Write the words and their connotations in the chart below. Then describe the effect the words had on the **tone** of the selection.

Word	Connotation	Effect on tone
1.		
2.		
3.		

Literary Skills Understand how a word's connotations can affect tone.

Reading Skills Analyze rhetorical devices.

READING FOCUS: ANALYZING RHETORICAL DEVICES

DIRECTIONS: On a separate sheet of paper, write two examples of **rhetorical devices** from each of the three selections, identify the type of rhetorical device, and explain how each supports the main idea of the selection.

Skills Review

Collection 6

LANGUAGE COACH

DIRECTIONS: In the right column, write one **antonym** for each of the words given. Remember that an antonym is a word that means the opposite of another word. Then, choose five more words from any of the three selections in this collection and write them in the left column. Provide an antonym for each word in the right column.

Word	Antonym
1. manifest	
2. profound	
3. knowledge	
4. tolerable	
5. haughty	
6.	
7.	
8.	
9.	
10.	

WRITING ACTIVITY

DIRECTIONS: Think of an issue with two or more points of view. The issue can be anything you have a strong opinion about. Write one paragraph about the issue in which you try to convince the reader to see your point of view. In the paragraph, use at least two of the five **rhetorical devices** you learned about—**rhetorical questions, analogies, historical allusions, repetition,** or **appeals to authority.**

Vocabulary Review

Unit 3

DIRECTIONS: Use context clues to figure out the meaning of each boldfaced word. Circle the letter of the correct answer.

1. For **sustenance**, the stranded camper picked berries and cooked fish that she caught.
   a. hiking shoes
   b. food for survival
   c. farm equipment
   d. cooking utensils
2. I want to **participate** in the singing contest, but I'm much too shy.
   a. create an atmosphere
   b. hold auditions
   c. avoid
   d. take part
3. It was **manifest** from the excellent grades on his report card that he had been studying hard.
   a. obvious
   b. choice
   c. unclear
   d. written
4. The two rivals will **vie** for the trophy at tomorrow's swim meet.
   a. hope
   b. debate
   c. allow
   d. compete
5. The **prodigious** construction project was by far the most expensive project the city had ever started.
   a. mediocre
   b. complicated
   c. huge
   d. average

Applying the Key Concepts

Unit 3

DIRECTIONS: Review the Key Concepts at the beginning of this unit. Then answer the following questions:

ORDER AND REASON

- During the period called the Enlightenment, writers appealed to reason to support their arguments. Did Mary Wollstonecraft, Daniel Defoe, and Mary, Lady Chudleigh use reason or emotion in their pleas for women's rights? Explain your answer.

SOCIAL CLASSES

- Although *Don Quixote* was originally written in Spanish, it was soon translated into English and influenced many English writers. Ever since then, *Don Quixote* has remained popular with people of different social classes. What do you think are some reasons for its lasting popularity?

VALUES AND BELIEFS

- In "A Modest Proposal," Jonathan Swift made an outrageous suggestion about what to do with Irish children. His essay is an example of satire. What do you think he was actually suggesting or stating?

Unit 4

The Romantic Period 1798–1832

Beaton Brown Fine Paintings, London/Fine Art Photographic Library, London/Art Resource, NY

Key Concepts

REVOLUTION SPREADS

History of the Times An age of revolution began in America in 1776. Revolutions then swept across western Europe, creating some of the most radical changes in human history. The violence of the French Revolution shocked Europe and spread fear that other kings and queens would also fall.

Literature of the Times Idealistic British writers who embraced the French Revolution rebelled against eighteenth-century rationalism. During the Romantic era, they created a literature based on imagination.

CONSERVATIVES CLAMP DOWN

History of the Times After the French Revolution, the English people suffered from strict government policies put in place by conservatives who feared political change. When England and its allies defeated Napoleon in 1815, many early supporters of the French Revolution felt that their own ruler was no better than Napoleon had been.

Literature of the Times Six poets led the Romantic movement: William Black, William Wordsworth, Samuel Taylor Coleridge, Lord Byron, Percy Bysshe Shelley, and John Keats. Their works are marked by idealism and emotion. Also important are an interest in nature, simplicity, and the past.

INDUSTRIALIZATION FINDS A FOOTHOLD

History of the Times England led the Industrial Revolution, when machines replaced much human labor. The business class adopted the policy of laissez faire economics. This policy let owners operate their factories without government regulation. The result was terrible abuse of the working poor.

Literature of the Times Gothic literature was popular during the Romantic era. With its eerie, supernatural style, this type of literature reflects the renewed interest in mysticism during the Romantic period.

ACADEMIC VOCABULARY

device (DIH VYS) *n.:* something made for a particular purpose. *Imagery is a common literary device in Romantic poetry.*

differentiate (DIHF UH REHN SHEE AYT) *v.:* distinguish; identify differences. *It is not difficult to differentiate between the two styles of poetry.*

function (FUNGK SHUHN) *n.:* the action for which a person or thing is specially fitted; purpose. *The poets believed that their function was to enlighten the masses.*

inherent (IHN HEHR UHNT) *adj.:* existing in something as a fixed, essential quality. *Many people now feel that abuse was inherent to unregulated economic policies.*

technique (TEHK NEEK) *n.:* method; way of using skills. *Evoking the powerful effect of nature was a popular Romantic technique.*

Collection 7

Truth and Imagination

© Pictorial Press, Ltd/Alamy

Preparing to Read

The Tyger *and* The Lamb

by William Blake

LITERARY FOCUS: SYMBOL

A **symbol** is a person, place, animal, thing, or event that stands for both itself and something more than itself. In literature, symbols have both a literal, or exact, meaning and a figurative, or metaphorical, one. The metaphorical meaning involves feelings and experiences, such as love, death, or hope.

The meanings of some symbols are well known, such as the dove as a symbol for peace. Writers may also create new symbols whose meaning can only be discovered by studying their work. As you read these poems, analyze what the tyger (tiger) and the lamb symbolize for William Blake.

Read the following sentences. In the space provided, write down the literal and symbolic meaning of the underlined word.

1. My heart goes out to them in their time of trouble.

____

____

2. Reach for the stars.

____

____

Literary Skills Understand symbols.

Reading Skills Use context clues.

READING FOCUS: USING CONTEXT CLUES

Sometimes you can figure out the meaning of a new word by looking for **clues** in the **context,** or the surrounding words. When a poet uses words symbolically, context clues can help you figure out the words' meanings. In the following poems, use context clues to uncover the meanings of Blake's symbols.

Vocabulary Development

The Tyger *and* The Lamb

SELECTION VOCABULARY

frame (FRAYM) *v.:* shape.

Blake's love and awe of nature frame his poetry.

aspire (UH SPYR) *v.:* reach upward to a goal.

His illustrated poems aspire to an understanding of human nature.

sinews (SIHN YOOZ) *n.:* powerful, tough connective tissues.

Can you see the strong sinews of the tiger in the photo?

dread (DREHD) *adj.:* inspiring fear and awe.

The dread face of the tiger terrified some viewers.

bid (BIHD) *v.:* commanded; asked.

The boy in the poem bid the gentle lamb to eat from his hand.

WORD STUDY

DIRECTIONS: Circle the letter of the correct synonym, or word with a similar meaning, for each vocabulary word.

1. aspire

a. lose

b. aim

c. create

2. bid

a. wondered

b. gave

c. ordered

3. dread

a. frightful

b. beloved

c. great

THE TYGER

by William Blake

BACKGROUND
William Blake (1757–1827) was a poet and artist. His poetry and art show his fascination with the Bible and his struggle to find answers to questions that bothered him, such as: What is the source of evil in the world? Can evil be overcome? Blake came to believe that good and evil must combat each other in order for progress to happen. He saw the world as a set of signs or symbols representing religious ideas. The symbols in his writing tend to have many different meanings.

Tyger! Tyger! burning bright
In the forests of the night,
What immortal hand or eye
Could frame thy fearful symmetry? A

In what distant deeps or skies B
Burnt the fire of thine eyes?
On what wings dare he aspire?
What the hand dare seize the fire?

And what shoulder, and what art,
Could twist the sinews of thy heart?
And when thy heart began to beat,
What dread hand? and what dread feet?

What the hammer? what the chain?
In what furnace was thy brain?
What the anvil? what dread grasp
Dare its deadly terrors clasp?

A VOCABULARY

Selection Vocabulary

To *frame* is to "shape." What do you think "frame thy fearful symmetry" means?

B LANGUAGE COACH

As a noun, *deep* has multiple meanings. What meaning do you think is used here?

A LITERARY ANALYSIS

The prefix *im–* means "not." Knowing this, what do you think *immortal* means? What is Blake saying about the origin of the tiger?

B READING FOCUS

Underline the **context clues** on this page that hint that this tiger stands for something beyond itself.

C LITERARY FOCUS

What is one thing you think the tiger is a **symbol** for? Explain your answer.

© Randy Wells/Corbis

When the stars threw down their spears,[1]
And watered heaven with their tears,
Did he smile his work to see?
Did he who made the Lamb make thee?

Tyger! Tyger! burning bright
In the forests of the night,
What immortal hand or eye, **A**
Dare frame thy fearful symmetry? **B** **C**

1. **stars . . . spears:** reference to the angels who fell with Satan and threw down their spears after losing the war in heaven.

THE LAMB

by William Blake

© Moodboard/Corbis

Little Lamb, who made thee?
Dost thou know who made thee?
Gave thee life, and bid thee feed
By the stream and o'er the mead,[1]
Gave thee clothing of delight,
Softest clothing, wooly, bright;
Gave thee such a tender voice,
Making all the vales[2] rejoice?
Little Lamb, who made thee?
Dost thou know who made thee?

Little Lamb, I'll tell thee,
Little Lamb, I'll tell thee:
He[3] is called by thy name,
For He calls himself a Lamb.
He is meek, and he is mild; (A)
He became a little child.
I a child, and thou a lamb,
We are called by his name.
Little Lamb, God bless thee!
Little Lamb, God bless thee! (B) (C)

1. **mead:** meadow.
2. **vales:** valleys.
3. **He:** Christ.

(A) READING FOCUS

What **context clues** in the poem support the definition of *He* given in the footnotes?

(B) LITERARY FOCUS

Underline the sections of the second stanza where Blake makes clear what the lamb is a **symbol** for.

(C) VOCABULARY

Academic Vocabulary
Differentiate, or identify the differences, between the tyger in the previous poem and the lamb here.

Applying Your Skills

The Tyger *and* The Lamb

VOCABULARY DEVELOPMENT

DIRECTIONS: Write the letter of each definition next to the correct vocabulary word.

_____ **1.** frame	**a.** inspiring fear
_____ **2.** aspire	**b.** connective tissues
_____ **3.** sinews	**c.** reach for a goal
_____ **4.** dread	**d.** command
_____ **5.** bid	**e.** shape

LITERARY FOCUS: SYMBOL

DIRECTIONS: In the space provided, describe what you think the tiger and the lamb are **symbols** of. Each may have more than one symbolic meaning.

1. Tiger ____

____

2. Lamb ____

____

READING FOCUS: USING CONTEXT CLUES

DIRECTIONS: In the chart below, list some of the **context clues** that helped you decide what the tiger and the lamb are symbols of.

The Tiger	The Lamb
1.	4.
2.	5.
3.	6.

Literary Skills Understand symbols.

Reading Skills Use context clues.

Preparing to Read

Lines Composed a Few Miles Above Tintern Abbey

by William Wordsworth

LITERARY FOCUS: BLANK VERSE

Blank verse is a natural-sounding, flowing style of poetry that echoes the rhythms of everyday speech. The lines do not rhyme, and each line contains five iambs. An **iamb** is a unit that consists of an unstressed syllable followed by a stressed syllable, as in the word *today*. A poet may vary this pattern slightly to draw attention to an idea or an image.

READING FOCUS: ANALYZING PATTERNS OF ORGANIZATION

Poets use different methods to organize their verse. Common **organizational patterns** in poetry include **meter**, a generally regular pattern of stressed and unstressed syllables, and **rhyme**.

Wordsworth organizes his poem into **stanzas**, or groups of consecutive lines that form units. He splits some lines and indents the second part of each line to signal the beginning of a new stanza. If you skim this poem, you can easily spot these stanza breaks; they fall in lines 22, 49, and 111. A stanza break that does not follow this pattern occurs at line 58, where the line is only indented, not split.

Within each stanza, Wordsworth repeats key words or details in order to call attention to an idea. For example: In stanza one (lines 1–22), the repetition of the word *again* in lines 4, 9, and 14 places emphasis on the idea of the passage of time.

Literary Skills Understand blank verse.

Reading Skills Analyze patterns of organization.

Lines Composed a Few Miles Above Tintern Abbey

SELECTION VOCABULARY

pastoral (PAS TUHR UHL) *adj.:* of simple or peaceful rural life.
The visit to the Wye Valley offered pastoral views of cottages and farms.

sublime (SUH BLYM) *adj.:* awe inspiring due to magesty or nobility.
He saw a sublime vision when he journeyed to the beautiful Wye Valley.

corporeal (KAWR PAWR EE UHL) *adj.:* of the body.
While our corporeal existence will someday end, Wordsworth believed that we will continue to exist in spirit.

recompense (REHK UHM PEHNS) *n.:* payment or compensation in return for something lost.
The wisdom of experience is ample recompense for the loss of the pleasures of youth.

impels (IHM PEHLZ) *v.:* forces; causes to move.
While visiting the Wye Valley, the speaker feels a presence that impels all things.

zeal (ZEEL) *n.:* eager enthusiasm.
They will remember with zeal the happy experience that they shared together.

WORD STUDY

DIRECTIONS: Write the vocabulary words from the list above next to their correct synonyms (words with a similar meaning).

1. ______________________ inspirational
2. ______________________ physical
3. ______________________ push
4. ______________________ rustic
5. ______________________ compensation
6. ______________________ energy

Lines Composed a Few Miles Above Tintern Abbey

On Revisiting the Banks of the Wye During a Tour. July 13, 1798

by William Wordsworth

BACKGROUND
Tintern Abbey, mentioned in the poem's title, refers to the ruins of an abbey, or church building. The poem records Wordsworth's reflections after he and his sister, Dorothy, took a vigorous walking tour in southern Wales. Wordsworth wrote the poem in his head over the period of four to five days as he and his sister left the area near Tintern Abbey to walk to Bristol. The poem was published almost immediately after Wordsworth wrote it down on paper.

Five years have past; five summers, with the length
Of five long winters! and again I hear
These waters, rolling from their mountain springs
With a soft inland murmur.—Once again
Do I behold these steep and lofty cliffs,
That on a wild secluded scene impress
Thoughts of more deep seclusion; and connect
The landscape with the quiet of the sky.
The day is come when I again repose
Here, under this dark sycamore, and view
These plots of cottage ground, these orchard tufts,
Which at this season, with their unripe fruits,
Are clad in one green hue, and lose themselves
'Mid groves and copses.[1] Once again I see **A** **B**
These hedgerows,[2] hardly hedgerows, little lines

A LITERARY FOCUS

How do the first 14 lines show that this poem is written in **blank verse**?

B QUICK CHECK

Underline key words on this page that tell what the speaker hears, and circle key words that show what he sees.

1. **copses:** areas densely covered with shrubs and small trees.
2. **hedgerows:** rows of bushes, shrubs, and small trees that serve as fences.

A VOCABULARY

Selection Vocabulary

Pastoral means "of simple or peaceful rural life." If you did not know the meaning of this word, what clues from the text could help you figure out its meaning? Circle these clues.

B LANGUAGE COACH

The suffix *–al* can mean "of" or "relating to." Something that is *corporeal* relates to the body. What do you think something that is *nocturnal* relates to?

C VOCABULARY

Word Study

Frame has multiple meanings. Knowing the meaning of *corporeal,* which definition of *frame* do you think is meant here? Use a dictionary if you need help.

Of sportive wood run wild: these pastoral farms, (A)
Green to the very door; and wreaths of smoke
Sent up, in silence, from among the trees!
With some uncertain notice, as might seem
Of vagrant dwellers in the houseless woods,
Or of some Hermit's cave, where by his fire
The Hermit sits alone.
These beauteous forms,
Through a long absence, have not been to me
As is a landscape to a blind man's eye:
But oft, in lonely rooms, and 'mid the din
Of towns and cities, I have owed to them
In hours of weariness, sensations sweet,
Felt in the blood, and felt along the heart;
And passing even into my purer mind,
With tranquil restoration:—feelings too
Of unremembered pleasure: such, perhaps,
As have no slight or trivial influence
On that best portion of a good man's life,
His little, nameless, unremembered acts
Of kindness and of love. Nor less, I trust,
To them I may have owed another gift,
Of aspect more sublime; that blessed mood,
In which the burden of the mystery,
In which the heavy and the weary weight
Of all this unintelligible world,
Is lightened:—that serene and blessed mood,
In which the affections[3] gently lead us on,—
Until, the breath of this corporeal frame (B) (C)
And even the motion of our human blood
Almost suspended, we are laid asleep
In body, and become a living soul:
While with an eye made quiet by the power

3. **affections:** feelings.

Of harmony, and the deep power of joy,
We see into the life of things. **D**
If this
Be but a vain belief, yet, oh! how oft—
In darkness and amid the many shapes
Of joyless daylight; when the fretful stir
Unprofitable, and the fever of the world,
Have hung upon the beatings of my heart—
How oft, in spirit, have I turned to thee,
O sylvan[4] Wye! thou wanderer through the woods,
How often has my spirit turned to thee! **E**

And now, with gleams of half-extinguished thought,
With many recognitions dim and faint,
And somewhat of a sad perplexity,
The picture of the mind[5] revives again:
While here I stand, not only with the sense
Of present pleasure, but with pleasing thoughts
That in this moment there is life and food
For future years. And so I dare to hope,
Though changed, no doubt, from what I was when first
I came among these hills; when like a roe[6]
I bounded o'er the mountains, by the sides
Of the deep rivers, and the lonely streams,
Wherever nature led: more like a man
Flying from something that he dreads, than one
Who sought the thing he loved. For nature then
(The coarser pleasures of my boyish days,
And their glad animal movements all gone by)
To me was all in all.—I cannot paint **F**
What then I was. The sounding cataract[7]
Haunted me like a passion: the tall rock,
The mountain, and the deep and gloomy wood,

---

4. **sylvan:** associated with the forest or woodlands.
5. **picture of the mind:** primarily the picture in the mind, but also the picture the individual mind has of itself.
6. **roe:** deer.
7. **cataract:** waterfall.

D READING FOCUS

What visual clue signals that a new **stanza** is beginning in line 49? Read to the end of line 57. How does the speaker's tone change in the next stanza?

E LITERARY ANALYSIS

The speaker talks directly to an element of nature in lines 49–57. Who—or what—is the "wanderer through the woods" (line 56) that the speaker addresses?

F QUICK CHECK

The speaker recalls his youth. At that time, what was it that he loved about nature?

A QUICK CHECK

Circle two things from the past that the speaker says are gone now. Restate in your own words how the speaker feels about this loss.

B VOCABULARY

Selection Vocabulary

Impels means "forces; causes to move." What is it that the speaker says "impels/All thinking things"?

C LITERARY FOCUS

Read lines 85–102 aloud, using the punctuation as a guide. Read the passage several times until you feel you have captured the natural rhythm of the **blank verse**.

Their colors and their forms, were then to me
An appetite; a feeling and a love,
That had no need of a remoter charm,[8]
By thought supplied, nor any interest
Unborrowed from the eye.—That time is past,
And all its aching joys are now no more.
And all its dizzy raptures. Not for this
Faint[9] I, nor mourn nor murmur; other gifts
Have followed; for such loss, I would believe,
Abundant recompense. **A** For I have learned
To look on nature, not as in the hour
Of thoughtless youth; but hearing oftentimes
The still, sad music of humanity,
Nor harsh nor grating, though of ample power
To chasten and subdue. And I have felt
A presence that disturbs me with the joy
Of elevated thoughts; a sense sublime
Of something far more deeply interfused,
Whose dwelling is the light of setting suns,
And the round ocean and the living air,
And the blue sky, and in the mind of man:
A motion and a spirit, that impels
All thinking things, all objects of all thought,
And rolls through all things. **B** **C** Therefore am I still
A lover of the meadows and the woods,
And mountains; and of all that we behold
From this green earth; of all the mighty world
Of eye, and ear—both what they half create,
And what perceive; well pleased to recognize
In nature and the language of the sense
The anchor of my purest thoughts, the nurse,
The guide, the guardian of my heart, and soul
Of all my moral being.
                    Nor perchance,

---

8. **remoter charm:** appeal other than the scene itself.
9. **faint:** become weak; lose heart.

If I were not thus taught, should I the more
Suffer[10] my genial[11] spirits to decay:
For thou art with me here upon the banks
Of this fair river; thou my dearest Friend,[12]
My dear, dear Friend; and in thy voice I catch
The language of my former heart, and read
My former pleasures in the shooting lights
Of thy wild eyes. Oh! yet a little while
May I behold in thee what I was once,
My dear, dear Sister! and this prayer I make, **D** **E**
Knowing that Nature never did betray
The heart that loved her; 'tis her privilege,
Through all the years of this our life, to lead
From joy to joy: for she can so inform
The mind that is within us, so impress
With quietness and beauty, and so feed
With lofty thoughts, that neither evil tongues,
Rash judgments, nor the sneers of selfish men,
Nor greetings where no kindness is, nor all
The dreary intercourse[13] of daily life,
Shall e'er prevail against us, or disturb
Our cheerful faith, that all which we behold
Is full of blessings. Therefore let the moon
Shine on thee in thy solitary walk;
And let the misty mountain winds be free
To blow against thee: and, in after years,
When these wild ecstasies shall be matured
Into a sober pleasure; when thy mind
Shall be a mansion for all lovely forms,
Thy memory be as a dwelling place
For all sweet sounds and harmonies; **F** oh! then,
If solitude, or fear, or pain, or grief,
Should be thy portion, with what healing thoughts

10. **suffer:** allow.
11. **genial:** creative.
12. **my dearest Friend:** Wordsworth's sister, Dorothy.
13. **intercourse:** dealings; social contacts.

D READING FOCUS

Re-read lines 111–121. How does the speaker's focus shift in this **stanza**?

E QUICK CHECK

The speaker compares his sister to how he once was. How is she similar?

F QUICK CHECK

The speaker offers a prayer for his sister. Underline the blessings he asks nature to bestow upon her.

 VOCABULARY

Selection Vocabulary

Zeal means "eager enthusiasm." For what does the speaker feel zeal?

 QUICK CHECK

What things does the speaker want his sister to always remember, even after the speaker has died?

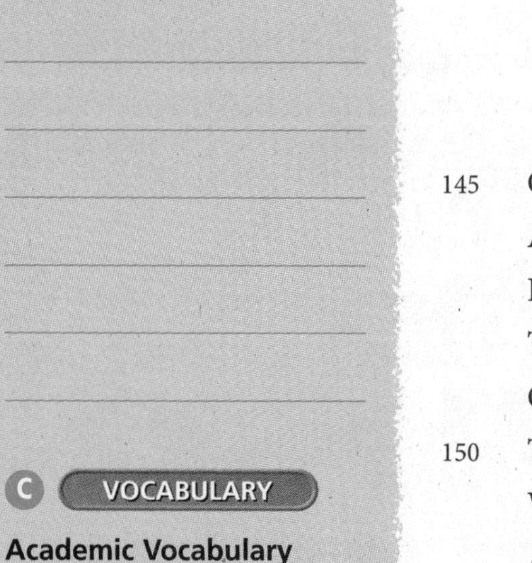

C VOCABULARY

Academic Vocabulary

Did you find the blank verse *technique*, or method, difficult to read? Why or why not?

Neil Setchfield/Alamy

Of tender joy wilt thou remember me,
And these my exhortations![14] Nor, perchance—
If I should be where I no more can hear
Thy voice, nor catch from thy wild eyes these gleams
Of past existence—wilt thou then forget
That on the banks of this delightful stream
We stood together; and that I, so long
A worshipper of Nature, hither came
Unwearied in that service: rather say
With warmer love—oh! with far deeper zeal
Of holier love. A Nor wilt thou then forget
That after many wanderings, many years
Of absence, these steep woods and lofty cliffs,
And this green pastoral landscape, were to me
More dear, both for themselves and for thy sake! B C

14. exhortations: strong advice.

Lines Composed a Few Miles Above Tintern Abbey

USE A RESTATEMENT CHART

DIRECTIONS: Choose the **stanza** in "Lines Composed a Few Miles Above Tintern Abbey" that you had the most difficulty understanding. In the rectangle below, write the line numbers of this stanza. Then, in the bottom oval, restate the stanza in your own words.

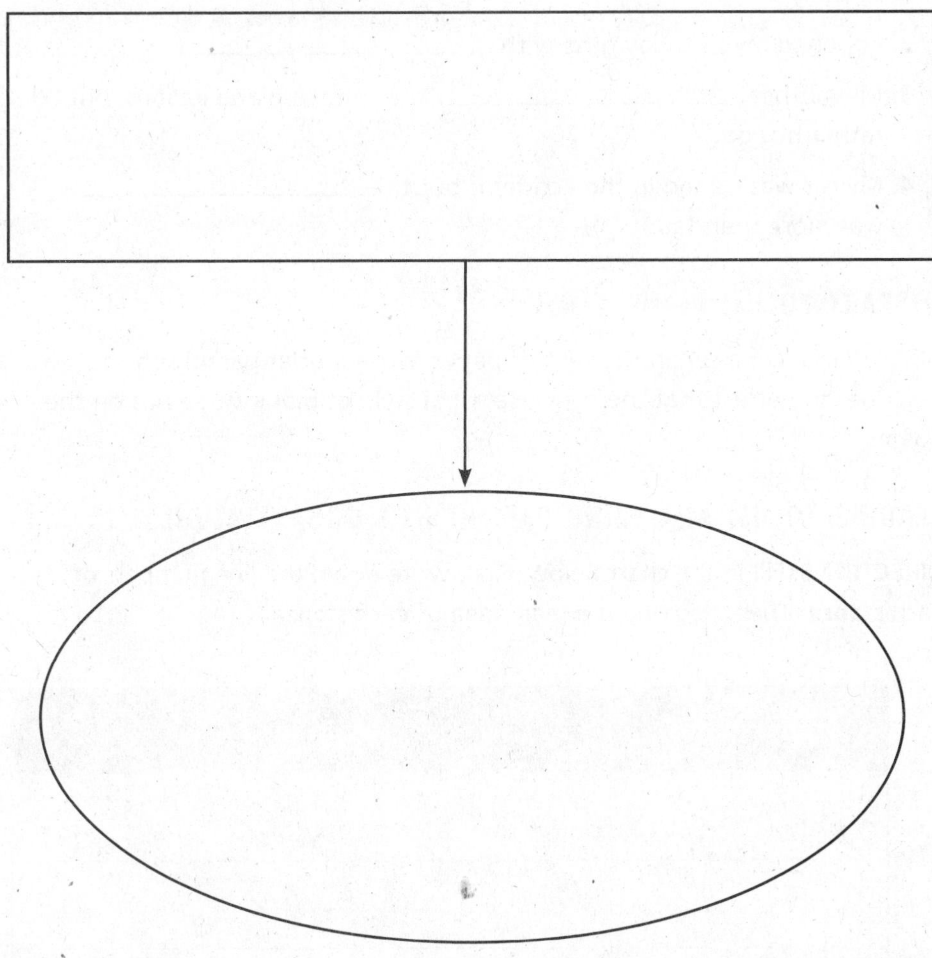

Applying Your Skills

Lines Composed a Few Miles Above Tintern Abbey

VOCABULARY DEVELOPMENT

DIRECTIONS: To complete each sentence, fill in the blanks with the correct vocabulary words from the Word Box. Some words will not be used.

Word Box
pastoral
sublime
corporeal
recompense
impels
zeal

1. We had a ____________________ view of the mountaintop from our balcony.
2. I opened my birthday gifts with ____________________.
3. My mother ____________________ me to take piano lessons, but I'd rather not go.
4. My car was ruined in the accident, but the ____________________ was more than fair.

LITERARY FOCUS: BLANK VERSE

DIRECTIONS: On a separate sheet of paper, write a brief paragraph that describes the effect that the conversational style of **blank verse** has on the poem.

READING FOCUS: ANALYZING PATTERNS OF ORGANIZATION

DIRECTIONS: Fill in the chart below. First, write down the line numbers of each **stanza**. Then, describe the main idea of each stanza.

Stanza (lines)	Main Idea
1.	2.
3.	4.
5.	6.
7.	8.
9.	10.

Literary Skills Understand blank verse.

Reading Skills Analyze patterns of organization.

Preparing to Read

Kubla Khan

by Samuel Taylor Coleridge

LITERARY FOCUS: ALLITERATION

Alliteration is the repetition of consonant sounds in words that are near each other. It occurs most often at the beginnings of words, but it can also happen in the middle or at the end of words. For example, the sound repeated in "*c*a*ck*ling *ch*i*ck*ens" is the *k* sound. This technique creates musical effects in a poem and makes certain lines easy to remember.

In "Kubla Khan," Coleridge uses alliteration to create a mood of enchantment, establish **rhythm**, and emphasize images or ideas. Alliteration can also suggest movement, as in line 25: "Five miles meandering with a mazy motion." The repeated *m* sound evokes the flow of a river.

Think of examples of alliteration. They could be tongue twisters, the names of cartoon characters, the lyrics of a song, a nursery rhyme, or some examples you create. Write your examples below, and then circle the sounds that are repeated.

Examples of alliteration
1.
2.

Literary Skills Understand alliteration.

Reading Skills Interpret imagery.

READING FOCUS: INTERPRETING IMAGERY

Imagery is language that appeals to the senses (sight, hearing, taste, touch, smell). The phrase "caverns measureless to man" (line 4 in "Kubla Khan"), for example, brings forth a powerful visual image. In this poem, you will encounter vivid images that help you imagine what is being described.

Vocabulary Development

Kubla Khan

SELECTION VOCABULARY

girdled (GUR DUHLD) *v.* used as *adj.:* enclosed or circled around.

The girdled garden had walls and towers on its perimeter.

sinuous (SIHN YOO UHS) *adj.:* winding; twisting.

Sinuous streams ran like snakes through Kubla Khan's gardens.

turmoil (TUR MOYL) *n.:* a state of agitation or commotion.

The water churning over the rocks in the valley was in constant turmoil.

meandering (MEE AN DUHR IHNG) *v.* used as *adj.:* wandering with no clear direction.

Coleridge describes a meandering river in a mystical forest.

WORD STUDY

DIRECTIONS: Write the vocabulary words from the list above next to their correct antonyms (words with the opposite meaning).

1. ______________________ peace
2. ______________________ focusing
3. ______________________ open
4. ______________________ straight

KUBLA KHAN

by Samuel Taylor Coleridge

BACKGROUND

The historical Kubla Khan (c. 1216–1294) was the Mongol conqueror of China and grandson of the famous Genghis Khan. The poem resembles a dream. Images in the poem collide and overlap as they do in dreams, and the story is interrupted before it reaches a real conclusion.

In Xanadu did Kubla Khan
A stately pleasure-dome decree:
Where Alph,[1] the sacred river, ran
Through caverns measureless to man
Down to a sunless sea.
So twice five miles of fertile ground
With walls and towers were girdled round: (A)
And there were gardens bright with sinuous rills,
Where blossomed many an incense-bearing tree;
And here were forests ancient as the hills,
Enfolding sunny spots of greenery. (B)

But oh! that deep romantic chasm which slanted
Down the green hill athwart a cedarn cover![2]
A savage place! as holy and enchanted
As e'er beneath a waning moon was haunted
By woman wailing for her demon-lover!
And from this chasm, with ceaseless turmoil seething,
As if this earth in fast thick pants were breathing,

1. **Alph:** probably a reference to the Greek river Alpheus, which flows into the Ionian Sea, and whose waters are fabled to rise up again in Sicily.
2. **athwart a cedarn cover:** crossing diagonally under a covering growth of cedar trees.

A LANGUAGE COACH

Girdled means "enclosed or circled around." Other forms of this verb include *girdle*, *girdles*, and *girdling*. Use one of these other forms in a sentence of your own.

B READING FOCUS

Underline the visual **imagery** the speaker uses to describe the setting. What effect do these images create?

A VOCABULARY

Selection Vocabulary

Turmoil (line 17) means "a state of agitation or commotion." In the poem, what is in turmoil?

B LITERARY FOCUS

Lines 25–28 contain examples of **alliteration**. Circle the letters that make the alliterative sounds.

C READING FOCUS

Underline **imagery** on this page that appeals to the sense of hearing. What sounds are being described?

© The Granger Collection, NY

A mighty fountain momently[3] was forced: **A**
Amid whose swift half-intermitted burst
Huge fragments vaulted like rebounding hail,
Or chaffy grain beneath the thresher's flail:[4]
And 'mid these dancing rocks at once and ever
It flung up momently the sacred river.
Five miles meandering with a mazy[5] motion
Through wood and dale the sacred river ran,
Then reached the caverns measureless to man,
And sank in tumult to a lifeless ocean: **B**
And 'mid this tumult Kubla heard from far
Ancestral voices prophesying war!
The shadow of the dome of pleasure
Floated midway on the waves;
Where was heard the mingled measure[6]
From the fountain and the caves. **C**
It was a miracle of rare device,
A sunny pleasure-dome with caves of ice!
A damsel with a dulcimer[7]

---

3. **momently:** at each moment.
4. **thresher's flail:** heavy, whiplike tool used to thresh, or beat, grain in order to separate the kernels from their chaff, or husks.
5. **mazy:** like a maze; having many turns.
6. **measure:** rhythmic sound.
7. **dulcimer:** musical instrument that is often played by striking the strings with small hammers.

Bibliothéque Nationalę de France, Paris.

In a vision once I saw:
It was an Abyssinian[8] maid,
And on her dulcimer she played,
Singing of Mount Abora.[9]
Could I revive within me
Her symphony and song,
To such a deep delight 'twould win me,
That with music loud and long,
I would build that dome in air,
That sunny dome! those caves of ice! **D**
And all who heard should see them there,
And all should cry, Beware! Beware!
His flashing eyes, his floating hair!
Weave a circle round him thrice,
And close your eyes with holy dread, **E**
For he on honeydew hath fed,
And drunk the milk of Paradise. **F**

8. **Abyssinian:** Ethiopian. Ethiopia is in northeast Africa.
9. **Mount Abora:** probably a reference to John Milton's (1608–1674) *Paradise Lost*, in which Mount Amara, in Ethiopia, is a mythical, earthly paradise.

D LITERARY ANALYSIS

Underline whom the speaker sees in his vision. What connection does he make between his memory of her and his dream-vision of the pleasure dome?

E VOCABULARY

Word Study

Dread means "great fear." What is a synonym (word with a similar meaning) that you could use in place of *dread*? Does the synonym have the same effect as *dread*? Why or why not?

F VOCABULARY

Academic Vocabulary

What is the *function*, or purpose, of the use of alliteration and imagery in this poem?

Applying Your Skills

Kubla Khan

VOCABULARY DEVELOPMENT

DIRECTIONS: Fill in the blanks with the correct vocabulary words from the Word Box.

Word Box

girdled
sinuous
turmoil
meandering

1. The ____________________ puppy was found walking in the forest.
2. Losing the schedule created an atmosphere of ____________________ in the office.
3. The ____________________ garbage cans were protected by a fence to keep raccoons away.
4. The ____________________ road was difficult to drive on during the storm.

LITERARY FOCUS: ALLITERATION

DIRECTIONS: Write four examples of **alliteration** from "Kubla Khan." Circle the sounds that are repeated.

1. ____
2. ____
3. ____
4. ____

READING FOCUS: INTERPRETING IMAGERY

DIRECTIONS: List four examples of visual **imagery** from "Kubla Khan."

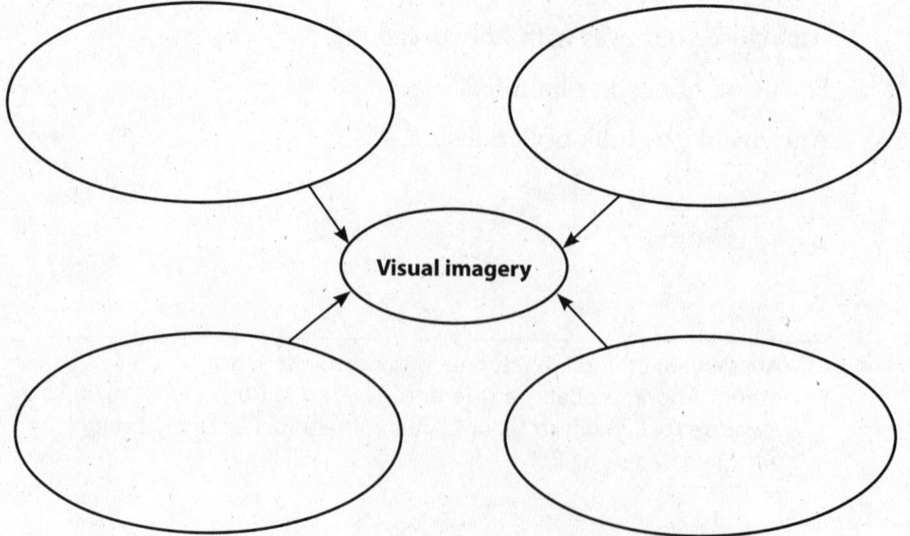

Literary Skills Understand alliteration.

Reading Skills Interpret imagery.

Preparing to Read

The Rime of the Ancient Mariner

by Samuel Taylor Coleridge

LITERARY FOCUS: LITERARY BALLAD

A **ballad** is a song or poem that tells a story. Coleridge's **literary ballad** imitates a traditional **folk ballad** in content and form. Both types of ballad blend real events with supernatural ones, use simple language and repetition, and have strong patterns of rhythm and rhyme. However, folk ballads are meant to be sung, and literary ballads are meant to be read. To add variety, Coleridge changes the meter and rhyme scheme throughout the poem. He also uses internal rhyme, or rhyming words within one line, as well as assonance, the repetition of vowel sounds in words that are close together.

Read these lines from "The Rime of the Ancient Mariner" and underline any examples of internal rhyme or assonance that you find.

The Sun came up upon the left,
Out of the sea came he!
And he shone bright, and on the right
Went down into the sea. (lines 25–28)

READING FOCUS: UNDERSTANDING ARCHAIC WORDS

To make his ballad seem like it was written long before his lifetime, Coleridge uses many **archaic**, or out-of-date, words. The meanings of many words appear in footnotes. In addition, summaries of the poem are shown in annotations next to some of the lines. In order to experience the flow and rhythm of the poem, try to read several stanzas at once, stopping only occasionally to check the annotations and footnotes. The rest of the time, use context clues to figure out the meanings of words you don't understand. For example, in the line "The glorious sun *uprist*" (line 98) your knowledge of the sun and of the prefix *up–* should help you guess that *uprist* means "rose."

Use the Skill This line from the poem contains an underlined archaic word. Use context clues to guess the word's meaning. Then, fill in the chart with the word's definition and a modern replacement.

Literary Skills Recognize the characteristics of a literary ballad.

Reading Skills Understand archaic words.

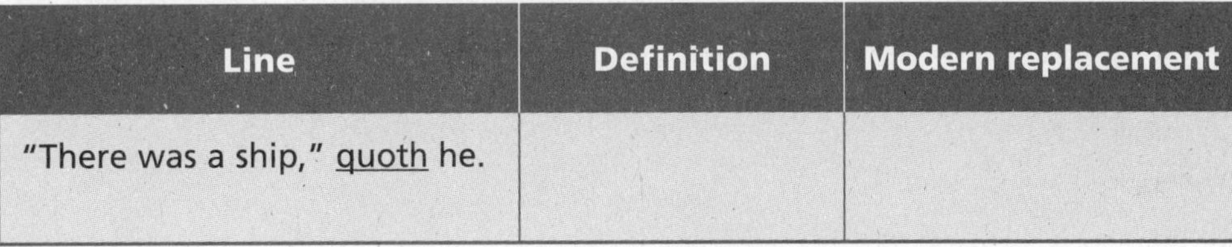

Line	Definition	Modern replacement
"There was a ship," quoth he.		

Vocabulary Development

The Rime of the Ancient Mariner

SELECTION VOCABULARY

tyrannous (TIHR UH NUHS) *adj.:* harsh; oppressive.
The storm that hit the Mariner's ship was tyrannous.

dismal (DIHZ MUHL) *adj.:* gloomy.
The light reflected from the cliffs cast a dismal glow on the crew.

ghastly (GAST LEE) *adj.:* dreadful; ghostly.
The Mariner's crew mates looked at him with ghastly eyes.

abated (UH BAYT IHD) *v.* used as *adj.:* lessened.
The ship would slow down once the Mariner's trance was abated.

wrenched (REHNCHT) *v.* used as *adj.:* anguished; grief-stricken.
The Mariner's expression was wrenched with the agony of his memories.

WORD STUDY

DIRECTIONS: To complete the sentences fill in the blanks with the correct vocabulary word from the list above.

1. The cold rainstorm made the day seem long and ______________________.
2. The ______________________ storm produced much less rain and wind than it had when it was stronger.
3. My ______________________ heart was greatly affected by the little girl's tears and complaints.
4. After the hurricane had passed, we stepped out to look over the ______________________ destruction it had caused.
5. After ten years of ______________________ and violent rule, the dictator was finally forced to leave power.

THE RIME OF THE ANCIENT MARINER

by Samuel Taylor Coleridge

BACKGROUND
Samuel Taylor Coleridge (1772–1834) was an English poet, critic, and philosopher. In this well-known poem, he presents strange, supernatural characters and events, hoping to create a suspension of disbelief for readers. As you read, remember that the story is told through the eyes of the Mariner. The annotations—the text to the right of the poem—will further explain what you are reading.

Argument

How a Ship having passed the Line was driven by storms to the cold Country toward the South Pole; and how from thence she made her course to the tropical Latitude of the Great Pacific Ocean; and of the strange things that befell; and in what manner the Ancient Mariner came back to his own Country.

PART I

It is an ancient Mariner,
And he stoppeth one of three.
"By thy long gray beard and glittering eye,
Now wherefore stopp'st thou me? (A)

An ancient Mariner meeteth three Gallants bidden to a wedding feast, and detaineth one.

The Bridegroom's doors are opened wide,
And I am next of kin;
The guests are met, the feast is set:
May'st hear the merry din." (B)

A READING FOCUS

Use context clues and your knowledge of modern English to guess the meanings of the **archaic** words *stoppeth*, *stopp'st*, and *thou*.

B QUICK CHECK

What happens in the first two stanzas of the poem?

A QUICK CHECK

What have you learned about the Mariner from his words, appearance, and actions?

View of a Harbour, 1815–16, by Caspar David Friedrich. Schloss Sanssouci/Potsdam, Germany/The Bridgeman Art Library.

He holds him with his skinny hand,
"There was a ship," quoth he.
"Hold off! unhand me, gray-beard loon!"
Eftsoons[1] his hand dropt he.

He holds him with his glittering eye—
The Wedding Guest stood still,
And listens like a three years' child:
The Mariner hath his will.

The Wedding Guest is spellbound by the eye of the old seafaring man, and constrained to hear his tale.

The Wedding Guest sat on a stone:
He cannot choose but hear;
And thus spake on that ancient man,
The bright-eyed Mariner. **A**

1. **eftsoons:** archaic word meaning "at once."

"The ship was cheered, the harbor cleared,
Merrily did we drop
Below the kirk,[2] below the hill,
Below the lighthouse top.

The Sun came up upon the left,
Out of the sea came he!
And he shone bright, and on the right
Went down into the sea.

The Mariner tells how the ship sailed southward with a good wind and fair weather, till it reached the Line.

Higher and higher every day,
Till over the mast at noon[3]—"
The Wedding Guest here beat his breast,
For he heard the loud bassoon.

The bride hath paced into the hall,
Red as a rose is she;
Nodding their heads before her goes
The merry minstrelsy.[4]

The Wedding Guest heareth the bridal music; but the Mariner continueth his tale.

The Wedding Guest he beat his breast,
Yet he cannot choose but hear;
And thus spake on that ancient man,
The bright-eyed Mariner. **B**

"And now the STORM-BLAST came, and he
Was tyrannous and strong: **C**
He struck with his o'ertaking wings,
And chased us south along.

The ship driven by a storm toward the South Pole.

With sloping masts and dipping prow,
As who[5] pursued with yell and blow

2. **kirk:** church.
3. **over . . . noon:** The ship has reached the equator, here called the Line.
4. **minstrelsy:** group of musicians.
5. **who:** one.

B LITERARY FOCUS

This line is a repetition of line 20. What other characteristics of a **literary ballad** are found in this stanza?

C VOCABULARY

Selection Vocabulary

Tyrannous means "harsh; oppressive." How do you think this tyrannous storm will affect the Mariner's journey?

A **LANGUAGE COACH**

One way to remember a word's definition is to think about a context in which you might use the word. For example, if you just learned the word *disrepair* ("a poor, run-down condition"), you might imagine a house that is falling apart. Describe a scene that can help you remember the meaning of the word *dismal* ("gloomy").

Still[6] treads the shadow of his foe,
And forward bends his head,
The ship drove fast, loud roared the blast,
And southward aye[7] we fled.

And now there came both mist and snow,
And it grew wondrous cold:
And ice, mast-high, came floating by,
As green as emerald.

And through the drifts[8] the snowy cliffs[9]
Did send a dismal sheen: **A**
Nor shapes of men nor beasts we ken[10]—
The ice was all between.

The land of ice, and of fearful sounds where no living thing was to be seen.

6. **still:** archaic word meaning "always."
7. **aye:** archaic word meaning "continually."
8. **drifts:** windblown snow and fog.
9. **cliffs:** icebergs.
10. **ken:** archaic word meaning "saw."

Dover Books

The ice was here, the ice was there,
The ice was all around:
It cracked and growled, and roared and howled, B
Like noises in a swound![11]

At length did cross an Albatross,
Through the fog it came;
As if it had been a Christian soul,
We hailed it in God's name.

Till a great seabird, called the Albatross, came through the snow fog, and was received with great joy and hospitality.

It ate the food it ne'er had eat,
And round and round it flew.
The ice did split with a thunder fit;
The helmsman steered us through!

And a good south wind sprung up behind;
The Albatross did follow,
And every day, for food or play,
Came to the mariner's hello!

And lo! the Albatross proveth a bird of good omen, and followeth the ship as it returned northward through fog and floating ice.

In mist or cloud, on mast or shroud,[12]
It perched for vespers[13] nine;
Whiles all the night, through fog-smoke white,
Glimmered the white Moonshine."

"God save thee, ancient Mariner!
From the fiends, that plague thee thus!—
Why look'st thou so?"—With my crossbow
I shot the ALBATROSS. C

The ancient Mariner inhospitably killeth the pious bird of good omen.

B LITERARY FOCUS

Find and underline any examples of internal rhyme in this page of the **literary ballad**.

C LITERARY ANALYSIS

The Ancient Mariner never explains why he killed the Albatross. For what reason do you think he might have killed it?

11. swound: swoon.
12. shroud: support rope that stretches from the top of the mast to the side of the ship.
13. vespers: evenings; also, evening prayers.

A QUICK CHECK

How do the sailors' opinions about the killing of the albatross change from the previous stanza to this one? Why?

B VOCABULARY

Word Study

The word *furrow*, as it is used here, means "ship's wake." Look up the word's other, more common, meaning in a dictionary and use it in a sentence.

PART II

The Sun now rose upon the right:
Out of the sea came he,
Still hid in mist, and on the left
Went down into the sea.

And the good south wind still blew behind,
But no sweet bird did follow,
Nor any day for food or play
Came to the mariner's hello!

And I had done a hellish thing,
And it would work 'em woe:
For all averred,[14] I had killed the bird
That made the breeze to blow.
Ah wretch! said they, the bird to slay,
That made the breeze to blow!

His shipmates cry out against the ancient Mariner, for killing the bird of good luck.

Nor dim nor red, like God's own head,
The glorious Sun uprist:
Then all averred, I had killed the bird
That brought the fog and mist.
'Twas right, said they, such birds to slay,
That bring the fog and mist. A

But when the fog cleared off, they justify the same, and thus make themselves accomplices in the crime.

The fair breeze blew, the white foam flew,
The furrow[15] followed free; B
We were the first that ever burst
Into that silent sea.

The fair breeze continues; the ship enters the Pacific Ocean, and sails northward, even till it reaches the Line.

Down dropt the breeze, the sails dropt down,
'Twas sad as sad could be;
And we did speak only to break
The silence of the sea!

The ship hath been suddenly becalmed.

14. averred: asserted; claimed.
15. furrow: ship's wake.

All in a hot and copper sky,
The bloody Sun, at noon,
Right up above the mast did stand,
No bigger than the Moon.

Day after day, day after day,
We stuck, nor breath nor motion;
As idle as a painted ship
Upon a painted ocean. C

Water, water, everywhere,
And all the boards did shrink;
Water, water, everywhere,
Nor any drop to drink. D

And the Albatross begins to be avenged.

The very deep did rot: O Christ!
That ever this should be!
Yea, slimy things did crawl with legs
Upon the slimy sea.

About, about, in reel and rout[16]
The death-fires[17] danced at night;
The water, like a witch's oils,
Burnt green, and blue and white.

And some in dreams assured were
Of the Spirit that plagued us so;
Nine fathom deep he had followed us
From the land of mist and snow.

A Spirit had followed them; one of the invisible inhabitants of this planet, neither departed souls nor angels; concerning whom the learned Jew, Josephus, and the Platonic Constantinopolitan, Michael Psellus, may be consulted. They are very numerous, and there is no climate or element without one or more.

And every tongue, through utter drought,
Was withered at the root;
We could not speak, no more than if
We had been choked with soot.

16. reel and rout: violent, whirling movement.
17. death-fires: firelike, luminous glow said to be seen over dead bodies.

C LITERARY FOCUS

Underline any examples of assonance that you find in this stanza of the **literary ballad**.

D QUICK CHECK

What problem do the sailors now face?

A READING FOCUS

Do you think the **archaic** word *welladay* is a better word choice for this ballad than *alas*? Why or why not?

B LITERARY ANALYSIS

Why do you think the word *weary* is repeated so often in this stanza? What effect does it have on the mood of the poem?

Ah! welladay![18] what evil looks **A**
Had I from old and young!
Instead of the cross, the Albatross
About my neck was hung.

The shipmates, in their sore distress, would fain throw the whole guilt on the ancient Mariner: in sign whereof they hang the dead seabird round his neck.

PART III

There passed a weary time. Each throat
Was parched, and glazed each eye.
A weary time! a weary time!
How glazed each weary eye,
When looking westward, I beheld
A something in the sky. **B**

The ancient Mariner beholdeth a sign in the element afar off.

At first it seemed a little speck,
And then it seemed a mist;
It moved and moved, and took at last
A certain shape, I wist.[19]

A speck, a mist, a shape, I wist!
And still it neared and neared:
As if it dodged a water sprite,
It plunged and tacked and veered.[20]

With throats unslaked,[21] with black lips baked,
We could not laugh nor wail;
Through utter drought all dumb we stood!
I bit my arm, I sucked the blood,
And cried, A sail! a sail!

At its nearer approach, it seemeth him to be a ship; and at a dear ransom, he freeth his speech from the bonds of thirst.

With throats unslaked, with black lips baked,
Agape[22] they heard me call:
Gramercy![23] they for joy did grin,

A flash of joy;

18. **welladay:** archaic word meaning "alas," an exclamation of sorrow.
19. **wist:** archaic word meaning "knew."
20. **tacked and veered:** turned toward and then away from the wind.
21. **unslaked:** unrelieved of thirst.
22. **agape:** with mouths wide open in wonder or fear.
23. **gramercy:** from Middle French *grand merci*, an exclamation of great thanks.

And all at once their breath drew in,
As they were drinking all. **C**

See! see! (I cried) she tacks no more!
Hither to work us weal;[24]
Without a breeze, without a tide,
She steadies with upright keel!

And horror follows. For can it be a ship that comes onward without wind or tide?

The western wave was all aflame.
The day was well nigh done!
Almost upon the western wave
Rested the broad bright Sun;
When that strange shape drove suddenly
Betwixt us and the Sun.

And straight the Sun was flecked with bars,
(Heaven's Mother send us grace!)
As if through a dungeon grate he peered
With broad and burning face.

It seemeth him but the skeleton of a ship.

And its ribs are seen as bars on the face of the setting Sun.

Alas! (thought I, and my heart beat loud)
How fast she nears and nears!
Are those *her* sails that glance in the Sun,
Like restless gossameres?[25] **D**

Are those *her* ribs through which the Sun
Did peer, as through a grate?
And is that Woman all her crew?
Is that a DEATH? and are there two?
Is DEATH that woman's mate?

The Specter Woman and her Deathmate, and no other onboard the skeleton ship.

Her lips were red, *her* looks were free,
Her locks were yellow as gold:
Her skin was as white as leprosy,

C READING FOCUS

What words give this stanza an **archaic** quality?

D LITERARY FOCUS

Underline the lines on this page that contain assonance. How does this assonance contribute to the musical quality of the **literary ballad**?

---

24. work us weal: do us good.
25. gossameres: filmy cobwebs.

A LITERARY FOCUS

Literary ballads blend real events with supernatural ones. What strange supernatural event has just taken place?

Dover Books

The Nightmare LIFE-IN-DEATH was she,
Who thicks man's blood with cold.

Like vessel, like crew!

The naked hulk alongside came,
And the twain were casting dice;
"The game is done! I've won! I've won!"
Quoth she, and whistles thrice.

Death and Life-in-Death have diced for the ship's crew, and she (the latter) winneth the ancient Mariner.

The Sun's rim dips; the stars rush out:
At one stride comes the dark;
With far-heard whisper, o'er the sea,
Off shot the specter bark.[26] A

No twilight within the courts of the Sun.

26. **specter bark:** ghost ship.

We listened and looked sideways up!
Fear at my heart, as at a cup,
My lifeblood seemed to sip!
The stars were dim, and thick the night,

At the rising of the Moon,

The steersman's face by his lamp gleamed white;
From the sails the dew did drip—
Till clomb[27] above the eastern bar
The hornèd[28] Moon, with one bright star
Within the nether tip.[29]

One after one, by the star-dogged Moon,
Too quick for groan or sigh,
Each turned his face with a ghastly pang, B
And cursed me with his eye.

One after another,

Four times fifty living men,
(And I heard nor sigh nor groan)
With heavy thump, a lifeless lump,
They dropped down one by one.

His shipmates drop down dead.

The souls did from their bodies fly,—
They fled to bliss or woe!
And every soul, it passed me by,
Like the whizz of my crossbow! C

But Life-in-Death begins her work on the ancient Mariner.

PART IV

"I fear thee, ancient Mariner!
I fear thy skinny hand!
And thou art long, and lank, and brown,
As is the ribbed sea sand.

The Wedding Guest feareth that a Spirit is talking to him;

27. **clomb:** archaic form of "climbed."
28. **hornèd:** crescent.
29. **star . . . tip:** A star dogging, or following, the moon is believed by sailors to be an evil omen.

B VOCABULARY

Selection Vocabulary

The word *ghastly* means "dreadful, ghostly." What do you think is happening to the men in this line?

 VOCABULARY

Academic Vocabulary

Differentiate, or identify differences, between one example of reality and one example of the supernatural in Part III.

A READING FOCUS

What words help give this stanza an **archaic** feel?

B LITERARY ANALYSIS

How does the Mariner feel in this stanza? How do you know?

I fear thee and thy glittering eye,
And thy skinny hand, so brown."—
Fear not, fear not, thou Wedding Guest!
This body dropt not down.

But the ancient Mariner assureth him of his bodily life, and proceedeth to relate his horrible penance.

Alone, alone, all, all alone,
Alone on a wide wide sea!
And never a saint took pity on
My soul in agony.

He despiseth the creatures of the calm,

The many men, so beautiful!
And they all dead did lie:
And a thousand thousand slimy things
Lived on; and so did I.

And envieth that they should live, and so many lie dead.

I looked upon the rotting sea,
And drew my eyes away;
I looked upon the rotting deck,
And there the dead men lay.

I looked to heaven, and tried to pray;
But or[30] ever a prayer had gusht,
A wicked whisper came, and made
My heart as dry as dust. **A**

I closed my lids, and kept them close,
And the balls like pulses beat;
For the sky and the sea, and the sea and the sky
Lay like a load on my weary eye,
And the dead were at my feet. **B**

But the curse liveth for him in the eye of the dead men.

The cold sweat melted from their limbs,
Nor rot nor reek did they:
The look with which they looked on me
Had never passed away.

30. or: before.

An orphan's curse would drag to hell
A spirit from on high;
But oh! more horrible than that
Is the curse in a dead man's eye!
Seven days, seven nights, I saw that curse,
And yet I could not die. **C**

In his loneliness and fixedness he yearneth toward the journeying Moon, and the stars that still sojourn, yet still move onward; and everywhere the blue sky belongs to them, and is their appointed rest, and their native country and their own natural homes, which they enter unannounced, as lords that are certainly expected and yet there is a silent joy at their arrival.

The moving Moon went up the sky,
And nowhere did abide:
Softly she was going up,
And a star or two beside—

Her beams bemocked the sultry main,[31]
Like April hoarfrost[32] spread;
But where the ship's huge shadow lay,
The charmèd water burnt alway[33]
A still and awful red. **D**

By the light of the Moon he beholdeth God's creatures of the great calm.

Beyond the shadow of the ship,
I watched the water snakes:
They moved in tracks of shining white,
And when they reared, the elfish light
Fell off in hoary[34] flakes.

Within the shadow of the ship
I watched their rich attire:
Blue, glossy green, and velvet black,
They coiled and swam; and every track
Was a flash of golden fire.

Their beauty and their happiness.

O happy, living things! no tongue
Their beauty might declare:

C QUICK CHECK

Why does the Mariner wish to die?

D LITERARY FOCUS

How does the combination of realistic and supernatural elements affect the believability of the **literary ballad**?

31. **main:** archaic word meaning "open sea."
32. **hoarfrost:** frost.
33. **alway:** archaic form of "always."
34. **hoary:** white or gray.

A VOCABULARY

Word Study

Based on your knowledge of the words *self* and *same*, what do you think the compound word *selfsame* means?

B LITERARY ANALYSIS

What causes the Albatross to fall from the Mariner's neck? What do you think this event symbolizes?

C READING FOCUS

Use context clues to write a definition for the **archaic** word *anear*?

A spring of love gushed from my heart,
And I blessed them unaware:
Sure my kind saint took pity on me,
And I blessed them unaware.

He blesseth them in his heart.

The selfsame moment I could pray; **A**
And from my neck so free
The Albatross fell off, and sank
Like lead into the sea. **B**

The spell begins to break.

PART V

Oh sleep! it is a gentle thing,
Beloved from pole to pole!
To Mary Queen the praise be given!
She sent the gentle sleep from Heaven,
That slid into my soul.

The silly[35] buckets on the deck,
That had so long remained,
I dreamt that they were filled with dew;
And when I awoke, it rained.

By grace of the holy Mother, the ancient Mariner is refreshed with rain.

My lips were wet, my throat was cold,
My garments all were dank;
Sure I had drunken in my dreams,
And still my body drank.

I moved, and could not feel my limbs:
I was so light—almost
I thought that I had died in sleep,
And was a blessèd ghost.

And soon I heard a roaring wind:
It did not come anear; **C**

He heareth sounds and seeth strange sights and commotions in the sky and the element.

35. **silly:** simple; plain.

But with its sound it shook the sails,
That were so thin and sere.[36]

The upper air burst into life!
And a hundred fire flags sheen,
To and fro they were hurried about!
And to and fro, and in and out,
The wan stars danced between.[37]

And the coming wind did roar more loud,
And the sails did sigh like sedge;[38]
And the rain poured down from one black cloud;
The Moon was at its edge.

The thick black cloud was cleft,[39] and still
The Moon was at its side:
Like waters shot from some high crag,
The lightning fell with never a jag,
A river steep and wide. **D**

The loud wind never reached the ship,
Yet now the ship moved on! **E**
Beneath the lightning and the Moon
The dead men gave a groan.

The bodies of the ship's crew are inspired, and the ship moves on;

They groaned, they stirred, they all uprose,
Nor spake, nor moved their eyes;
It had been strange, even in a dream,
To have seen those dead men rise.

The helmsman steered, the ship moved on;
Yet never a breeze up-blew;

36. sere: archaic word meaning "worn."
37. The upper . . . danced between: apparently a description of the shifting lights of an aurora, which sometimes resemble waving, luminous folds of fabric.
38. sedge: reedy plants.
39. cleft: split.

D QUICK CHECK

A *jag* is a sharp, projecting point. What is unusual about the lightning that the Mariner sees?

E LITERARY ANALYSIS

What has just happened to rescue the Mariner? What do you think caused this?

A LITERARY ANALYSIS

Why do you think the wedding guest fears the Ancient Mariner?

B LITERARY FOCUS

Underline all examples of internal rhyme and circle all examples of assonance in this stanza of the **literary ballad**.

The mariners all 'gan work the ropes,
Where they were wont[40] to do;
They raised their limbs like lifeless tools—
We were a ghastly crew.

The body of my brother's son
Stood by me, knee to knee:
The body and I pulled at one rope,
But he said nought to me.

"I fear thee, ancient Mariner!"
Be calm, thou Wedding Guest!
'Twas not those souls that fled in pain,
Which to their corses[41] came again,
But a troop of spirits blest: A

But not by the souls of the men, nor by demons of earth or middle air, but by a blessed troop of angelic spirits, sent down by the invocation of the guardian saint.

For when it dawned—they dropt their arms,
And clustered round the mast;
Sweet sounds rose slowly through their mouths,
And from their bodies passed.

Around, around, flew each sweet sound,
Then darted to the Sun;
Slowly the sounds came back again,
Now mixed, now one by one. B

Sometimes a-dropping from the sky
I heard the skylark sing;
Sometimes all little birds that are,
How they seemed to fill the sea and air
With their sweet jargoning![42]

---

40. wont: accustomed.

41. corses: archaic form of "corpses."

42. jargoning: archaic word meaning "twittering."

And now 'twas like all instruments,
Now like a lonely flute;
And now it is an angel's song,
That makes the heavens be mute.

It ceased; yet still the sails made on
A pleasant noise till noon,
A noise like of a hidden brook
In the leafy month of June,
That to the sleeping woods all night
Singeth a quiet tune. **C**

Till noon we quietly sailed on,
Yet never a breeze did breathe:
Slowly and smoothly went the ship,
Moved onward from beneath.

Under the keel nine fathom deep, **D**
From the land of mist and snow,
The spirit slid: and it was he
That made the ship to go.
The sails at noon left off their tune,
And the ship stood still also.

The lonesome Spirit from the South Pole carries on the ship as far as the Line, in obedience to the angelic troop, but still requireth vengeance.

The Sun, right up above the mast,
Had fixed her[43] to the ocean:
But in a minute she 'gan stir,
With a short uneasy motion—
Backwards and forwards half her length
With a short uneasy motion.

Then like a pawing horse let go,
She made a sudden bound:
It flung the blood into my head,
And I fell down in a swound. **E**

43. fixed her: seemed to hold the ship motionless.

C LITERARY ANALYSIS

How has the mood of the poem shifted in the last few stanzas?

D VOCABULARY

Word Study

The word *fathom* has two common meanings. Find the word in a dictionary, and use context clues to decide which definition is used here. Write the definition below.

E READING FOCUS

Why do you think Coleridge chose to use the **archaic** word *swound* instead of the modern *swoon*?

A **LITERARY ANALYSIS**

The last four stanzas summarize what happened earlier in the poem, and foreshadow, or predict, what is to come. Based on what you have read, what do you think will happen to the Mariner?

Dover Books

How long in that same fit I lay,
I have not to declare;
But ere my living life returned,
I heard and in my soul discerned
Two voices in the air.

The Polar Spirit's fellow demons, the invisible inhabitants of the element, take part in his wrong; and two of them relate, one to the other, that penance long and heavy for the ancient Mariner hath been accorded to the Polar Spirit, who returneth southward.

"Is it he?" quoth one, "Is this the man?
By him who died on cross,
With his cruel bow he laid full low
The harmless Albatross.

The spirit who bideth by himself
In the land of mist and snow,
He loved the bird that loved the man
Who shot him with his bow."

The other was a softer voice,
As soft as honeydew:
Quoth he, "The man hath penance done,
And penance more will do." A

Dover Books

PART VI

FIRST VOICE

"But tell me, tell me! speak again,
Thy soft response renewing—
What makes that ship drive on so fast?
What is the ocean doing?"

SECOND VOICE

"Still as a slave before his lord,
The ocean hath no blast;[44]
His great bright eye most silently
Up to the Moon is cast— **B**

If he may know which way to go;
For she guides him smooth or grim.
See, brother, see! how graciously
She looketh down on him."

The Mariner hath been cast into a trance; for the angelic power causeth the vessel to drive northward faster than human life could endure.

FIRST VOICE

"But why drives on that ship so fast,
Without or wave or wind?"[45]

44. blast: wind.
45. without . . . wind: with neither wave nor wind.

B LITERARY ANALYSIS

Who do you think are the speakers of the "first voice" and "second voice"?

A LITERARY FOCUS

What elements of a **literary ballad** can you find in this stanza?

B VOCABULARY

Selection Vocabulary

Abated means "lessened." If you were told that someone's thirst had abated, what would you think he or she had just done?

SECOND VOICE

"The air is cut away before,
And closes from behind.

Fly, brother, fly! more high, more high!
Or we shall be belated:
For slow and slow that ship will go,
When the Mariner's trance is abated." A B

The supernatural motion is retarded; the Mariner awakes, and his penance begins anew.

I woke, and we were sailing on
As in a gentle weather:
'Twas night, calm night, the Moon was high;
The dead men stood together.

All stood together on the deck,
For a charnel dungeon[46] fitter:
All fixed on me their stony eyes,
That in the Moon did glitter.

The pang, the curse, with which they died,
Had never passed away:
I could not draw my eyes from theirs,
Nor turn them up to pray.

The curse is finally expiated [removed, after penance is done].

And now this spell was snapt: once more
I viewed the ocean green,
And looked far forth, yet little saw
Of what had else[47] been seen—

Like one, that on a lonesome road
Doth walk in fear and dread,
And having once turned round walks on,

46. charnel dungeon: burial vault.
47. had else: would otherwise have.

And turns no more his head;
Because he knows, a frightful fiend **C**
Doth close behind him tread.

But soon there breathed a wind on me,
Nor sound nor motion made:
Its path was not upon the sea,
In ripple or in shade.

It raised my hair, it fanned my cheek
Like a meadow gale of spring—
It mingled strangely with my fears,
Yet it felt like a welcoming. **D**

Swiftly, swiftly flew the ship,
Yet she sailed softly too:
Sweetly, sweetly blew the breeze—
On me alone it blew.

Oh! dream of joy! is this indeed
The lighthouse top I see?
Is this the hill? is this the kirk?
Is this mine own countree?

And the ancient Mariner beholdeth his native country.

We drifted o'er the harbor bar,
And I with sobs did pray—
O let me be awake, my God!
Or let me sleep alway.

The harbor bay was clear as glass,
So smoothly it was strewn![48]
And on the bay the moonlight lay,
And the shadow of the Moon.

48. strewn: stretched out; calmed.

C VOCABULARY

Word Study

Think of a synonym, or word with a similar meaning, for the word *frightful*. Use the synonym in a sentence of your own.

D QUICK CHECK

How did the wind affect the Mariner?

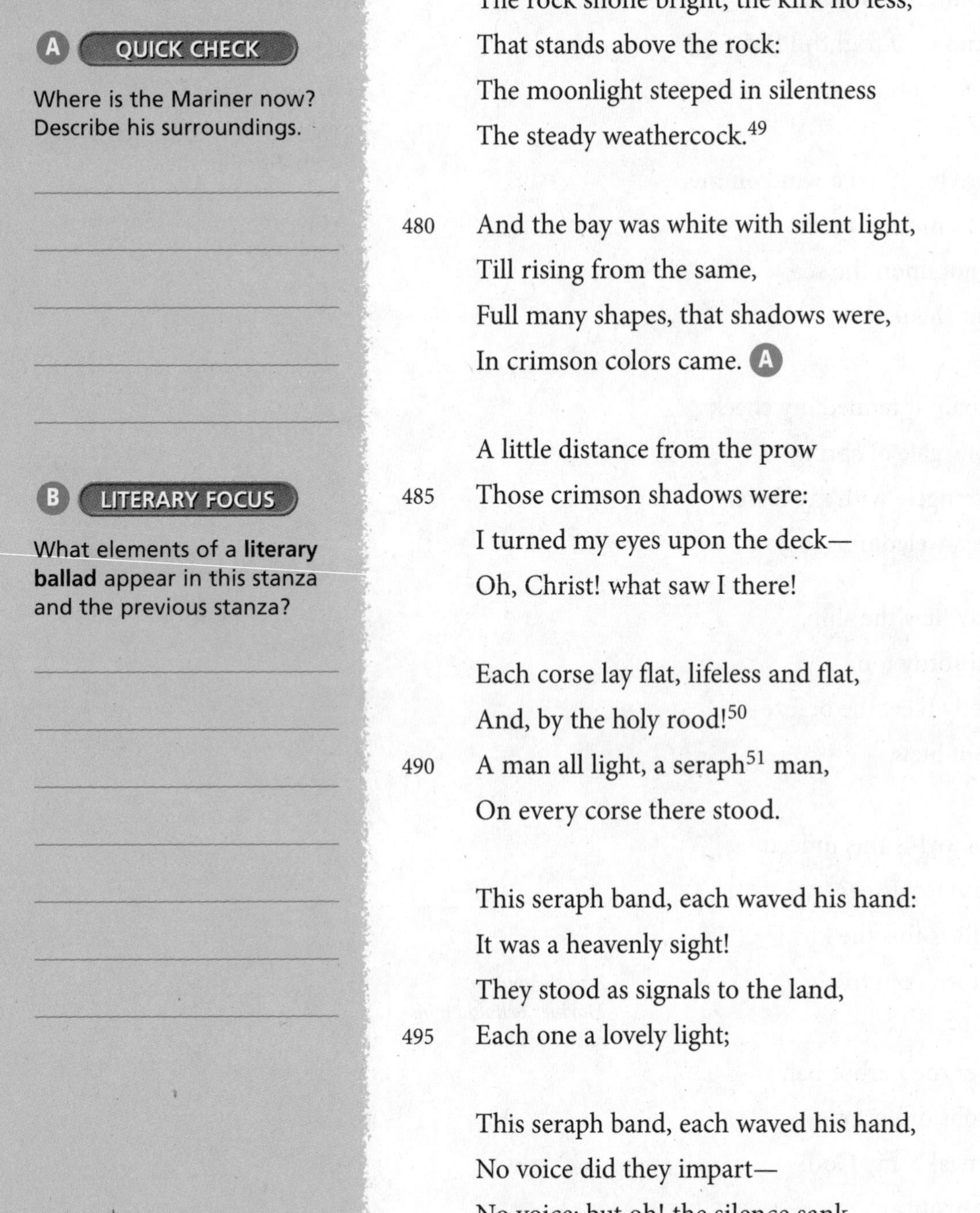

A QUICK CHECK

Where is the Mariner now? Describe his surroundings.

B LITERARY FOCUS

What elements of a **literary ballad** appear in this stanza and the previous stanza?

The rock shone bright, the kirk no less,
That stands above the rock:
The moonlight steeped in silentness
The steady weathercock.[49]

And the bay was white with silent light,
Till rising from the same,
Full many shapes, that shadows were,
In crimson colors came. **A**

The angelic spirits leave the dead bodies,

A little distance from the prow
Those crimson shadows were:
I turned my eyes upon the deck—
Oh, Christ! what saw I there!

And appear in their own forms of light.

Each corse lay flat, lifeless and flat,
And, by the holy rood![50]
A man all light, a seraph[51] man,
On every corse there stood.

This seraph band, each waved his hand:
It was a heavenly sight!
They stood as signals to the land,
Each one a lovely light;

This seraph band, each waved his hand,
No voice did they impart—
No voice; but oh! the silence sank
Like music on my heart. **B**

But soon I heard the dash of oars,
I heard the Pilot's cheer;
My head was turned perforce away
And I saw a boat appear.

49. **weathercock:** rooster-shaped weather vane.
50. **rood:** crucifix.
51. **seraph:** angel of the highest rank.

The Pilot and the Pilot's boy,
I heard them coming fast:
Dear Lord in Heaven! it was a joy
The dead men could not blast.

I saw a third—I heard his voice:
It is the Hermit good!
He singeth loud his godly hymns
That he makes in the wood.
He'll shrieve[52] my soul, he'll wash away
The Albatross's blood. C

PART VII

The Hermit of the Wood,

This Hermit good lives in that wood
Which slopes down to the sea.
How loudly his sweet voice he rears!
He loves to talk with marineres
That come from a far countree. D

He kneels at morn, and noon, and eve—
He hath a cushion plump:
It is the moss that wholly hides
The rotted old oak stump.

The skiff boat[53] neared: I heard them talk,
"Why, this is strange, I trow![54]
Where are those lights so many and fair,
That signal made but now?"

Approacheth the ship with wonder.

"Strange, by my faith!" the Hermit said—
"And they answered not our cheer!
The planks looked warped! and see those sails,

C QUICK CHECK

Why is the Mariner happy to see these three men approaching?

D LITERARY FOCUS

Which line in this stanza of the **literary ballad** contains an internal rhyme?

---

52. shrieve: archaic word meaning "release from guilt after hearing confession."

53. skiff boat: rowboat.

54. trow: archaic word meaning "believe."

A QUICK CHECK

What do the three approaching men think of the Mariner's ship?

B LITERARY ANALYSIS

What do you think causes the ship to sink? Do you think Coleridge wanted his readers to think of a natural or a supernatural reason for its sinking?

How thin they are and sere!
I never saw aught[55] like to them,
Unless perchance it were

Brown skeletons of leaves that lag[56]
My forest brook along;
When the ivy tod[57] is heavy with snow,
And the owlet whoops to the wolf below,
That eats the she-wolf's young."

"Dear Lord! it hath a fiendish look—
(The Pilot made reply)
I am afeared"—"Push on, push on!"
Said the Hermit cheerily. **A**

The boat came closer to the ship,
But I nor spake nor stirred;
The boat came close beneath the ship,
And straight[58] a sound was heard.

Under the water it rumbled on,
Still louder and more dread:
It reached the ship, it split the bay;
The ship went down like lead. **B**

The ship suddenly sinketh.

Stunned by that loud and dreadful sound,
Which sky and ocean smote,[59]
Like one that hath been seven days drowned
My body lay afloat;
But swift as dreams, myself I found
Within the Pilot's boat.

The ancient Mariner is saved in the Pilot's boat.

55. **aught:** anything.
56. **lag:** drift; move more slowly than the current.
57. **ivy tod:** clump of ivy.
58. **straight:** straightaway; at once.
59. **smote:** struck.

Upon the whirl, where sank the ship,
The boat spun round and round;
And all was still, save that the hill
Was telling of the sound.

I moved my lips—the Pilot shrieked
And fell down in a fit;
The holy Hermit raised his eyes,
And prayed where he did sit. **C**

I took the oars: the Pilot's boy,
Who now doth crazy go,
Laughed loud and long, and all the while
His eyes went to and fro.
"Ha! ha!" quoth he, "full plain I see,
The Devil knows how to row."

And now, all in my own countree,
I stood on the firm land!
The Hermit stepped forth from the boat,
And scarcely he could stand.

"O shrieve me, shrieve me, holy man!" **D**
The Hermit crossed[60] his brow.
"Say quick," quoth he, "I bid thee say—
What manner of man art thou?"

The ancient Mariner earnestly entreateth the Hermit to shrieve him; and the penance of life falls on him.

Forthwith[61] this frame of mine was wrenched **E**
With a woeful agony,
Which forced me to begin my tale;
And then it left me free.

Since then, at an uncertain hour,
That agony returns:
And till my ghastly tale is told,
This heart within me burns.

And ever and anon throughout his future life an agony constraineth him to travel from land to land;

60. crossed: made the sign of the cross.
61. forthwith: at once.

C QUICK CHECK

Why does the motion of the Mariner's lips frighten the Pilot and the Hermit?

D READING FOCUS

If necessary, use a dictionary to look up the **archaic** word *shrieve*. What is the Mariner asking the Hermit to do here?

E VOCABULARY

Selection Vocabulary

Wrenched means "anguished" or "grief-stricken." Use the word in a sentence of your own.

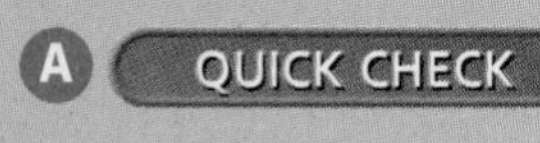

QUICK CHECK

Why has the Mariner told his story to the Wedding Guest?

I pass, like night, from land to land;
I have strange power of speech;
That moment that his face I see,
I know the man that must hear me:
To him my tale I teach. (A)

What loud uproar bursts from that door!
The wedding guests are there:
But in the garden bower the bride
And bridemaids singing are:
And hark the little vesper bell,
Which biddeth me to prayer!

O Wedding Guest! this soul hath been
Alone on a wide wide sea:
So lonely 'twas, that God himself
Scarce seemed there to be.

O sweeter than the marriage feast,
'Tis sweeter far to me,
To walk together to the kirk
With a goodly company!—

To walk together to the kirk,
And all together pray,
While each to his great Father bends,
Old men, and babes, and loving friends
And youths and maidens gay!

Farewell, farewell! but this I tell
To thee, thou Wedding Guest!
He prayeth well, who loveth well
Both man and bird and beast.

And to teach, by his own example, love and reverence to all things that God made and loveth.

Dover Books

He prayeth best, who loveth best
All things both great and small;
For the dear God who loveth us,
He made and loveth all. **B**

The Mariner, whose eye is bright,
Whose beard with age is hoar,
Is gone: and now the Wedding Guest
Turned from the bridegroom's door.

He went like one that hath been stunned,
And is of sense forlorn:[62]
A sadder and a wiser man,
He rose the morrow morn. **C**

62. **forlorn:** deprived.

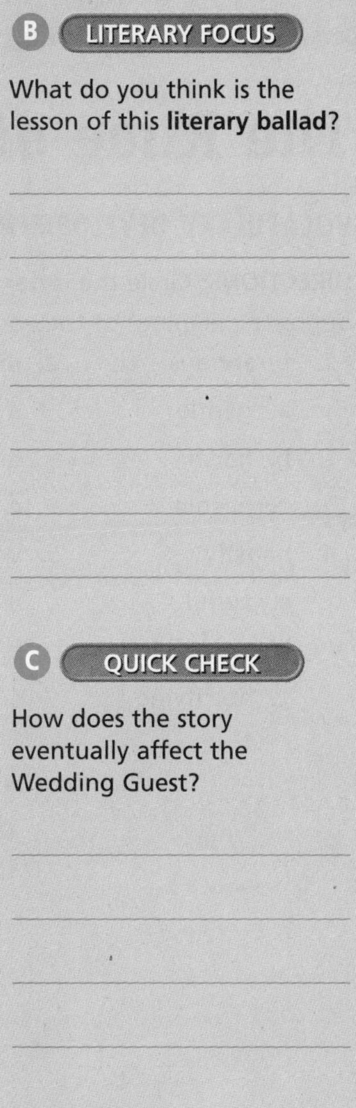

B LITERARY FOCUS

What do you think is the lesson of this **literary ballad**?

C QUICK CHECK

How does the story eventually affect the Wedding Guest?

Applying Your Skills

The Rime of the Ancient Mariner

VOCABULARY DEVELOPMENT

DIRECTIONS: Circle the letter of the word that is an antonym (word with the opposite meaning) of the vocabulary word.

1. tyrannous
- **a.** gentle
- **b.** harsh
- **c.** hostile

2. dismal
- **a.** gloomy
- **b.** plain
- **c.** pleasant

3. abated
- **a.** increased
- **b.** lessened
- **c.** maintained

4. ghastly
- **a.** awful
- **b.** wonderful
- **c.** horrifying

5. wrenched
- **a.** cheerful
- **b.** miserable
- **c.** distressed

LITERARY FOCUS: LITERARY BALLAD

DIRECTIONS: List all of the elements of a **literary ballad** that you can find in this stanza:

Water, water, everywhere,
And all the boards did shrink;
Water, water, everywhere,
Nor any drop to drink. (lines 119–122)

____

____

READING FOCUS: UNDERSTANDING ARCHAIC WORDS

DIRECTIONS: These lines contain **archaic** words. Rewrite the lines in modern English.

1. The day was well nigh done! (line 172)

____

____

2. This body dropt not down. (line 231)

____

____

Literary Skills Recognize the characteristics of a literary ballad.

Reading Skills Understand archaic words.

Skills Review

Collection 7

LANGUAGE COACH

DIRECTIONS: A word's meaning determines how it is used in a sentence. Some words have **multiple meanings,** so they can be used in two or more different ways. The words listed below have multiple meanings. Write two sentences of your own for each word. Use the word correctly, depending on which definition and part of speech (verb, noun, adjective, or adverb) is given. The first sentence has been done for you.

1. bid

   noun: an offer of money. I made a bid of twenty dollars for the painting.

   verb: demanded; asked. ____________________

2. patch

   verb: to repair. ____________________

   noun: a covering worn over an injury. ____________________

3. dash

   verb: to move with speed. ____________________

   noun: a small amount. ____________________

4. crane

   verb: to stretch out the neck. ____________________

   noun: a large bird with long legs, neck, and bill. ____________________

5. frame

   verb: shape. ____________________

   noun: skeletal structure around which something is built. ____________________

ORAL LANGUAGE ACTIVITY

DIRECTIONS: Write a short poem (about two stanzas) about any subject. You can write the poem in blank verse or you can use a rhyming pattern. In your poem, use at least three of the following elements of poetry: symbols, internal rhymes, assonance, imagery, and alliteration. Read your poem to the class. Have your classmates try to identify all of the elements of poetry in your poem.

Collection

8

The Quest for Beauty

The Interior of the British Institution Gallery, 1829, by John Scarlett Davis/Yale Center for British Art, Paul Mellon Collection, USA/The Bridgeman Art Library

Preparing to Read

Ozymandias

by Percy Bysshe Shelley

LITERARY FOCUS: IRONY

Irony is created when expectations do not match reality. "Ozymandias" (AHZ UH MAHN DEE UHS) contains a kind of irony called situational irony. **Situational irony** occurs when what happens is the opposite of what we expect to happen.

In "Ozymandias" you'll meet the speaker, a traveler, and a king who lived centuries ago. As you read, identify which character expects one thing to happen only to have something else occur.

READING FOCUS: COMPARING AND CONTRASTING

To **compare** is to see how things are alike; to **contrast** is to see how they are different. Both skills help us differentiate and categorize things around us. Irony requires us to compare and contrast, because we must compare what is expected with what really happens, and note any differences.

Use the Skill As you read "Ozymandias," compare and contrast the condition of the statue today with its condition when it was first built. Use the chart below to organize your thoughts.

Now	Then

Literary Skills Understand situational irony.

Reading Skills Compare and contrast details.

Vocabulary Development

Ozymandias

SELECTION VOCABULARY

antique (AN TEEK) *adj.:* ancient.
The antique and decaying ruins fascinated the traveler.

sneer (SNIHR) *n.:* proud, unkind facial expression.
The king's sneer caused his servants to tremble with fear.

passions (PASH UHNZ) *n. pl.:* strong emotions.
Passions ran high as the candidates debated the hot topic.

colossal (KUH LAHS UHL) *adj.:* magnificently huge.
The colossal statue towered over the people who came to view it.

boundless (BOWND LEHS) *adj.:* limitless.
The boundless reach of time is difficult to imagine.

WORD STUDY

DIRECTIONS: Write "Yes" after each sentence if the vocabulary word is being used correctly. Write "No" if it is being used incorrectly, and rewrite the sentence so that the word is used correctly.

1. This necklace is an *antique* heirloom; it has been passed down in my family for generations. _______

   ____

2. I got paint on my hands and had to *sneer* it off on a towel. _______

   ____

3. The old mansion had many secret *passions* to hidden rooms. _______

   ____

4. The ocean seemed *colossal* to Timmy, especially since he was accustomed to swimming in a small pool. _______

   ____

5. My cousin's imagination is *boundless;* he can daydream for hours. _______

   ____

OZYMANDIAS

by Percy Bysshe Shelley

BACKGROUND

"Ozymandias" was inspired by fragments from ancient Egypt that had been exhibited at the British Museum in the early 1800s. Some of the fragments were from the empire of one of Egypt's greatest pharaohs, or kings, Ramses II. Ozymandias is the Greek name for Ramses II.

© Michael Juno/Alamy

I met a traveler from an antique land
Who said: Two vast and trunkless legs[1] of stone
Stand in the desert . . . Near them, on the sand,
Half sunk, a shattered visage[2] lies, whose frown,
And wrinkled lip, and sneer of cold command, **A**
Tell that its sculptor well those passions read
Which yet survive, stamped on these lifeless things,

1. **trunkless legs:** that is, the legs without the rest of the body.
2. **visage:** face.

A VOCABULARY

Selection Vocabulary

Use context clues to write a definition of the word *sneer*. Circle the words that helped you figure out the meaning.

____

____

The hand that mocked them, and the heart[3] that fed; **A**
And on the pedestal these words appear:
"My name is Ozymandias, king of kings:
Look on my works, ye Mighty, and despair!" **B**
Nothing beside remains. Round the decay
Of that colossal wreck, boundless and bare **C**
The lone and level sands stretch far away.

A READING FOCUS

Compare and **contrast** the statue's remains with its original form. Note at least one similarity and one difference.

B LITERARY FOCUS

What is **ironic** about this inscription?

C LANGUAGE COACH

Notice how the double *s* in *passions* (line 6) is pronounced with a "sh" sound, while *colossal* and *boundless* (line 13) are pronounced with an "ess" sound. Come up with two more words with double *s's*—one with a "sh" sound and one with an "ess" sound.

3. **the hand . . . heart:** the hand of the sculptor who, with his art, ridiculed the passions to which Ozymandias gave himself wholeheartedly.

Skills Practice

Ozymandias

USE A SITUATIONAL IRONY CHART

DIRECTIONS: To help you identity the **situational irony** in "Ozymandias," fill in the chart with what the king thinks will happen and what actually happens.

What the king thinks will happen	What actually happens

Applying Your Skills

Ozymandias

VOCABULARY DEVELOPMENT

DIRECTIONS: Complete each of the following sentences with the correct word from the Word Box. Some words will be not used.

Word Box

- antique
- sneer
- passions
- colossal
- boundless

1. King Ozymandias could often be seen with a ______________ upon his lips.
2. The ______________ statue stood high above the passing travelers.
3. Ozymandias ruled with ______________ power; he seized lands wherever he wished.

LITERARY FOCUS: IRONY

DIRECTIONS: Look back at the chart you filled out on the Skills Practice page. What sort of expectations did Ozymandias have for himself and his kingdom? Did things turn out as he expected? Write a brief paragraph answering these questions and discussing the **irony** of the poem.

____

____

____

____

____

READING FOCUS: COMPARING AND CONTRASTING

DIRECTIONS: Complete the following chart by **comparing** and **contrasting** the remains of the statue of Ozymandias with its original state. Include adjectives from the poem that describe the statue now and as it was centuries ago.

Literary Skills Understand situational irony.

Reading Skills Compare and contrast details.

Statue now	Statue long ago

Preparing to Read

Ode on a Grecian Urn

by John Keats

LITERARY FOCUS: METAPHOR

A **metaphor** is a figure of speech that compares two unlike things without using a connecting word such as *like* or *as*. Often a metaphor describes one thing as if it were another. Notice how two dissimilar objects are compared in the metaphor below.

Object 1: dancer	Object 2: gazelle
Metaphor: She was a gazelle, leaping with ease and joy across the stage.	

Keats begins this poem with three metaphors that describe a Greek urn. In line 1, he calls the urn a "still unravished bride of quietness." By comparing the urn with a virgin bride, he implies that the urn has remained untouched through the ages. By adding "of quietness," he implies that it has been silent through the centuries and long awaited contact with the world. As you read, look for other metaphors that describe the urn.

READING FOCUS: VISUALIZING IMAGERY

Imagery is language that appeals to the senses. Most images appeal to the senses of sight and hearing, but they may also appeal to the senses of touch, taste, or smell. Poets often use imagery to bring their subject matter to life. When you visualize imagery, you create mental pictures of what is being described—people, objects, settings, or experiences.

Use the Skill As you read "Ode on a Grecian Urn," look for imagery that helps you to visualize the scenes painted on the urn.

Literary Skills Understand metaphor.

Reading Skills Visualize imagery.

Vocabulary Development

Ode on a Grecian Urn

SELECTION VOCABULARY

deities (DEE UH TEEZ) *n. pl.:* gods or goddesses.

Keats wonders what story of deities or mortals is represented on the vase.

loath (LOHTH) *adj.:* unwilling or reluctant.

Keats imagines that the maidens on the vase are loath to be caught by the men and gods who pursue them.

sensual (SEHN SHOO UHL) *adj.:* having to do with the five senses.

Keats says that the musicians on the vase play not for the sensual ear but for the imagination.

WORD STUDY

DIRECTIONS: When you don't know the meaning of a word, you can often find hints in its context, the words or sentences that surround it. Read the sentences below and underline any clues that hint at the vocabulary words' definitions.

1. In Greek mythology, men and women are often visited by the gods; interaction between mortals and *deities* is perfectly normal.
2. My cousins are *loath* to do their laundry—in fact, they protest any household chores.
3. This cake appeals to my senses of taste and smell; it's a *sensual* delight.

ODE ON A GRECIAN URN

by John Keats

BACKGROUND

Like other Romantic poets, Keats wrote a number of odes. An ode is a type of long poem that presents a reflection on a serious subject. The speaker in "Ode on a Grecian Urn" studies a beautiful urn, or vase, and thinks about its meaning.

© British Museum, London/Erich Lessing/Art Resource, NY

1

Thou still unravished bride of quietness,
Thou foster child of silence and slow time,
Sylvan[1] historian, who canst thus express (A)
A flowery tale more sweetly than our rhyme:
What leaf-fringed legend haunts about thy shape
Of deities or mortals, or of both, (B)
In Tempe or the dales of Arcady?[2]
What men or gods are these? What maidens loath?

1. **sylvan:** of the forest. (The urn is decorated with a rural scene.)
2. **Tempe** (TEHM PEE) . . . **Arcady** (AHR KUH DEE): valleys in ancient Greece; ideal types of rural beauty.

A LITERARY FOCUS

Restate the **metaphor** in this line in your own words. What does it mean?

B LANGUAGE COACH

The wording of this line suggests that the words *deities* and *mortals* are **antonyms** (words with opposite meanings). If *deities* means "gods or goddesses," what do you think *mortals* means?

A READING FOCUS

Describe the scene you visualize from the **imagery** in lines 5–10.

B VOCABULARY

Academic Vocabulary

What is the *predominant*, or most noticeable, image for you in this stanza? What sense does this imagery appeal to?

C VOCABULARY

Word Study

A *bough* (BOU) is a branch of a tree. *Bow* (BOU) is a homophone of *bough*—they are pronounced the same but have different spellings and meanings. What is one definition of *bow*?

What mad pursuit? What struggle to escape?
What pipes and timbrels?[3] What wild ecstasy? A

2

Heard melodies are sweet, but those unheard
Are sweeter; therefore, ye soft pipes, play on;
Not to the sensual ear, but, more endeared,
Pipe to the spirit ditties[4] of no tone:
Fair youth, beneath the trees, thou canst not leave
Thy song, nor ever can those trees be bare;
Bold Lover, never, never canst thou kiss,
Though winning near the goal—yet, do not grieve;
She cannot fade, though thou hast not thy bliss,
Forever wilt thou love, and she be fair! B

3

Ah, happy, happy boughs! that cannot shed C
Your leaves, nor ever bid the Spring adieu;[5]
And, happy melodist, unwearied,
Forever piping songs forever new;
More happy love! more happy, happy love!
Forever warm and still to be enjoyed,
Forever panting, and forever young;
All breathing human passion far above,
That leaves a heart high-sorrowful and cloyed,[6]
A burning forehead, and a parching tongue.

4

Who are these coming to the sacrifice?
To what green altar, O mysterious priest,

3. **timbrels:** tambourines.
4. **ditties:** short, simple songs.
5. **adieu** (UH DYOO): French for "goodbye."
6. **cloyed** (KLOID): filled; satisfied; wearied with excess.

Lead'st thou that heifer lowing[7] at the skies,
And all her silken flanks[8] with garlands dressed?
What little town by river or seashore,
Or mountain-built with peaceful citadel,[9]
Is emptied of this folk, this pious morn?
And, little town, thy streets forevermore
Will silent be; and not a soul to tell
Why thou art desolate, can e'er return.

5

O Attic[10] shape! Fair attitude![11] with brede[12]
Of marble men and maidens overwrought,[13]
With forest branches and the trodden weed; **D**
Thou, silent form, dost tease us out of thought
As doth eternity: Cold Pastoral![14]
When old age shall this generation waste,
Thou shalt remain, in midst of other woe
Than ours, a friend to man, to whom thou say'st,
"Beauty is truth, truth beauty,"—that is all
Ye know on earth, and all ye need to know. **E**

---

7. **lowing:** mooing.
8. **flanks:** sides between the ribs and the hips.
9. **citadel** (SIHT UH DEL): fortress.
10. **Attic:** Athenian; classically elegant.
11. **attitude:** disposition or feeling conveyed by the postures of the figures on the urn.
12. **brede:** interwoven design.
13. **overwrought:** decorated to excess; also, in reference to the men and maidens, overexcited.
14. **Pastoral:** artwork depicting idealized rural life.

D READING FOCUS

How do you picture the urn from the **imagery** in the first three lines of this stanza?

E QUICK CHECK

Re-read lines 46–50. What does the speaker say will happen to the urn?

Applying Your Skills

Ode on a Grecian Urn

VOCABULARY DEVELOPMENT

DIRECTIONS: Decide if the following pairs of words are synonyms (words with similar meanings) or antonyms (words with opposite meanings). Write your answers on the blank lines.

1. deities; humans ________________

2. loath; opposed ________________

3. sensual; spiritual ________________

LITERARY FOCUS: METAPHOR

DIRECTIONS: Complete the chart below by deciding what each of the following **metaphors** means.

Metaphor	Meaning
"Thou foster child of silence and slow time," (line 2)	**1.**
"Bold Lover, never, never canst thou kiss," (line 17)	**2.**

READING FOCUS: VISUALIZING IMAGERY

DIRECTIONS: There are many descriptive phrases in "Ode on a Grecian Urn" that help the reader visualize the poem's **imagery**. Complete the chart below by describing how you visualize the selected scenes.

Scenes on the urn	How I visualize the scenes
"Ah, happy, happy boughs! that cannot shed / Your leaves, nor ever bid the Spring adieu;" (lines 21–22)	**1.**
"To what green altar, O mysterious priest, / Lead'st thou that heifer lowing at the skies," (lines 32–33)	**2.**

Literary Skills Understand metaphor.

Reading Skills Visualize imagery.

Skills Review

Collection 8

LANGUAGE COACH

DIRECTIONS: Antonyms are words that have opposite meanings. Match each word in the first column with its correct antonym in the second column. Write the letter of the correct antonym on the line.

______	1. ambitious	a. smile
______	2. sneer	b. strong
______	3. colossal	c. needy
______	4. antique	d. unmotivated
______	5. loath	e. selfish
______	6. wealthy	f. new
______	7. generous	g. irresponsible
______	8. frail	h. small
______	9. boundless	i. willing
______	10. dependable	j. limited

WRITING ACTIVITY

DIRECTIONS: The poems "Ozymandias" and "Ode on a Grecian Urn" both speak about a piece of art from the ancient past. Write a paragraph in which you **compare** and **contrast** the two poems. In your paragraph, answer the following questions: What works of art are the authors writing about? How are their styles of writing similar and how are they different? How are the tones of the two works similar and how are they different?

Vocabulary Review

Unit 4

DIRECTIONS: Write the correct vocabulary words from the Word Box on the blank lines below. Some words will not be used.

Word Box

abated
antique
aspire
bid
boundless
colossal
deities
device
differentiate
dismal
girdled
impels
inherent
loath
meandering
pastoral
recompense
sinews
sneer
tyrannous

1. I hate cleaning out the garage, and I am ________________ to do it every spring.
2. The ________________ vase in the museum is more than 2,000 years old!
3. To the pioneers, the ________________ mountain range seemed much too large to cross.
4. The high-spirited child has ________________ energy and never tires out.
5. The ________________ king limited the citizens' freedoms.
6. After a few days, the pain in Matt's shoulder ________________ and he was able to play football again.
7. The cowboys ________________ the cattle in order to keep them from running away.
8. The ________________ scene in the painting included a simple farmhouse, some cattle, and a forest.
9. Sara has an ________________ ability to tell when someone is lying.
10. Alex's ________________ story jumped from topic to topic and had absolutely no point.
11. The students at the film school ________________ to be movie directors some day.
12. I cannot ________________ between the two photos; they look exactly the same to me.
13. The dark, ________________ rain clouds left me feeling sad.
14. The father ________________ the boy to take his hand before they crossed the street.
15. The thought of winning the marathon ________________ me to keep training daily.

Applying the Key Concepts

Unit 4

DIRECTIONS: Review the Key Concepts at the beginning of this unit. Then answer the following questions:

REVOLUTION SPREADS

- Writers of the Romantic era reacted against the ugliness of revolution by turning to worlds and events that existed only in their imaginations. Find at least one example of such a world or event in this unit's selections.

CONSERVATIVES CLAMP DOWN

- In "Lines Composed a Few Miles Above Tintern Abbey," Wordsworth tells of the healing power of nature. In what natural place—either real or in your imagination—do you or might you find a similar feeling?

INDUSTRIALIZATION FINDS A FOOTHOLD

- What are some elements of "The Rime of the Ancient Mariner" that connect the poem to the Gothic style of literature?

Unit 5

The Victorian Period 1832–1901

Victoria & Albert Museum, London/Art Resource, NY

Key Concepts

RIOTS AND REFORMS

History of the Times The Reform Bill of 1832 gave more power to middle class Englishmen. When widespread unemployment and high bread prices gave way to an economic crisis, riots broke out. The tax that had caused bread prices to rise was ended, though, and England did not have a revolution.

Literature of the Times The extremely popular novels of Charles Dickens described the suffering of poor people and helped move the nation toward reform.

PROGRESS BRINGS PROSPERITY

History of the Times In the mid-1800s, the English people felt hopeful. Free trade within Europe made some people rich, while better control of the factory system improved the lives of the working class.

Literature of the Times Many writers believed that history, technology, free markets, and God were working toward the betterment of human beings.

DECORUM AND DOUBT

History of the Times Middle-class society followed strict codes of manners and morality. Many people believed that life would be better if it were more cultured and better controlled. However, some people mocked these notions and argued that wealth did not fulfill human needs.

Literature of the Times Matthew Arnold's poem "Dover Beach" expressed the doubts and anxieties of the late Victorian period.

ACADEMIC VOCABULARY

benefit (BEHN UH FIHT) *n.:* anything that is for the good of a person or thing. *The Reform Bill of 1832 was a benefit for middle-class Englishmen.*

respond (RIH SPAHND) *v.:* react. *Can you respond to the writer's complaint?*

statistics (STUH TIHS TIHKS) *n. pl.:* numerical facts. *Statistics show that Victorians did not live as long on average as we do.*

publish (PUHB LIHSH) *v.:* print and issue for the public. *Do you hope to publish your own poetry?*

complex (KAHM PLEHKS) *adj.:* hard to understand; complicated. *The factors causing the crisis were complex.*

Collection 9

Love and Loss

© Christie's Images/Corbis

The Lady of Shalott

by Alfred, Lord Tennyson

LITERARY FOCUS: SOUND DEVICES IN POETRY

Poets use many different **sound devices** to create musical effects in their poems. In "The Lady of Shalott," Tennyson uses **meter**, or rhythm, and sound repetitions such as **rhyme, alliteration** (the repetition of the beginning consonants of words), and **assonance** (the repetition of vowel sounds), to create a musical flow that carries the reader through the poem. The rhythms and repetitions help to create a dreamy, almost supernatural mood.

Use the Skill Read the following lines from the poem. Circle one example of rhyme, underline one example of alliteration, and double underline one example of assonance.

Only reapers, reaping early
In among the bearded barley,
Hear a song that echoes cheerly
From the river winding clearly,
  Down to towered Camelot; (lines 28–32)

READING FOCUS: IDENTIFYING CONTRASTING IMAGES

Poets sometimes use **contrasting images** (images that are opposite of each other) to add tension to their poems. "The Lady of Shalott" has many contrasting images, such as the flat, flowing river and the tall, unchanging tower; the busy lives of the villagers and the lonely life of the Lady; the weary whisper of the reaper and the energetic song of Sir Lancelot. As you read the poem, pay attention to the contrasting images in setting, actions, or imagery. Notice how they affect the mood.

Use the Skill Read these lines from "The Lady of Shalott." Find a set of contrasting images in the lines and list them in the space provided. Explain whether you think they are in opposition in setting, action, or imagery.

Lying, robed in snowy white
That loosely flew to left and right—
The leaves upon her falling light—
Through the noises of the night (lines 136–139)

____

____

____

____

Literary Skills Understand and analyze sound devices in poetry.

Reading Skills Identify contrasting images.

Vocabulary Development

The Lady of Shalott

SELECTION VOCABULARY

surly (SUR LEE) *adj.:* rude or unfriendly.

The Lady of Shalott watches surly peasants traveling along the highway toward Camelot.

brazen (BRAY ZUHN) *adj.:* made of brass.

Sir Lancelot is wearing brazen armor.

burnished (BUHR NIHSHT) *v.* used as *adj.:* bright and smooth.

The knights of Camelot wear burnished helmets.

waning (WAYN IHNG) *v.:* fading gradually.

As night falls, the Lady weaves in the waning light.

countenance (KOWN TUH NUHNS) *n.:* facial appearance.

The Lady's blank countenance suggests that she is in a trance.

WORD STUDY

DIRECTIONS: Some words have strong connotations, or feelings and associations attached to a word. Read each sentence below. List at least two of the connotations that the underlined vocabulary word has for you.

1. The burnished metal of the car hood shone in the sun.

   ____

2. He answered my question with a surly tone.

   ____

3. It grew increasingly difficult to read in the waning light.

   ____

4. Her countenance gave no clues as to how she really felt about the situation.

   ____

THE LADY OF SHALOTT

by Alfred, Lord Tennyson

BACKGROUND
Alfred, Lord Tennyson (1809–1892) was a very popular poet during his lifetime, and is still well known today. This poem is set near the legendary court of King Arthur at Camelot. According to English legend, King Arthur and his knights would travel to and from Camelot on their heroic adventures. Sir Lancelot is the most famous of Arthur's knights.

Part I

On either side the river lie **A**
Long fields of barley and of rye,
That clothe the wold[1] and meet the sky;
And through the field the road runs by
To many-towered Camelot;[2]
And up and down the people go,
Gazing where the lilies blow[3]
Round an island there below,
The island of Shalott. **B**

Willows whiten,[4] aspens quiver,
Little breezes dusk and shiver
Through the wave that runs forever
By the island in the river
Flowing down to Camelot.
Four gray walls, and four gray towers,
Overlook a space of flowers,

1. **wold:** rolling plain.
2. **Camelot:** legendary city, site of King Arthur's court and Round Table.
3. **blow:** blossom.
4. **whiten:** show the white undersides of their leaves when blown by the wind.

A LANGUAGE COACH

The word *lie* has multiple meanings. Which definition do you think is intended here?

B READING FOCUS

What **contrasting images** can you find in the first stanza?

And the silent isle imbowers[5]
  The Lady of Shalott. **A**

By the margin, willow-veiled,
Slide the heavy barges trailed
By slow horses; and unhailed
The shallop[6] flitteth silken-sailed
  Skimming down to Camelot:
But who hath seen her wave her hand?
Or at the casement seen her stand?
Or is she known in all the land,
  The Lady of Shalott?

Only reapers, reaping early
In among the bearded barley,
Hear a song that echoes cheerly[7]
From the river winding clearly,
  Down to towered Camelot;
And by the moon the reaper weary,
Piling sheaves in uplands airy,
Listening, whispers "'Tis the fairy
  Lady of Shalott." **B** **C**

Part II

There she weaves by night and day
A magic web with colors gay.
She has heard a whisper say,
A curse is on her if she stay
  To look down to Camelot.
She knows not what the curse may be,
And so she weaveth steadily,
And little other care hath she,
  The Lady of Shalott.

5. **imbowers:** covers with trees, gardens, and flowers.
6. **shallop:** small, open boat.
7. **cheerly:** archaic for "cheerily."

A LITERARY FOCUS

Underline each example of **alliteration** in this stanza.

B LITERARY ANALYSIS

Part I of the poem describes the Lady's environment, without telling us much about the Lady herself. Why do you think Tennyson chose to begin the poem this way?

C LITERARY FOCUS

Underline all examples of the **assonance** of one vowel sound of your choice in this stanza.

And moving through a mirror clear[8]
That hangs before her all the year,
Shadows of the world appear.
There she sees the highway near
Winding down to Camelot;
There the river eddy whirls,
And there the surly village churls,[9] D
And the red cloaks of market girls,
Pass onward from Shalott. E

Sometimes a troop of damsels glad,
An abbot on an ambling pad,[10] F
Sometimes a curly shepherd lad,
Or long-haired page in crimson clad,
Goes by to towered Camelot;
And sometimes through the mirror blue
The knights come riding two and two:
She hath no loyal knight and true,
The Lady of Shalott.

But in her web she still delights
To weave the mirror's magic sights,
For often through the silent nights
A funeral, with plumes and lights
And music, went to Camelot;
Or when the moon was overhead,
Came two young lovers lately wed:
"I am half sick of shadows," said
The Lady of Shalott. G

Part III

A bowshot from her bower eaves,
He rode between the barley sheaves,

8. mirror clear: Weavers worked on the back of the tapestry so that they could easily knot their yarns. To see the front of their designs, weavers looked in a mirror that reflected the front of the tapestry.
9. churls: peasants; country folk.
10. pad: easy-gaited horse.

D VOCABULARY

Selection Vocabulary

Surly is an adjective meaning "rude or unfriendly." Based on this knowledge, describe how you visualize the villagers.

E LITERARY FOCUS

Find and circle at least one example of **assonance** in this stanza.

F VOCABULARY

Word Study

Use a thesaurus to find a synonym, or word with a similar meaning, for *ambling*. Use the synonym in a sentence.

G READING FOCUS

List the **contrasting images** that appear in the last two stanzas of Part II.

A LANGUAGE COACH

The word *brazen* has **multiple meanings**. As it is used here, it means "made of brass." It can also mean "bold." How is the use of *brazen* especially appropriate here, given its multiple meanings?

B LITERARY FOCUS

Which consonant is used the most in the **alliteration** in this stanza?

The sun came dazzling through the leaves,
And flamed upon the brazen greaves[11]
Of bold Sir Lancelot. **A**
A red-cross knight[12] forever kneeled
To a lady in his shield,
That sparkled on the yellow field,
Beside remote Shalott.

The gemmy[13] bridle glittered free,
Like to some branch of stars we see
Hung in the golden Galaxy.[14]
The bridle bells rang merrily
As he rode down to Camelot;
And from his blazoned baldric[15] slung
A mighty silver bugle hung,
And as he rode his armor rung,
Beside remote Shalott. **B**

All in the blue unclouded weather
Thick-jeweled shone the saddle leather,
The helmet and the helmet feather
Burned like one burning flame together,
As he rode down to Camelot;
As often through the purple night,
Below the starry clusters bright,
Some bearded meteor, trailing light,
Moves over still Shalott.

His broad clear brow in sunlight glowed;
On burnished hooves his war horse trode;
From underneath his helmet flowed
His coal-black curls as on he rode,

11. **greaves:** armor for the lower legs.
12. **red-cross knight:** The red cross is the emblem of Saint George, England's patron saint.
13. **gemmy:** set with jewels.
14. **Galaxy:** Milky Way galaxy.
15. **blazoned baldric:** richly decorated sash worn diagonally across the chest.

As he rode down to Camelot.
From the bank and from the river
He flashed into the crystal mirror,
"Tirra lirra," by the river
Sang Sir Lancelot.

She left the web, she left the loom,
She made three paces through the room,
She saw the waterlily bloom,
She saw the helmet and the plume,
She looked down to Camelot.
Out flew the web and floated wide;
The mirror cracked from side to side;
"The curse is come upon me," cried
The Lady of Shalott. **C**

Part IV

In the stormy east wind straining,
The pale yellow woods were waning, **D**
The broad stream in his banks complaining,
Heavily the low sky raining
Over towered Camelot;
Down she came and found a boat
Beneath a willow left afloat,
And round about the prow[16] she wrote
The Lady of Shalott.

And down the river's dim expanse
Like some bold seër[17] in a trance,
Seeing all his own mischance—
With a glassy countenance
Did she look to Camelot.
And at the closing of the day
She loosed the chain, and down she lay;

16. **prow:** front part of a boat.
17. **seër:** prophet.

C VOCABULARY

Academic Vocabulary
How does the Lady *respond*, or react, to Lancelot?

D VOCABULARY

Selection Vocabulary
Waning means "fading gradually." What do you think Tennyson means by saying that the "woods were waning"?

A READING FOCUS

Describe the **contrasting images** of the Lady of Shalott and Sir Lancelot.

The Lady of Shalott, 1888, by John William Waterhouse/Tate Gallery, London/Art Resource, NY

The broad stream bore her far away,
    The Lady of Shalott.

Lying, robed in snowy white
That loosely flew to left and right—
The leaves upon her falling light—
Through the noises of the night
    She floated down to Camelot; **A**
And as the boat head wound along
The willowy hills and fields among,
They heard her singing her last song,
    The Lady of Shalott.

    Heard a carol, mournful, holy,
Chanted loudly, chanted lowly,
Till her blood was frozen slowly,
And her eyes were darkened wholly,
    Turned to towered Camelot.
For ere she reached upon the tide
The first house by the waterside,

Singing in her song she died,
  The Lady of Shalott. B

Under tower and balcony,
By garden wall and gallery,
A gleaming shape she floated by,
Dead-pale between the houses high,
  Silent into Camelot.
Out upon the wharfs they came,
Knight and burgher,[18] lord and dame,
And round the prow they read her name,
  The Lady of Shalott.

Who is this? and what is here?
And in the lighted palace near
Died the sound of royal cheer;
And they crossed themselves for fear,
  All the knights at Camelot:
But Lancelot mused a little space;
He said, "She has a lovely face;
God in his mercy lend her grace,
  The Lady of Shalott." C D

18. **burgher:** townsperson.

B QUICK CHECK

Underline the fate of the Lady.

C LITERARY FOCUS

What mood do the **sound devices** in this stanza create, and how?

D LITERARY ANALYSIS

What do you think is the message of this poem? Explain.

The Lady of Shalott

VOCABULARY DEVELOPMENT

DIRECTIONS: Match the vocabulary words in the left column with their synonyms in the right column.

_______	**1.** surly	**a.** decreasing
_______	**2.** burnished	**b.** grouchy
_______	**3.** waning	**c.** expression
_______	**4.** countenance	**d.** polished

LITERARY FOCUS: SOUND DEVICES IN POETRY

DIRECTIONS: Review "The Lady of Shalott" to find two examples of each of the **sound devices** listed below. Include the numbers of the lines where you find each example.

1. alliteration ______________________________

____

2. rhyme ______________________________

____

3. assonance ______________________________

____

READING FOCUS: IDENTIFYING CONTRASTING IMAGES

DIRECTIONS: Review "The Lady of Shalott" to find three sets of **contrasting images** and list them below.

1. ______________________________

____

2. ______________________________

____

3. ______________________________

____

Literary Skills Understand sound devices in poetry.

Reading Skills Identify contrasting images.

Preparing to Read

My Last Duchess

by Robert Browning

LITERARY FOCUS: DRAMATIC MONOLOGUE

"My Last Duchess" is one of Browning's most popular dramatic monologues. A **dramatic monologue** is a poem in which a speaker who is not the poet addresses one or more listeners who remain silent. The poet sets a scene in which the speaker reveals information about himself or herself, the other characters, and the situation by dropping indirect clues that we must piece together.

READING FOCUS: DRAWING INFERENCES FROM TEXTUAL CLUES

Sometimes you must draw inferences in order to understand things a writer has not stated directly. An **inference** is a guess based on information in the text and on your own knowledge and experience. To draw an inference, focus on important details in the text, and then combine that information with what you already know.

Use the Skill As you read, look for details in the poem that provide clues to the questions below. These details will help you infer answers to the questions after you read the poem.

Questions
What kind of a person is the Duke?
What impression of the Duchess does the Duke give in his description of her?
What happened to the Duke's "last Duchess"?

Literary Skills
Understand the characteristics of dramatic monologue.

Reading Skills
Draw inferences from textual clues.

Vocabulary Development

My Last Duchess

SELECTION VOCABULARY

officious (UH FIHSH UHS) *adj.:* eager to give unwanted help.
My officious neighbor interferes in everyone's business.

munificence (MYOO NIHF UH SUHNS) *n.:* generosity.
I was impressed by her munificence when she bought toys for all the children in the orphanage.

pretense (PREE TEHNS) *n.:* weakly supported claim; deception.
He excused himself from the business meeting on the pretense of an urgent phone call.

object (AHB JEHKT) *n.:* goal or purpose.
My object in jogging everyday is to prepare for the upcoming marathon.

WORD STUDY

DIRECTIONS: Write "Yes" after each sentence if the italicized vocabulary word is being used correctly. Write "No" if it is being used incorrectly, and rewrite the sentence so that the word is used correctly.

1. My *officious* brother never helps out around the house. ________

   ____

2. The baseball players showed their *munificence* by donating money to charity for every homerun they hit. ________

   ____

3. His shoulders were *pretense* for days following the afternoon of rock climbing. ________

   ____

4. The *object* of this homework is for students to continue practicing the skills they develop in the classroom. ________

   ____

My Last Duchess

by Robert Browning

BACKGROUND

The speaker in "My Last Duchess" is not named, but Browning identified him as Alfonso II, the fifth Duke of Ferrara, who was a powerful nobleman in Renaissance Italy. The first of the Duke's three wives was a young girl. She died in 1561, about three years after they were married. Many believed that she had been poisoned. In "My Last Duchess," the Duke is making plans to marry the daughter of a count, and he is making arrangements with the Count's representative.

That's my last Duchess painted on the wall,
Looking as if she were alive. I call
That piece a wonder, now; Frà Pandolf's[1] hands
Worked busily a day, and there she stands.
Will 't please you sit and look at her? I said
"Frà Pandolf" by design, for never read
Strangers like you that pictured countenance, **A**
The depth and passion of its earnest glance,
But to myself they turned (since none puts by
the curtain I have drawn for you, but I) **B**
And seemed as they would ask me, if they durst,
How such a glance came there; so, not the first
Are you to turn and ask thus. Sir, 'twas not
Her husband's presence only, called that spot
Of joy into the Duchess' cheek; perhaps
Frà Pandolf chanced to say, "Her mantle[2] laps
Over my lady's wrist too much," or, "Paint
Must never hope to reproduce the faint

A LITERARY FOCUS

What clues so far tell you that this is a **dramatic monologue**?

B READING FOCUS

Considering that the Duke keeps the painting of his former wife hidden behind a curtain, what can you **infer** about him?

1. **Frà Pandolf's:** Brother Pandolf, a fictitious painter and monk.
2. **mantle:** cloak.

A LANGUAGE COACH

The word *flush* can have multiple meanings. What part of speech is *flush* as it is used here and what does it mean?

B VOCABULARY

Word Study

Favor comes from the Latin *favorem*, meaning "good will or support." How is the definition of *favor* related to the definition of its root?

Half flush that dies along her throat." **A** Such stuff
Was courtesy, she thought, and cause enough
For calling up that spot of joy. She had
A heart—how shall I say?—too soon made glad,
Too easily impressed; she liked whate'er
She looked on, and her looks went everywhere.
Sir, 'twas all one! My favor[3] at her breast, **B**
The dropping of the daylight in the West,
The bough of cherries some officious fool
Broke in the orchard for her, the white mule

3. **favor:** gift; token of love.

La Donna Velata, 1516, by Raphael/Palazzo pitti, Florence, Italy/Alinari/The Bridgeman Art Library

She rode with round the terrace—all and each
Would draw from her alike the approving speech,
Or blush, at least. She thanked men—good! but thanked
Somehow—I know not how—as if she ranked
My gift of a nine-hundred-years-old name
With anybody's gift. **C** Who'd stoop to blame
This sort of trifling? Even had you skill
In speech—(which I have not)—to make your will
Quite clear to such an one, and say, "Just this
Or that in you disgusts me; here you miss,
Or there exceed the mark"—and if she let
Herself be lessoned so, nor plainly set
Her wits to yours, forsooth,[4] and made excuse,
—E'en then would be some stooping; and I choose
Never to stoop. Oh sir, she smiled, no doubt,
Whene'er I passed her; but who passed without
Much the same smile? This grew; I gave commands;
Then all smiles stopped together. There she stands
As if alive. Will 't please you rise? **D** We'll meet
The company below, then. I repeat,
The Count your master's known munificence
Is ample warrant[5] that no just pretense
Of mine for dowry will be disallowed;
Though his fair daughter's self, as I avowed
At starting, is my object. **E** Nay, we'll go
Together down, sir. Notice Neptune,[6] though,
Taming a seahorse, thought a rarity,
Which Claus of Innsbruck[7] cast in bronze for me! **F**

4. **forsooth:** archaic for "in truth."
5. **warrant:** guarantee.
6. **Neptune:** in Roman mythology, god of the sea.
7. **Claus of Innsbruck:** fictional sculptor.

C READING FOCUS

What can you **infer** about the Duke's personality based on these complaints about his late wife?

D LITERARY ANALYSIS

What do you suspect happened to the Duchess?

E VOCABULARY

Selection Vocabulary

The Duke says that the Count's "fair daughter's self" is his *object*. What does *object* mean here?

F VOCABULARY

Academic Vocabulary

For the Duke, what *benefit*, or advantage, is there of including this last sentence?

Applying Your Skills

My Last Duchess

VOCABULARY DEVELOPMENT

DIRECTIONS: Select the correct vocabulary words from the Word Box to complete the following sentences. One word will not be used.

Word Box

- officious
- munificence
- pretense
- object

1. To show his ____________________, the Count offered the Duke a large amount of money for marrying his daughter.
2. The Count's ____________________ in sending a representative to meet the Duke was to allow them to discuss the marriage arrangements.
3. While the Duchess appreciated her various gift-givers, the Duke considered them to be ____________________ fools.

LITERARY FOCUS: DRAMATIC MONOLOGUE

DIRECTIONS: One important component of a **dramatic monologue** is that the listener remains silent. In "My Last Duchess," the Duke asks many questions, but he never allows the Count's representative to answer. Write a brief paragraph explaining the meaning of the following quotation and the effect of the Duke's unanswered question:

Lines 43–45: "Oh sir, she smiled, no doubt, / Whene'er I passed her; but who passed without / Much the same smile?"

____

____

____

READING FOCUS: DRAWING INFERENCES FROM TEXTUAL CLUES

DIRECTIONS: Write a brief paragraph describing the type of person the Duke is, based on the **inferences** you made while reading the poem. Consider the following questions as you respond: What was the Duke's relationship with his late wife like? What does he think of women? Why is he looking to remarry?

____

____

____

SKILLS FOCUS

Literary Skills Understand the characteristics of dramatic monologue.

Reading Skills Draw inferences from textual clues.

Sonnet 43

by Elizabeth Barrett Browning

LITERARY FOCUS: PETRARCHAN SONNET

"Sonnet 43," like many of Elizabeth Barrett Browning's poems, is a **Petrarchan sonnet**. A Petrarchan, or Italian, sonnet is divided into a group of eight lines (an octave) followed by a group of six lines (a sestet). It is written in **iambic pentameter**, an alternating pattern of unstressed and stressed syllables with a total of ten syllables per line, and rhymes in the following way: *abbaabba* (the octave) and *cdcdcd* (the sestet). Petrarchan sonnets also usually have a break in thought, or **turn**, between the octave and the sestet. "Sonnet 43," however, lacks a turn and is instead broken into short units of thought.

Use the Skill As you read, keep the following chart in mind and notice how Browning's rhyme scheme meets the requirements of a Petrarchan sonnet:

Sonnet section	Rhyme scheme
Octave: Line 1	*a*
2	*b*
3	*b*
4	*a*
5	*a*
6	*b*
7	*b*
8	*a*
Sestet: Line 9	*c*
10	*d*
11	*c*
12	*d*
13	*c*
14	*d*

Literary Skills Understand the Petrarchan sonnet form.

Preparing to Read

Sonnet 43

READING FOCUS: PARAPHRASING

When you **paraphrase** a poem, you restate it using your own words. You do not use quotations from the work. A paraphrase is often as long as, or even longer than, the original text. A paraphrase differs from a summary, which is shorter than the original text and includes only its main ideas.

The chart below contains a paraphrase of the first three lines of William Shakespeare's "Sonnet 116."

Lines from Sonnet 116	Paraphrase
"Let me not to the marriage of true minds / Admit impediments. Love is not love / Which alters when it alterations finds,"	I will not allow any obstacles to stand in the way of true love. True love is not changeable.

Reading Skills
Paraphrase to clarify meaning.

Notice that when you paraphrase, you not only replace the original words with your own, but you also use your own grammar and sentence structure. While reading "Sonnet 43," you may need to consult a dictionary to define some terms to help you more accurately paraphrase the poem.

SONNET 43

by Elizabeth Barrett Browning

BACKGROUND
The following is one of the many love poems that Elizabeth Barrett Browning (1806–1861) addressed to her future husband, Robert Browning, during their courtship.

Love Among the Ruins by Sir Edward Burne-Jones/Wightwick Manor, Staffordshire UK/National Trust Photographic Library/Derrick E. Witty/The Bridgeman Art Library

How do I love thee? Let me count the ways.
I love thee to the depth and breadth and height
My soul can reach, when feeling out of sight
For the ends of Being and ideal Grace. **A**
I love thee to the level of everyday's
Most quiet need, by sun and candlelight.
I love thee freely, as men strive for Right;
I love thee purely, as they turn from Praise. **B**
I love thee with the passion put to use
In my old griefs, and with my childhood's faith.
I love thee with a love I seemed to lose
With my lost saints[1]—I love thee with the breath,
Smiles, tears, of all my life!—and, if God choose,
I shall but love thee better after death. **C** **D**

1. **lost saints:** childhood faith.

A READING FOCUS

Paraphrase lines 1–4.

B LANGUAGE COACH

Write a **synonym** (word with a similar meaning) for *praise*.

C LITERARY FOCUS

Draw brackets around the sestet of this **Petrarchan sonnet**. Then, underline the *c* rhymes and circle the *d* rhymes in the sestet.

D VOCABULARY

Academic Vocabulary

Do you find this poem to be *complex*, or hard to understand? Why or why not?

Applying Your Skills

Sonnet 43

LITERARY FOCUS: PETRARCHAN SONNET

DIRECTIONS: Review the elements of a **Petrarchan sonnet.** Then decide whether each statement below is "True" or "False".

1. A Petrarchan sonnet is made up of three parts: an octave, a sestet, and a rhymed couplet. ________
2. The rhyme scheme of a Petrarchan sonnet's octave is *abbaabba*. ________
3. Traditional Petrarchan sonnets are written in iambic hexameter. ________
4. A Petrarchan sonnet has more lines than an Italian sonnet. ________

READING FOCUS: PARAPHRASING

DIRECTIONS: **Paraphrase** the following passages from "Sonnet 43":

Passages from the poem	Paraphrase
"I love thee to the level of everyday's / Most quiet need, by sun and candlelight." (lines 5–6)	1.
"I love thee freely, as men strive for Right; / I love thee purely, as they turn from Praise." (lines 7–8)	2.
"I love thee with the passion put to use / In my old griefs, and with my childhood's faith." (lines 9–10)	3.
"I love thee with a love I seemed to lose / With my lost saints" (lines 11–12)	4.
"I love thee with the breath, / Smiles, tears, of all my life!" (lines 12–13)	5.

Literary Skills Understand the Petrarchan sonnet form.

Reading Skills Paraphrase to clarify meaning.

Skills Review

Collection 9

LANGUAGE COACH

DIRECTIONS: Remember that **synonyms** are words that have similar meanings. Match each word in the first column with its correct synonym in the second column. Write the letter of the correct synonym on the line.

_______	**1.** munificence	**a.** expression
_______	**2.** surly	**b.** charity
_______	**3.** countenance	**c.** challenging
_______	**4.** respond	**d.** polished
_______	**5.** object	**e.** hostile
_______	**6.** officious	**f.** deceit
_______	**7.** waning	**g.** reply
_______	**8.** pretense	**h.** decreasing
_______	**9.** complex	**i.** intrusive
_______	**10.** burnished	**j.** goal

ORAL LANGUAGE ACTIVITY

DIRECTIONS: Re-read "My Last Duchess" by Robert Browning. Remember that the speaker of the poem is talking to a Count's representative about a possible marriage. Suppose that you are the Count's representative. Prepare a short speech in which you try to convince the Count why he should or should not allow the marriage between his daughter and the Duke. Include a description of the Duke's characteristics, supported by examples from the text. Then, read your speech in front of the class.

Collection 10

The Paradox of Progress

Matthew Arnold by George Frederic Watts/ National Portrait Gallery, London

Preparing to Read

Dover Beach

by Matthew Arnold

LITERARY FOCUS: MOOD

Mood is the feeling, or emotional **atmosphere**, in a literary work. It is created by the writer's choice of descriptive details, images, and sounds. The mood can change within a single work. Arnold creates a mood in "Dover Beach" that shifts at certain points like the ebb and flow of the tide that he describes.

Use the Skill As you read "Dover Beach," use a chart like the one below to analyze the mood of each sentence in the poem. List examples of details, images, and sounds the author uses to create the mood.

Lines	Mood	Details/images/sounds

READING FOCUS: VISUALIZING SETTING

Writers like Matthew Arnold fill their writing with visual details to help their readers imagine a particular place at a particular time. As you read, focus on descriptive words that give you a sense of the **setting**, the time and place of the events in a literary work. You may find it useful to pause every few lines and summarize the specific details of the setting. While details are often visual, the writer may also appeal to other senses, such as hearing, smell, or touch.

Use the Skill To visualize the setting of "Dover Beach," make a concept map like the one below. Write each element of the setting outside the center oval. Then, circle the element and draw a line connecting it to the central oval. The first two have been provided for you.

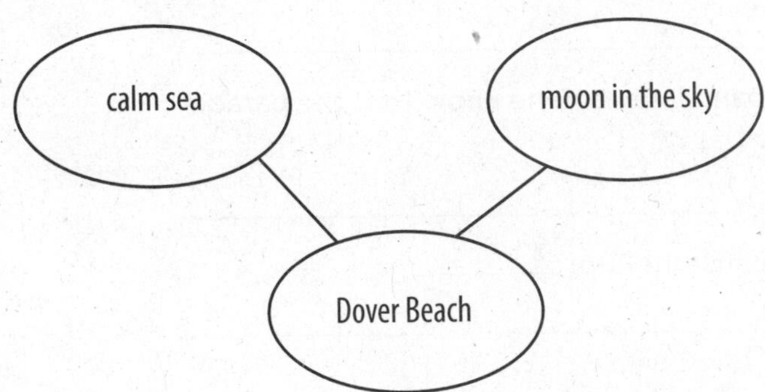

Literary Skills Understand mood.

Reading Skills Visualize setting.

Vocabulary Development

Dover Beach

SELECTION VOCABULARY

blanched (BLANCHT) *v.* used as *adj.:* made white or pale.
The pale light of the moon creates a blanched scene.

tremulous (TREHM YUH LUHS) *adj.:* quivering; wavering.
The tremulous waves beat back and forth.

cadence (KAY DUHNS) *n.:* the beat of a repetitive motion; a sound that rises and falls.
The sea beats on the shore with a steady cadence.

turbid (TUHR BIHD) *adj.:* cloudy; confused.
In the turbid waves, Sophocles sees a metaphor for human suffering.

melancholy (MEHL UHN KAHL EE) *adj.:* sad or causing sadness.
The loss of faith leaves the speaker feeling melancholy.

certitude (SUHR TUH TOOD) *n.:* feeling of sureness.
Changes in values and ideas leave the speaker without certitude.

WORD STUDY

DIRECTIONS: Write "Yes" after each sentence if the vocabulary word is being used correctly. Write "No" if it is being used incorrectly, and rewrite the sentence so the vocabulary word is used correctly.

1. The *tremulous* dog was nervous about her new surroundings. ________

   ____

2. After winning first prize, he felt overjoyed and *melancholy*. ________

   ____

3. Even though we were lost, the scout leader's *certitude* reassured the group. ________

   ____

4. I bought a *turbid* for my mother at the gift store. ________

   ____

5. The *cadence* from the marching band let everyone know that the parade was about to begin. ________

   ____

6. I painted my room *blanched* to match the sun. ________

   ____

Dover Beach

by Matthew Arnold

BACKGROUND
Matthew Arnold (1822–1888) wrote at a time when science and technology were changing traditional beliefs. Just three years before Arnold wrote this poem, several European nations had faced civil rebellions. Arnold was concerned that rapid changes in technology and politics were weakening cultural ties among people. He believed that the arts could unify people in the future, just as religion had done in the past.

The sea is calm tonight.
The tide is full, the moon lies fair
Upon the straits[1]—on the French coast the light
Gleams and is gone; the cliffs of England stand,
Glimmering and vast, out in the tranquil bay.
Come to the window, sweet is the night air!
Only, from the long line of spray
Where the sea meets the moon-blanched land, (A)
Listen! you hear the grating roar
Of pebbles which the waves draw back, and fling,
At their return, up the high strand,[2]
Begin, and cease, and then again begin,
With tremulous cadence slow, and bring
The eternal note of sadness in. (B)

Sophocles[3] long ago
Heard it on the Aegean,[4] and it brought
Into his mind the turbid ebb and flow

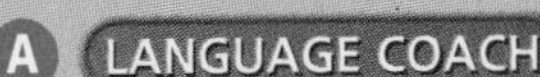

Blanched comes from the **French root** *blanc*, meaning "white." Knowing this, what do you think *blanched* means? What do you think *moon-blanched* means?

B READING FOCUS

Underline the sights and sounds of the **setting** that the author describes in lines 1–14.

1. **straits:** Strait of Dover, a body of water separating southeastern England and northwestern France.
2. **strand:** shore.
3. **Sophocles** (SAHF UH KLEEZ) (c. 496–406 B.C.): writer of tragedies in ancient Greece.
4. **Aegean** (UH JEE UHN): sea between Greece and Turkey.

A VOCABULARY

Word Study

Misery means "extreme unhappiness." Circle all of the synonyms (words with similar meanings) for *misery* in this poem.

B VOCABULARY

Selection Vocabulary

Melancholy means "sad or causing sadness." What is being described as melancholy?

C LITERARY FOCUS

How does the **mood** change from the beginning of the poem to the end?

____

____

____

____

D VOCABULARY

Academic Vocabulary

Arnold waited sixteen years to *publish* this poem, or print and issue it for the public. Considering the subject matter, why do you think he waited so long?

____

____

____

____

Pegwell Bay, Kent -- A Recollection of October 5, 1858 by William Dyce/ Tate Gallery, London/Art Resource, NY

Of human misery; we **A**
Find also in the sound a thought,
Hearing it by this distant northern sea.
The Sea of Faith
Was once, too, at the full, and round earth's shore
Lay like the folds of a bright girdle[5] furled.
But now I only hear
Its melancholy, long, withdrawing roar, **B**
Retreating, to the breath
Of the night wind, down the vast edges drear
And naked shingles[6] of the world.

Ah, love, let us be true
To one another! for the world, which seems
To lie before us like a land of dreams,
So various, so beautiful, so new,
Hath really neither joy, nor love, nor light,
Nor certitude, nor peace, nor help for pain;
And we are here as on a darkling[7] plain
Swept with confused alarms of struggle and flight,
Where ignorant armies clash by night. **C** **D**

5. **girdle:** belt.
6. **shingles:** here, beaches covered with pebbles.
7. **darkling:** growing gloomy or dark.

Skills Practice

Dover Beach

USE AN IMAGERY CHART

DIRECTIONS: Use the chart below to list the details from "Dover Beach" that appeal to the reader's senses of sight and hearing. Then, on the lines below, explain which details contributed most to the poem's **mood**. Explain your answer.

Sight	Hearing

Applying Your Skills

Dover Beach

VOCABULARY DEVELOPMENT

DIRECTIONS: Next to each pair of words, write whether the two words are "antonyms" (words with opposite meanings) or "synonyms" (words with similar meanings).

1. blanched; lightened ________________________

2. tremulous; steady ________________________

3. cadence; rhythm ________________________

4. turbid; clear ________________________

5. melancholy; ecstatic ________________________

6. certitude; confidence ________________________

LITERARY FOCUS: MOOD

DIRECTIONS: Review the chart you made on the previous page. Then, write a short summary that describes the overall **mood** of the entire poem.

____

____

____

____

____

READING FOCUS: VISUALIZING SETTING

DIRECTIONS: Re-read "Dover Beach" carefully. Describe in detail how you visualized each element of the **setting** listed below.

Setting	My visualization
sea	**1.**
straits	**2.**
beach	**3.**

Literary Skills Understand mood.

Reading Skills Visualize setting.

Collection 10

LANGUAGE COACH

Although English belongs to the same language family as German, Dutch, Norwegian, Danish, and Swedish, many English words have **Latin** or **French roots**. Knowing the meanings of the original Latin and French words can help you understand the English words that are based on them.

DIRECTIONS: Look at the list of modern English words below. Match each word with its Latin or French root. Write the letter of the original word next to the correct English word.

Modern English word	Root word
_____ **1.** sequence	**a.** from the Latin word *turbidus*, meaning "muddy"
_____ **2.** rich	**b.** from the Latin word *leg* meaning "read"
_____ **3.** regret	**c.** from the Latin word *sequ*, meaning "follow"
_____ **4.** turbid	**d.** from the Old French word *riche*, meaning "wealthy"
_____ **5.** illegible	**e.** from the Old French word *regreter*, meaning "bewail"

WRITING ACTIVITY

DIRECTIONS: In the poem "Dover Beach," Matthew Arnold describes some of the negative effects of progress and technology. Write a paragraph that explains why you agree or disagree with Arnold's point of view about progress. Include examples from the text, as well as examples from modern-day life, in your paragraph.

Vocabulary Review

Unit 5

DIRECTIONS: Use context clues to figure out the meaning of each boldfaced word. Circle the letter of the correct meaning.

1. The math problem was too **complex** for me, and I needed help solving it.
   - **a.** easy
   - **b.** short
   - **c.** hard to see
   - **d.** complicated
2. The **surly** man didn't even say "thank you" when I held the door open for him.
   - **a.** rude
   - **b.** friendly
   - **c.** shy
   - **d.** quiet
3. My **object** in taking the summer job is to earn enough money to buy a car by September.
   - **a.** approval
   - **b.** loan
   - **c.** goal
   - **d.** subject
4. I was struck by her **munificence** when she paid for everyone's dinner.
   - **a.** stinginess
   - **b.** generosity
   - **c.** checkbook
   - **d.** disinterest
5. The **tremulous** stray dog had been out in the cold all night and was freezing, so I took him in.
   - **a.** quivering
   - **b.** bold
   - **c.** exhausted
   - **d.** warm-blooded

Applying the Key Concepts

Unit 5

DIRECTIONS: Review the Key Concepts at the beginning of this unit. Then answer the following questions:

RIOTS AND REFORMS

- During times of economic hardship, people often try to "escape" by reading about idealistic worlds. Why might Lord Tennyson's "The Lady of Shallot" represent an ideal society for the people in England in the early 1800s?

PROGRESS BRINGS PROSPERITY

- As you have learned, people living in England in the middle 1800s began to feel hopeful about the future. In what ways is "Sonnet 43" by Elizabeth Barrett Browning a hopeful poem?

DECORUM AND DOUBT

- Tell how Matthew Arnold's poem "Dover Beach" expresses concerns about advancement, technology, and the loss of social codes. Find specific evidence from the poem to help support your answer.

Unit 6

The Modern World 1900 to the Present

© Dominic Burke/Alamy

Key Concepts

WORLD WAR I: THE GREAT WAR

History of the Times In the early 1900s in Europe, rising nationalism, competition for colonies, and growing military power helped create deep tensions between countries. By its end in 1918, World War I (called The Great War at the time) had cost Britain not only 750,000 lives but also Britain's confidence and hope for the future.

Literature of the Times Writers experimented with form and content. Literature reflected the disappointment and doubt that people felt after the war.

WORLD WAR II AND ITS AFTERMATH

History of the Times Poverty caused by economic problems in the 1930s helped bring dictators to power in Germany, Italy, and Russia. The German dictator Hitler invaded Poland in 1939, setting off World War II. The horrors of this war, particularly the use of nuclear weapons and the Nazi death camps, changed the world forever.

Literature of the Times Much of the literature written after World War II has been a sharply critical response to war and the limits set on freedom.

IDENTITY AND DIVERSITY

History of the Times After World War II, most of Britain's remaining colonies declared independence. Changes in political situations affected many nations in Europe and Latin America. Groups that had previously had little power, such as women and ethnic minorities, began demanding more control over their own lives. All of these changes were marked by conflict.

Literature of the Times Globalization has become extremely important in literature and in economics. Writers from all around the world, especially from Britain's former colonies, explore issues of the time in an honest fashion.

ACADEMIC VOCABULARY

perspective (PUHR SPEHK TIHV) *n.:* particular way of looking at something. *Many poets changed their perspective on World War I when they saw the terrible suffering it caused.*

inevitable (IHN EHV UH TUH BUHL) *adj.:* unavoidable. *By late 1944, Germany's defeat was inevitable.*

considerably (KUHN SIHD UHR UH BLEE) *adv.:* by a large amount. *Great Britain became considerably weaker after World War II.*

adapt (UH DAPT) *v.:* adjust for a new purpose. *Millions of people had to adapt to a wartime economy.*

exhibit (EHG ZIHB IHT) *v.:* show, demonstrate. *Former colonies still exhibit the effects of being ruled by other countries.*

Collection

11

The World at War

Popperfoto/Alamy

Preparing to Read

On the Bottom
from Survival in Auschwitz

by Primo Levi, translated by Stuart Woolf

LITERARY FOCUS: MEMOIR

A **memoir** is a record of the memories of its author. It is one kind of **autobiography**, or something an author writes about him- or herself. While autobiographies generally cover a large span of time, such as a person's entire adulthood, a memoir usually focuses on a particular time period in the writer's life, often one of historical importance.

READING FOCUS: EVALUATING HISTORICAL CONTEXT

Memoirs are usually shaped by their **historical context**—the political, ethical, and social influences that set apart a particular time and place. As you read this selection, think about this historical context:

During World War II, Nazi Germany sent Jews, homosexuals, gypsies, Poles, political protestors, and the disabled to death camps. This is known as the Holocaust, the largest mass murder in human history. As many as eleven million people, six million of them Jews, were killed.

Use the Skill Read these details from Levi's memoir, and then in the space provided, describe what they tell you about the Holocaust:

Detail	What it tells me
"We have a terrible thirst . . . we have had nothing to drink for four days. But there is also a tap—and above it a card which says that it is forbidden to drink as the water is dirty." (lines 6–10)	
"Mr. Levi asks me if I think that our women are like us at this moment, and where they are, and if we will be able to see them again." (lines 79–81)	

Literary Skills Understand characteristics of a memoir.

Reading Skills Evaluate historical context.

Vocabulary Development

On the Bottom

from Survival in Auschwitz

SELECTION VOCABULARY

taciturn (TAS UH TURN) *adj.:* not talkative.

The taciturn soldiers spoke little to the men and did not answer their questions.

disconcerted (DIHS KUHN SUR TIHD) *v.* used as *adj.:* confused.

The unwillingness of the soldiers to tell what was about to happen left the men feeling disconcerted.

livid (LIHV IHD) *adj.:* pale; grayish.

The men's livid faces showed their fright.

sordid (SAWR DIHD) *adj.:* filthy; foul.

The sordid conditions of the camp allowed the spread of disease.

demolition (DEHM UH LIHSH UHN) *n.:* destruction.

The demolition of the men's identities began when they had to give up all of their possessions.

affinity (UH FIHN UH TEE) *n.:* kinship; bond.

Their isolation and despair left the men feeling no affinity with one another.

WORD STUDY

DIRECTIONS: Synonyms are words with the same or nearly the same meaning. Antonyms are words with opposite meanings. Use the vocabulary words listed above to complete each of the sentences listed below.

1. ______________________ is a synonym for *ashen*.
2. ______________________ is an antonym for *chatty*.
3. ______________________ is a synonym for *connection*.
4. ______________________ is an antonym for *construction*.
5. ______________________ is an antonym for *clean*.
6. ______________________ is a synonym for *bewildered*.

ON THE BOTTOM
from Survival in Auschwitz

by Primo Levi, translated by Stuart Woolf

BACKGROUND
In this memoir, Primo Levi (1919–1987) describes his arrival in 1944 in Auschwitz, one of the Nazi prison camps. Of the 649 people with whom he was deported during World War II, only twenty-three survived.

The journey did not last more than twenty minutes. Then the lorry[1] stopped, and we saw a large door, and above it a sign, brightly illuminated (its memory still strikes me in my dreams): *Arbeit Macht Frei,*[2] work gives freedom.

We climb down, they make us enter an enormous empty room that is poorly heated. We have a terrible thirst. The weak gurgle of water in the radiators makes us ferocious; we have had nothing to drink for four days. But there is also a tap—and above it a card which says that it is forbidden to drink as the water is dirty. Nonsense. It seems obvious that the card is a joke, "they" know that we are dying of thirst and they put us in a room, and there is a tap, and *Wassertrinken Verboten.*[3] I drink and I incite my companions to do likewise, but I have to spit it out, the water is tepid and sweetish, with the smell of a swamp. **A**

This is hell. Today, in our times, hell must be like this. A huge, empty room: we are tired, standing on our feet, with a tap which drips while we cannot drink the water, and we wait for

A READING FOCUS

How does knowing the **historical context** of this memoir affect your understanding of what is happening so far?

1. **lorry** (LOHR REE): British for "truck."
2. ***Arbeit Macht Frei*** (AHR BYT MAHKHT FRY)
3. ***Wassertrinken Verboten*** (VAH SAYR TRIHNK EHN FAYR BOH TEHN): German for "Drinking water is forbidden."

A LANGUAGE COACH

In English, the letter *c* can have a soft "s" sound or a hard "k" sound. Usually a *c* sounds like a soft "s" when it occurs before the letters e, *i*, or *y*; otherwise it has a hard "k" sound. Which of the following words from the previous sentence has a soft *c*: *cannot*, *certainly*, or *continues*?

B LITERARY FOCUS

From what you have read so far, what parts of this **memoir** might be of use to a historian writing a book about the Holocaust?

C LITERARY FOCUS

What personal details make this **memoir** more than a strictly historical account?

something which will certainly be terrible, and nothing happens and nothing continues to happen. **A** What can one think about? One cannot think any more; it is like being already dead. Someone sits down on the ground. The time passes drop by drop.

We are not dead. The door is opened and an SS[4] man enters, smoking. He looks at us slowly and asks, "*Wer kann Deutsch*?"[5] One of us whom I have never seen, named Flesch, moves forward; he will be our interpreter. The SS man makes a long, calm speech; the interpreter translates. We have to form rows of five, with intervals of two yards between man and man; then we have to undress and make a bundle of the clothes in a special manner, the woolen garments on one side, all the rest on the other; we must take off our shoes but pay great attention that they are not stolen. **B**

Stolen by whom? Why should our shoes be stolen? And what about our documents, the few things we have in our pockets, our watches? We all look at the interpreter, and the interpreter asks the German, and the German smokes and looks him through and through as if he were transparent, as if no one had spoken.

I had never seen old men naked. Mr. Bergmann wore a truss[6] and asked the interpreter if he should take it off, and the interpreter hesitated. But the German understood and spoke seriously to the interpreter pointing to someone. We saw the interpreter swallow and then he said: "The officer says, take off the truss, and you will be given that of Mr. Coen." One could see the words coming bitterly out of Flesch's mouth; this was the German manner of laughing. **C**

Now another German comes and tells us to put the shoes in a certain corner, and we put them there, because now it is all over and we feel outside this world and the only thing is to obey.

4. **SS:** abbreviation for *Schutzstaffel* ("elite guard"), the Nazi units in charge of the extermination camps during World War II.
5. ***Wer kann Deutsch?*** (VAYR KOHN DOYCH): German for "Who knows German?"
6. **truss:** belt with a pad, worn to support a hernia, a rupture of the intestine through the abdominal wall.

Someone comes with a broom and sweeps away all the shoes, outside the door in a heap. He is crazy, he is mixing them all together, ninety-six pairs, they will be all unmatched. The outside door opens; a freezing wind enters and we are naked and cover ourselves up with our arms. The wind blows and slams the door; the German reopens it and stands watching with interest how we writhe to hide from the wind, one behind the other. Then he leaves and closes it. **D**

Now the second act begins. Four men with razors, soapbrushes, and clippers burst in; they have trousers and jackets with stripes, with a number sewn on the front; perhaps they are the same sort as those others of this evening (this evening or yesterday evening?), but these are robust and flourishing. We ask many questions but they catch hold of us and in a moment we find ourselves shaved and sheared. What comic faces we have without hair! The four speak a language which does not seem of this world. It is certainly not German, for I understand a little German.

Finally another door is opened: here we are, locked in, naked, sheared and standing, with our feet in water—it is a shower room. We are alone. Slowly the astonishment dissolves, and we speak, and everyone asks questions and no one answers. If we are naked in a shower room, it means that we will have a shower. If we have a shower it is because they are not going to kill us yet. But why then do they keep us standing, and give us nothing to drink, while nobody explains anything, and we have no shoes or clothes, but we are all naked with our feet in the water, and we have been traveling five days and cannot even sit down.

And our women?

Mr. Levi asks me if I think that our women are like us at this moment, and where they are, and if we will be able to see them again. I say yes, because he is married and has a daughter; certainly we will see them again. But by now my belief is that all this is a game to mock and sneer at us. Clearly they will kill us, whoever thinks he is going to live is mad, it means that he has

D **LITERARY ANALYSIS**

How have experiences of the prisoners thus far begun to dehumanize them (deprive them of their human qualities and individuality)?

A VOCABULARY

Academic Vocabulary

Why does the author believe that his death at the hands of the Nazis is *inevitable*, or unavoidable?

B LITERARY ANALYSIS

What do the details so far tell you about what the Nazis thought about their victims?

C VOCABULARY

Selection Vocabulary

Taciturn means "not talkative." Why is it ironic (unexpected or contradictory) that the interpreter is a taciturn man?

swallowed the bait, but I have not; I have understood that it will soon all be over, perhaps in this same room, when they get bored of seeing us naked, dancing from foot to foot and trying every now and again to sit down on the floor. **A** But there are two inches of cold water and we cannot sit down. **B**

We walk up and down without sense, and we talk, everybody talks to everybody else, we make a great noise. The door opens, and a German enters; it is the officer of before. He speaks briefly, the interpreter translates. "The officer says you must be quiet, because this is not a rabbinical[7] school." One sees the words which are not his, the bad words, twist his mouth as they come out, as if he was spitting out a foul taste. We beg him to ask what we are waiting for, how long we will stay here, about our women, everything; but he says no, that he does not want to ask. This Flesch, who is most unwilling to translate into Italian the hard, cold German phrases and refuses to turn into German our questions because he knows that it is useless, is a German Jew of about fifty, who has a large scar on his face from a wound received fighting the Italians on the Piave.[8] He is a closed, taciturn man, for whom I feel an instinctive respect as I feel that he has begun to suffer before us. **C**

The German goes and we remain silent, although we are a little ashamed of our silence. It is still night and we wonder if the day will ever come. The door opens again, and someone else dressed in stripes comes in. He is different from the others, older, with glasses, a more civilized face, and much less robust. He speaks to us in Italian.

By now we are tired of being amazed. We seem to be watching some mad play, one of those plays in which the witches, the Holy Spirit, and the devil appear. He speaks Italian badly, with a strong foreign accent. He makes a long speech, is very polite, and tries to reply to all our questions.

---

7. **rabbinical** (RUH BIHN UH KUHL): of or relating to rabbis, teachers of Jewish law.
8. **Italians on the Piave:** During World War I, Austria and Germany defeated 600,000 Italian troops in the Battle of Caporetto; the Italian forces were pushed back to the Piave River near Venice.

We are at Monowitz, near Auschwitz, in Upper Silesia,[9] a region inhabited by both Poles and Germans. This camp is a workcamp, in German one says *Arbeitslager*,[10] all the prisoners (there are about ten thousand) work in a factory which produces a type of rubber called Buna, so that the camp itself is called Buna.

We will be given shoes and clothes—no, not our own—other shoes, other clothes, like his. We are naked now because we are waiting for the shower and disinfection, which will take place immediately after the reveille,[11] because one cannot enter the camp without being disinfected.

Certainly there will be work to do; everyone must work here. But there is work and work: he, for example, acts as a doctor. He is a Hungarian doctor who studied in Italy and he is the dentist of the Lager.[12] He has been in the Lager for four and a half years (not in this one: Buna has only been open for a year and a half), but we can see that he is still quite well, not very thin. Why is he in the Lager? Is he Jewish like us? "No," he says simply, "I am a criminal." **D**

We ask him many questions. He laughs, replies to some and not to others, and it is clear that he avoids certain subjects. He does not speak of the women: he says they are well, that we will see them again soon, but he does not say how or where. Instead he tells us other things, strange and crazy things, perhaps he too is playing with us. Perhaps he is mad—one goes mad in the Lager. He says that every Sunday there are concerts and football matches. He says that whoever boxes well can become cook. **E** He says that whoever works well receives prize coupons with which to buy tobacco and soap. He says that the water is really not drinkable, and that instead a coffee substitute is distributed every day, but

---

9. **Upper Silesia:** region including parts of southwestern Poland, eastern Germany, and the northern Czech Republic. After World War I, Germany and Poland divided northern Silesia; southern Silesia fell under the rule of Czechoslovakia.
10. ***Arbeitslager*** (AHR BYTS LAHG AYR)
11. **reveille** (REHV UH LEE): early-morning bugle call to waken military troops.
12. **Lager:** short for *Arbeitslager*.

D LITERARY FOCUS

How does the writing style of this **memoir** illustrate the emotions of the prisoners? What emotions are most obvious?

E LANGUAGE COACH

As you read this paragraph, find one word containing a hard *c*, one containing a soft *c*, and one word that has both. Write them below.

A LITERARY ANALYSIS

Do you think that the dentist was talking to the prisoners against SS orders? Why or why not?

B VOCABULARY

Word Study

The word *livid*, as it is used here, means "pale; grayish." Use a dictionary to look up another common meaning for *livid* that might also describe the men, and write it below.

C VOCABULARY

Selection Vocabulary

Demolition means "destruction." How have the events that you have read about caused the "demolition" of these men?

generally nobody drinks it as the soup itself is sufficiently watery to quench thirst. We beg him to find us something to drink, but he says he cannot, that he has come to see us secretly, against SS orders, as we still have to be disinfected, and that he must leave at once; he has come because he has a liking for Italians, and because, he says, he "has a little heart." We ask him if there are other Italians in the camp and he says there are some, a few, he does not know how many; and he at once changes the subject. Meanwhile a bell rang and he immediately hurried off and left us stunned and disconcerted. Some feel refreshed but I do not. I still think that even this dentist, this incomprehensible person, wanted to amuse himself at our expense, and I do not want to believe a word of what he said. **A**

At the sound of the bell, we can hear the still dark camp waking up. Unexpectedly the water gushes out boiling from the showers—five minutes of bliss; but immediately after, four men (perhaps they are the barbers) burst in yelling and shoving and drive us out, wet and steaming, into the adjoining room which is freezing; here other shouting people throw at us unrecognizable rags and thrust into our hands a pair of broken-down boots with wooden soles; we have no time to understand and we already find ourselves in the open, in the blue and icy snow of dawn, barefoot and naked, with all our clothing in our hands, with a hundred yards to run to the next hut. There we are finally allowed to get dressed.

When we finish, everyone remains in his own corner and we do not dare lift our eyes to look at one another. There is nowhere to look in a mirror, but our appearance stands in front of us, reflected in a hundred livid faces, in a hundred miserable and sordid puppets. **B** We are transformed into the phantoms glimpsed yesterday evening.[13]

Then for the first time we became aware that our language lacks words to express this offense, the demolition of a man. **C** In a moment, with almost prophetic intuition, the reality was

13. **We are transformed . . . evening:** Levi is referring to the inmates at Auschwitz whom he and the other new prisoners witnessed briefly upon arriving at the camp on the previous evening.

1935...1940 by Russian School/Private Collection//Roger Perrin/The Bridgeman Art Library

revealed to us: we had reached the bottom. It is not possible to sink lower than this; no human condition is more miserable than this, nor could it conceivably be so. Nothing belongs to us any more; they have taken away our clothes, our shoes, even our hair; if we speak, they will not listen to us, and if they listen, they will not understand. They will even take away our name: and if we want to keep it, we will have to find ourselves the strength to do so, to manage somehow so that behind the name something of us, of us as we were, still remains.

We know that we will have difficulty in being understood, and this is as it should be. But consider what value, what meaning is enclosed even in the smallest of our daily habits, in the hundred possessions which even the poorest beggar owns: a handkerchief, an old letter, the photo of a cherished person. These things are part of us, almost like limbs of our body; nor is it conceivable that we can be deprived of them in our world, for we immediately find others to substitute the old ones, other objects which are ours in their personification and evocation of our memories. **D**

Imagine now a man who is deprived of everyone he loves, and at the same time of his house, his habits, his clothes, in short, of everything he possesses: he will be a hollow man, reduced to suffering and needs, forgetful of dignity and restraint, for he who loses all often easily loses himself. He will be a man whose life or death can be lightly decided with no sense of human affinity, in the most fortunate of cases, on the basis of a pure judgment of utility. **E** It is in this way that one can understand the double sense of the term "extermination camp," and it is now clear what we seek to express with the phrase: "to lie on the bottom." **F**

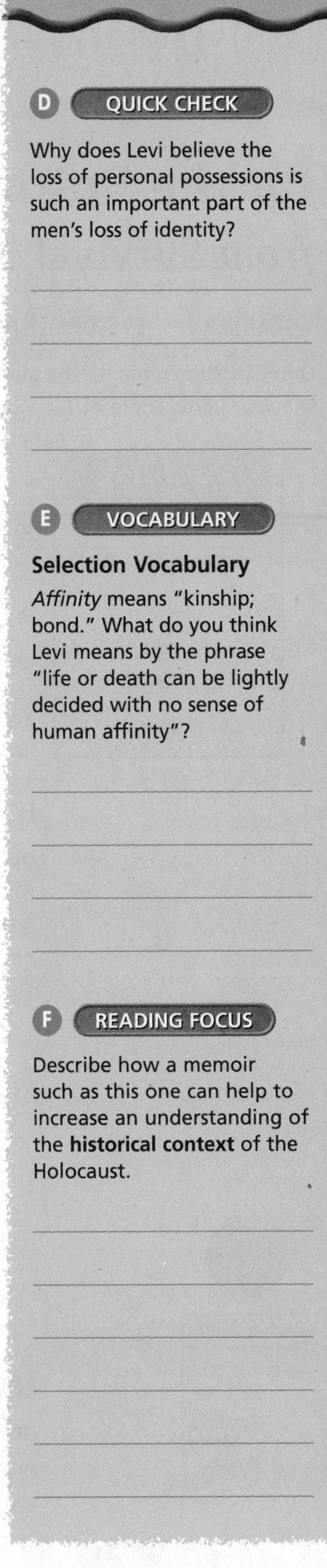

D QUICK CHECK

Why does Levi believe the loss of personal possessions is such an important part of the men's loss of identity?

E VOCABULARY

Selection Vocabulary

Affinity means "kinship; bond." What do you think Levi means by the phrase "life or death can be lightly decided with no sense of human affinity"?

F READING FOCUS

Describe how a memoir such as this one can help to increase an understanding of the **historical context** of the Holocaust.

Applying Your Skills

On the Bottom
from Survival in Auschwitz

VOCABULARY DEVELOPMENT

DIRECTIONS: Complete the paragraph with the correct vocabulary words from the Word Box. Some of the words will not be used.

Word Box
taciturn
disconcerted
livid
sordid
demolition
affinity

From the moment they arrived at the camp, the men were subjected to a series of actions whose purpose was the (1) ________________ of the prisoners' individuality. The (2) ________________ guards did not answer any of their questions. What little information they were given only (3) ________________ the men further, and the (4) ________________ conditions in the camp told them just how horrible their time there was going to be.

LITERARY FOCUS: MEMOIR

DIRECTIONS: A **memoir** usually conveys information in a very different way from other historical sources. Describe how each of the sources listed below might differ from Primo Levi's memoir.

1. A newspaper article about the death camps: ________________

____

____

2. A movie about the Holocaust: ________________

____

____

3. A chapter about World War II in a history textbook: ________________

____

____

Literary Skills Understand the characteristics of a memoir.

Reading Skills Evaluate historical context.

READING FOCUS: EVALUATING HISTORICAL CONTEXT

DIRECTIONS: Choose three details from "On the Bottom" and, on a separate sheet of paper, briefly explain what these details tell you about the **historical context** of the Holocaust.

Preparing to Read

Blood, Sweat, and Tears

by Winston Churchill

LITERARY FOCUS: ORATORY

The art of public speech is **oratory**. Winston Churchill, who was Prime Minister of Great Britain during World War II, was especially famous for his skills as an orator. Because listeners cannot return to an oral speech if they miss a point, orators often state their main ideas and then use **repetition** of words, phrases, and sentence structures to emphasize their key points. Repetition also creates **rhythm** in speaking. Try to find the phrases that Churchill repeats in his speech.

READING FOCUS: IDENTIFYING AND CRITIQUING AN AUTHOR'S ARGUMENT

To persuade listeners or readers to agree with their arguments, orators and writers use two types of appeals. **Logical appeals** offer facts and reasons as evidence to support an argument. Logical appeals show credibility, or reliability, and appeal to listeners' intellect. **Emotional appeals** use rousing language to create an emotional response in the audience. Churchill begins his speech by listing the methodical, reasonable steps he took to form his government. He then arouses strong feelings in his audience by using emotionally charged words like *ordeal*, *struggle*, and *tyranny*.

Use the Skill Make a graphic organizer like the one below, and list words, phrases, and sentences from Churchill's speech that appeal to logic and emotions.

Logical appeals	Emotional appeals

Literary Skills Understand oratory.

Reading Skills Identify and critique an author's argument.

Vocabulary Development

Blood, Sweat, and Tears

SELECTION VOCABULARY

rigor (RIHG UHR) *n.:* severity.
Churchill explained that the rigor of the situation called for speedy action.

grievous (GREEV VUHS) *adj.:* outrageous; horrible.
The grievous acts of German troops as they invaded their neighbors horrified British citizens.

lamentable (LUH MEHN TUH BUHL) *adj.:* regrettable; unfortunate.
Sending young troops to war was lamentable but necessary.

buoyancy (BOY UHN SEE) *n.:* lightness of spirit; cheerfulness.
Despite the hard task ahead of him, Chruchill felt a sense of buoyancy about the future.

WORD STUDY

DIRECTIONS: Pair each vocabulary word in the left column with the correct synonym (word with a similar meaning) from the right column. Write the letter of each synonym on the blank line.

_______ **1.** rigor
_______ **2.** grievous
_______ **3.** lamentable
_______ **4.** buoyancy

a. awful
b. disappointing
c. harshness
d. liveliness

Blood, Sweat, and Tears

by Winston Churchill

BACKGROUND

When Hitler's army invaded Poland on September 1, 1939, World War II officially began. Two days later, Britain declared war on Germany and began to manufacture weapons, ships, and planes. Over the next few months, Germany overran Holland and Belgium, and moved into France. By May 13, 1940, when Churchill gave this speech, it was clear that Germany's next target was Britain.

Churchill was the newly elected prime minister, or head of the British government (which is referred to as Parliament). He had just formed a new government that included all the political parties, even those that had opposed him. This speech, in which he addressed the Houses of Parliament, was broadcast on the radio. Churchill knew he had to unite the country to meet this terrible threat and inspire people to believe they could survive and triumph. No one who heard Churchill's radio speeches during the war ever forgot them.

On Friday evening last I received His Majesty's Commission[1] to form a new Administration. It was the evident wish and will of Parliament and the nation that this should be conceived on the broadest possible basis and that it should include all Parties, both those who supported the last Government and also the Parties of the Opposition.[2] I have completed the most important part of this task. A War Cabinet has been formed of five Members, representing, with the Opposition Liberals,[3] the unity of the nation. **(A)** The three Party Leaders have agreed to serve,

A VOCABULARY

Academic Vocabulary

How does Churchill *exhibit*, or show, his credibility to his listeners in the opening paragraph?

---

1. **His Majesty's Commission:** The king at the time was George VI; after his party is elected, the Prime Minister is officially appointed by the monarch.
2. **Parties of the Opposition:** political parties in the parliament other than the one(s) making up the ruling administration.
3. **Opposition Liberals:** Churchill was a member of the Conservative Party; those belonging to the Liberal Party were in the opposition, not the government.

A LITERARY ANALYSIS

What does the involvement of the leaders of rival parties suggest about the situation?

B VOCABULARY

Selection Vocabulary

Use context clues to write a definition for *rigor*.

C QUICK CHECK

Underline what Churchill wants the House to approve.

D READING FOCUS

In this paragraph, is Churchill using **logical appeals** or **emotional appeals**? How do you know?

Estate of Robert Elliot/National Portrait Gallery, London

either in the War Cabinet or in high executive office. **A** The three Fighting Services have been filled. It was necessary that this should be done in one single day, on account of the extreme urgency and rigor of events. **B** A number of other key positions were filled yesterday, and I am submitting a further list to His Majesty tonight. I hope to complete the appointment of the principal Ministers during tomorrow. The appointment of the other Ministers usually takes a little longer, but I trust that, when Parliament meets again, this part of my task will be complete in all respects.

I considered it in the public interest to suggest that the House should be summoned to meet today. Mr. Speaker agreed, and took the necessary steps, in accordance with the powers conferred[4] upon him by the Resolution of the House. At the end of the proceedings today, the Adjournment of the House will be proposed until Tuesday, 21st May, with, of course, provision for earlier meeting if need be. The business to be considered during that week will be notified to Members at the earliest opportunity. I now invite the House, by the Resolution which stands in my name, to record its approval of the steps taken and to declare its confidence in the new Government.[5] **C** **D**

4. **conferred:** granted.
5. **the new Government:** the recently elected administration led by Churchill.

To form an Administration of this scale and complexity is a serious undertaking in itself, but it must be remembered that we are in the preliminary stage of one of the greatest battles in history, that we are in action at many points in Norway and in Holland, that we have to be prepared in the Mediterranean, that the air battle is continuous, and the many preparations have to be made here at home. In this crisis I hope I may be pardoned if I do not address the House at any length today. I hope that any of my friends and colleagues, or former colleagues, who are affected by the political reconstruction, will make all allowance for any lack of ceremony with which it has been necessary to act. I would say to the House, as I said to those who have joined this Government: "I have nothing to offer but blood, toil, tears, and sweat."

We have before us an ordeal of the most grievous kind. **E** We have before us many, many long months of struggle and of suffering. You ask, What is our policy? I will say: "It is to wage war, by sea, land and air, with all our might and with all the strength that God can give us: to wage war against a monstrous tyranny, never surpassed in the dark, lamentable catalogue of human crime. **F** That is our policy." You ask, What is our aim? I can answer in one word: Victory—victory at all costs, victory in spite of all terror, victory however long and hard the road may be; for without victory there is no survival. Let that be realized; no survival for the British Empire; no survival for all that the British Empire has stood for; no survival for the urge and impulse of the ages, that mankind will move forward towards its goal. But I take up my task with buoyancy and hope. I feel sure that our cause will not be suffered to fail among men. At this time I feel entitled to claim the aid of all, and I say, "Come, then, let us go forward together with our united strength." **G** **H**

E LANGUAGE COACH

The suffix *–ous* is added to the verb *grieve* to make the adjective *grievous* (the *e* is dropped first). Write another word to which you can add the suffix *–ous* to make a new adjective.

____

F VOCABULARY

Word Study

Use a dictionary to look up the multiple meanings of *monstrous*. Which definition do you think is used in this sentence?

____

____

G LITERARY FOCUS

Underline examples of **repetition** in this paragraph.

H READING FOCUS

Re-read the final paragraph, in which Churchill uses **emotional appeals**. What powerful point does he make about the connection between "victory" and "survival"?

____

____

____

____

____

Applying Your Skills

Blood, Sweat, and Tears

VOCABULARY DEVELOPMENT

DIRECTIONS: Complete the paragraph with vocabulary words from the Word Box.

Word Box

rigor
grievous
lamentable
buoyancy

It is a sorry, (1) ______________ fact that nations often resort to war to achieve their goals. During World War II, Germany launched horrendous, (2) ______________ attacks upon neighboring countries. Winston Churchill knew that victory would require extreme discipline and (3) ______________, but that the English people would unite and face the challenges ahead with great (4) ______________ and hopefulness.

LITERARY FOCUS: ORATORY

DIRECTIONS: List three examples of **repetition** in Winston Churchill's speech "Blood, Sweat, and Tears."

1. ______________________________
2. ______________________________
3. ______________________________

READING FOCUS: IDENTIFYING AND CRITIQUING AN AUTHOR'S ARGUMENT

DIRECTIONS: Decide whether each of the following phrases from Churchill's speech is an example of a **logical appeal** or an **emotional appeal** and write your answers in the second column.

Phrase	Logical or emotional appeal?
"Victory—victory at all costs, victory in spite of all terror, victory however long and hard the road may be; for without victory there is no survival." (lines 51–53)	1.
"'Come, then, let us go forward together with our united strength.'" (lines 59–60)	2.
"It was necessary that this should be done in one single day, or account of the extreme urgency and rigor of events." (lines 11–13)"	3.

Literary Skills Understand oratory.

Reading Skills Identify and critique an author's argument.

Preparing to Read

from A Room of One's Own

by Virginia Woolf

LITERARY FOCUS: ESSAY

An **essay** is a short piece of nonfiction writing that examines a single subject from a limited point of view. Formal essays are usually serious in tone and full of facts. **Informal essays,** on the other hand, mostly reflect the beliefs, feelings, and attitudes of the author. Their language is more casual and informal, and their tone may be humorous. Despite their informality, informal essays like this one by Virginia Woolf often deal with controversial issues or serious subjects.

READING FOCUS: IDENTIFYING THE AUTHOR'S BELIEFS

As you read this essay, look for beliefs that Woolf states directly and other beliefs that she only hints at. To **identify the author's beliefs**, look for words, such as "I think" and "I agree," that show an opinion. Also look for **loaded language**, language with strong emotional connotations, and for evidence that supports the author's beliefs.

Use the Skill Each time you identify one of Woolf's beliefs, write it in the chart below.

Virginia Woolf believes that . . .

Literary Skills Understand the characteristics of an essay.

Reading Skills Identify an author's beliefs.

Vocabulary Development

from A Room of One's Own

SELECTION VOCABULARY

servile (SUR VYL) *adj.:* like a slave; submissive.

Some people believed women should set aside their own wants and be servile.

suppressed (SUH PREHST) *v.* used as an *adj.:* kept from being known.

Many women had suppressed talents that they were not allowed to exercise.

propitious (PRUH PIHSH UHS) *adj.:* favorable.

The most propitious place for a writer is a quiet room of one's own.

prodigious (PRUH DIHJ UHS) *adj.:* enormous.

It took prodigious energy to write, so Woolf was often exhausted by the time she finished.

notorious (NOH TAWR EE UHS) *adj.:* widely but unfavorably known.

Some writers are notorious for turning in manuscripts late.

formidable (FAWR MUH DUH BUHL) *adj.:* difficult to handle or overcome.

Finding time to write was a formidable task for married women with small children.

WORD STUDY

DIRECTIONS: Write "Yes" if the vocabulary word in each sentence is being used correctly. Write "No" if it is being used incorrectly.

1. It took almost a decade to complete the *prodigious* building project on Main Street. _______
2. I easily beat my *formidable* opponent at tennis. _______
3. She was known as a confident, *servile*, and strong leader. _______
4. During the question-and-answer session, the audience member's *suppressed* comment caught the politician of guard. _______
5. The *propitious* weather conditions made it impossible for us to finish our picnic. _______
6. The actor was *notorious* for his difficult behavior on set. _______

from A Room of One's Own

by Virginia Woolf

BACKGROUND

In 1929, Virginia Woolf published a collection of essays called *A Room of One's Own*, from which this essay is taken. In it, Woolf uncovers forgotten women writers and reveals how gender affects subjects, themes, and even style.

Woolf begins this essay by asking questions about the lives of women in sixteenth-century England, when Elizabeth I was on the throne, a period known as the Elizabethan Age. It was also the age of Shakespeare, when men were writing some of the most important plays and poems in the English language. Why then, asks Woolf, were women not writing poetry, too?

Virginia Woolf in a Deck Chair by Vanessa Bell/Permission of Angelica Garnett/Sotheby's Transparency Library, London

Here am I asking why women did not write poetry in the Elizabethan age, and I am not sure how they were educated; whether they were taught to write; whether they had sitting rooms to themselves; how many women had children before they were twenty-one; what, in short, they did from eight in the morning till eight at night. They had no money evidently; according to Professor Trevelyan[1] they were married whether they liked it or not before they were out of the nursery, at fifteen or sixteen very likely. It would have been extremely odd, even upon this showing, had one of them suddenly written the plays of Shakespeare, I concluded, and I thought of that old gentleman, who is dead now, but was a bishop, I think, who declared that it was impossible for any woman, past, present, or to come, to have the genius of Shakespeare. **A** **B** He wrote to the papers about it. He also told a lady who applied to him for information that cats do not as a matter of fact go to heaven,

A LITERARY FOCUS

What evidence in the opening paragraph indicates that this is an **informal essay?**

B LITERARY ANALYSIS

What belief is implied in the statement that it is "impossible for any woman . . . to have the genius of Shakespeare"?

1. **Professor Trevelyan:** G. M. Trevelyan, author of *The History of England* (1926).

A **LITERARY FOCUS**

How might the tone and content of this paragraph be different if this were a formal **essay**?

B **QUICK CHECK**

Who is the imaginary person Woolf introduces here?

C **LITERARY ANALYSIS**

What do you think Woolf is setting up with this story?

though they have, he added, souls of a sort. How much thinking those old gentlemen used to save one! How the borders of ignorance shrank back at their approach! Cats do not go to heaven. Women cannot write the plays of Shakespeare. A

Be that as it may, I could not help thinking, as I looked at the works of Shakespeare on the shelf, that the bishop was right at least in this; it would have been impossible, completely and entirely, for any woman to have written the plays of Shakespeare in the age of Shakespeare. Let me imagine, since facts are so hard to come by, what would have happened had Shakespeare had a wonderfully gifted sister, called Judith, let us say. B Shakespeare himself went, very probably—his mother was an heiress—to the grammar school, where he may have learnt Latin—Ovid, Virgil, and Horace—and the elements of grammar and logic. He was, it is well known, a wild boy who poached rabbits, perhaps shot a deer, and had, rather sooner than he should have done, to marry a woman in the neighborhood, who bore him a child rather quicker than was right. That escapade sent him to seek his fortune in London. He had, it seemed, a taste for the theater; he began by holding horses at the stage door. Very soon he got work in the theater, became a successful actor, and lived at the hub of the universe, meeting everybody, knowing everybody, practicing his art on the boards, exercising his wits in the streets, and even getting access to the palace of the queen. Meanwhile his extraordinarily gifted sister, let us suppose, remained at home. She was as adventurous, as imaginative, as agog to see the world as he was. But she was not sent to school. She had no chance of learning grammar and logic, let alone of reading Horace and Virgil. She picked up a book now and then, one of her brother's perhaps, and read a few pages. But then her parents came in and told her to mend the stockings or mind the stew and not moon about with books and papers. C They would have spoken sharply but kindly, for they were substantial people who knew the conditions of life for a woman and loved their daughter—indeed, more likely than not she was the apple of her father's eye. Perhaps she scribbled some pages up in an apple loft on the sly, but was careful to hide them or set fire to them. Soon, however, before she was out of her teens, she was to be betrothed to the son of a neighboring wool stapler.[2] She cried out that marriage was hateful to her, and for that she was severely beaten by her father. Then he ceased to scold her. He begged her instead not to hurt him, not to shame him in this matter of her marriage. He would give her a chain of beads or a fine petticoat, he said; and there were tears in his eyes. How could she disobey him? How could she break his heart? The force of her own gift alone drove her to it. **D** She made up a small parcel of her belongings, let herself down by a rope one summer's night, and took the road to London. She was not seventeen. The birds that sang in the hedge were not more musical than she was. She had the quickest fancy, a gift like her brother's, for the tune of words. Like him, she had a taste for the theater. She stood at the stage door; she wanted to act, she said. Men laughed in her face. The manager—a fat, loose-lipped man—guffawed. He bellowed something about poodles dancing and women acting—no woman, he said, could possibly be an actress. He hinted—you can imagine what. She could get no training in her craft. Could she even seek her dinner in a tavern or roam the streets at midnight? Yet her genius was for fiction and lusted to feed abundantly upon the lives of men and women and the study of their ways. At last—for she was very young, oddly like Shakespeare the poet in her face, with the same gray eyes and rounded brows—at last Nick Greene the actor-manager took pity on her; she found herself with child by that gentleman and so—who shall measure the heat and violence of the poet's heart when caught and tangled in a woman's body?—killed herself one winter's night and lies buried at some crossroads where the omnibuses now stop outside the Elephant and Castle.[3] **E**

2. **wool stapler:** dealer in wool, a product sorted according to its fiber, or "staple."
3. **buried . . . Elephant and Castle:** Suicides, who were for years not permitted church burials, were commonly buried at a crossroads as a kind of punishment, perhaps to ensure that their souls would wander forever. The Elephant and Castle is a pub at a busy crossroads in south London.

D QUICK CHECK

Woolf speculates that Judith didn't want to hurt her father, but that a powerful reason caused her to leave home. State the reason in your own words.

E READING FOCUS

Circle five examples of **loaded language** in this paragraph. **Identify the author's beliefs** that are expressed in this paragraph based on both the loaded language she uses and the main idea of the story of Judith.

A READING FOCUS

Woolf mentions the English novelist and poet Emily Brontë and the Scottish poet Robert Burns, who was a farmer. Underline the **belief** of Woolf's that these two examples support.

B VOCABULARY

Word Study

Anon is an abbreviation for *anonymous*, which comes from the Greek *an–*, meaning "without," and *onyma*, meaning "name." Works of literature for which the name of the author is unknown or withheld carry the word *anonymous* to designate unknown authorship. Why do you think some authors would leave out their name?

That, more or less, is how the story would run, I think, if a woman in Shakespeare's day had had Shakespeare's genius. But for my part, I agree with the deceased bishop, if such he was—it is unthinkable that any woman in Shakespeare's day should have had Shakespeare's genius. For genius like Shakespeare's is not born among laboring, uneducated, servile people. It was not born in England among the Saxons and the Britons. It is not born today among the working classes. How, then, could it have been born among women whose work began, according to Professor Trevelyan, almost before they were out of the nursery, who were forced to it by their parents and held to it by all the power of law and custom? Yet genius of a sort must have existed among women as it must have existed among the working classes. Now and again an Emily Brontë or a Robert Burns blazes out and proves its presence. But certainly it never got itself onto paper. **A** When, however, one reads of a witch being ducked, of a woman possessed by devils, of a wise woman selling herbs, or even of a very remarkable man who had a mother, then I think we are on the track of a lost novelist, a suppressed poet, of some mute and inglorious[4] Jane Austen, some Emily Brontë who dashed her brains out on the moor or mopped and mowed about the highways crazed with the torture that her gift had put her to. Indeed, I would venture to guess that Anon, who wrote so many poems without signing them, was often a woman. **B** It was a woman Edward Fitzgerald,[5] I think, suggested who made the ballads and the folk songs, crooning them to her children, beguiling her spinning with them, or the length of the winter's night.

This may be true or it may be false—who can say?—but what is true in it, so it seemed to me, reviewing the story of Shakespeare's sister as I had made it, is that any woman born with a great gift in the sixteenth century would certainly have gone crazed, shot herself, or ended her days in some lonely cottage

4. **mute and inglorious:** allusion to line 59 of Thomas Gray's poem "Elegy Written in a Country Churchyard."
5. **Edward Fitzgerald** (1809–1883): English translator and poet.

outside the village, half witch, half wizard, feared and mocked at. For it needs little skill in psychology to be sure that a highly gifted girl who had tried to use her gift for poetry would have been so thwarted and hindered by other people, so tortured and pulled asunder by her own contrary instincts, that she must have lost her health and sanity to a certainty. No girl could have walked to London and stood at a stage door and forced her way into the presence of actor-managers without doing herself a violence and suffering an anguish which may have been irrational—for chastity may be a fetish invented by certain societies for unknown reasons—but were nonetheless inevitable. **C** Chastity had then, it has even now, a religious importance in a woman's life, and has so wrapped itself round with nerves and instincts that to cut it free and bring it to the light of day demands courage of the rarest. To have lived a free life in London in the sixteenth century would have meant for a woman who was poet and playwright a nervous stress and dilemma which might well have killed her. Had she survived, whatever she had written would have been twisted and deformed, issuing from a strained and morbid imagination. And undoubtedly, I thought, looking at the shelf where there are no plays by women, her work would have gone unsigned. **D** That refuge she would have sought certainly. It was the relic of the sense of chastity that dictated anonymity to women even so late as the nineteenth century. Currer Bell, George Eliot, George Sand,[6] all the victims of inner strife as their writings prove, sought ineffectively to veil themselves by using the name of a man. Thus they did homage to the convention, which if not implanted by the other sex was liberally encouraged by them (the chief glory of a woman is not to be talked of, said Pericles,[7] himself a much-talked-of man), that publicity in women is detestable. Anonymity runs in their blood. The desire to be veiled still possesses them.

6. **Currer Bell, George Eliot, George Sand:** male pseudonyms for the female writers Charlotte Brontë, Mary Ann Evans, and Amantine-Aurore-Lucile Dupin.
7. **Pericles** (c. 495–429 B.C.): Athenian legislator and general.

C LITERARY ANALYSIS

Do you agree with Woolf's explanation about what is "true" in her story about Judith? Why or why not?

D QUICK CHECK

If a woman in the sixteenth century had written, what two things does Woolf say would have been true of her writing?

A QUICK CHECK

According to Woolf, how do men's feelings toward fame differ from women's feelings toward fame?

____

____

____

____

____

____

They are not even now as concerned about the health of their fame as men are, and, speaking generally, will pass a tombstone or a signpost without feeling an irresistible desire to cut their names on it, as Alf, Bert, or Chas. must do in obedience to their instinct, which murmurs if it sees a fine woman go by, or even a dog, *Ce chien est à moi.*[8] And, of course, it may not be a dog, I thought, remembering Parliament Square, the Sieges Allee,[9] and other avenues; it may be a piece of land or a man with curly black hair. It is one of the great advantages of being a woman that one can pass even a very fine negress without wishing to make an Englishwoman of her. **A**

That woman, then, who was born with a gift of poetry in the sixteenth century, was an unhappy woman, a woman at strife against herself. All the conditions of her life, all her own instincts, were hostile to the state of mind which is needed to set free whatever is in the brain. But what is the state of mind that is most propitious to the act of creation, I asked. Can one come by any notion of the state that furthers and makes possible that strange activity? Here I opened the volume containing the Tragedies of Shakespeare. What was Shakespeare's state of mind, for instance, when he wrote *Lear* and *Antony and Cleopatra*? It was certainly the state of mind most favorable to poetry that there has ever existed. But Shakespeare himself said nothing about it. We only know casually and by chance that he "never blotted a line." Nothing indeed was ever said by the artist himself about his state of mind until the eighteenth century perhaps. Rousseau[10] perhaps began it. At any rate, by the nineteenth century self-consciousness had developed so far that it was the habit for men of letters to describe their minds in confessions and autobiographies. Their lives also were written, and their

8. ***Ce chien est à moi*** (SUH SHEE EHN AYT A MWA): French for "This dog is mine."
9. **Sieges Allee** (ZEE GUHS AH LAY): busy thoroughfare in Berlin. The name—more commonly written as one word, *Siegesallee*—is German for "Avenue of Victory."
10. **Rousseau:** Jean-Jacques Rousseau (1712–1778), French author whose candid, autobiographical *Confessions* began a vogue in literature for confessional accounts.

© Michael Boys/Corbis

letters were printed after their deaths. Thus, though we do not know what Shakespeare went through when he wrote Lear, we do know what Carlyle went through when he wrote *The French Revolution*; what Flaubert went through when he wrote *Madame Bovary*; what Keats was going through when he tried to write poetry against the coming of death and the indifference of the world.

And one gathers from this enormous modern literature of confession and self-analysis that to write a work of genius is almost always a feat of prodigious difficulty. **B** Everything is against the likelihood that it will come from the writer's mind whole and entire. Generally material circumstances are against it. Dogs will bark; people will interrupt; money must be made; health will break down. Further, accentuating all these difficulties and making them harder to bear is the world's notorious indifference. **C** It does not ask people to write poems and novels and histories; it does not need them. It does not care whether Flaubert finds the right word or whether Carlyle scrupulously verifies this or that fact. Naturally, it will not pay for what it does not want. And so the writer, Keats, Flaubert, Carlyle, suffers, especially in the creative years of youth, every form of distraction and discouragement. A curse, a cry of agony, rises from those

B VOCABULARY

Selection Vocabulary

Prodigious means "enormous." List three synonyms, or words with similar meanings, for *prodigious*. Use a thesaurus if you need help.

____

____

____

C LANGUAGE COACH

Prodigious and *notorious* have the suffix *–ious*, which means "full of" or "characterized by." List two other words that have the suffix *–ious*.

____

____

books of analysis and confession. "Mighty poets in their misery dead"[11]—that is the burden of their song. If anything comes through in spite of all this, it is a miracle, and probably no book is born entire and uncrippled as it was conceived.

But for women, I thought, looking at the empty shelves, these difficulties were infinitely more formidable. In the first place, to have a room of her own, let alone a quiet room or a soundproof room, was out of the question, unless her parents were exceptionally rich or very noble, even up to the beginning of the nineteenth century. Since her pin money,[12] which depended on the goodwill of her father, was only enough to keep her clothed, she was debarred from such alleviations[13] as came even to Keats or Tennyson or Carlyle, all poor men, from a walking tour, a little journey to France, from the separate lodging which, even if it were miserable enough, sheltered them from the claims and tyrannies of their families. Such material difficulties were formidable; but much worse were the immaterial. The indifference of the world which Keats and Flaubert and other men of genius have found so hard to bear was in her case not indifference but hostility. The world did not say to her as it said to them, Write if you choose; it makes no difference to me. The world said with a guffaw, Write? What's the good of your writing? A B C

A QUICK CHECK

In this paragraph, underline one "material difficulty" women writers face and put brackets around an "immaterial" one.

B VOCABULARY

Academic Vocabulary

How would you describe Virginia Woolf's *perspective*, or particular way of looking at something, about women writers?

C READING FOCUS

Circle three examples of **loaded language** on this page. Choose one of the words and explain its connotations below.

11. **"Mighty poets . . . dead":** line from William Wordsworth's poem "Resolution and Independence."
12. **pin money:** small allowance given for personal expenses.
13. **alleviations** (UH LEE VEE AY SHUHNZ): things that lighten, relieve, or make easier to bear.

from A Room of One's Own

USE A COMPARISON TABLE

Woolf's concerns, principles, and beliefs are directly reflected in this **informal essay**. The left column below lists some of her beliefs about the special difficulties faced by women writers. Review the essay, and complete the chart with details, examples, or other evidence Woolf uses to express and support her beliefs.

Woolf's beliefs	Evidence from the essay
Sixteenth-century women lacked the education, money, privacy, and time to become writers.	
A woman who tried to write would have suffered great personal misery and public scorn.	
Women probably wrote many of the works that are marked "Anonymous."	
All writing demands a prodigious amount of work and is largely unappreciated.	
Society is hostile, not just indifferent, toward women writers.	

Applying Your Skills

from A Room of One's Own

VOCABULARY DEVELOPMENT

DIRECTIONS: Complete the paragraph with vocabulary words from the Word Box. One word will not be used.

Word Box

servile
suppressed
propitious
prodigious
notorious
formidable

Virginia Woolf imagines the role of sixteenth-century women as primarily (1) ____________________ : cooking, cleaning, and sewing. She observes that society did not create (2) ____________________ circumstances to support women who had literary talent. In any era, even male writers face huge obstacles and need to exert (3) ____________________ effort to write anything worthwhile. In the sixteenth century, however, women faced obstacles so (4) ____________________, or difficult, that most of them probably (5) ____________________ the urge to write—or settled for composing ballads to sing to their children.

LITERARY FOCUS: ESSAY

DIRECTIONS: On a separate sheet of paper, write a paragraph explaining why "*from* A Room of One's Own" is considered an **informal essay**. Include examples from the selection.

READING FOCUS: IDENTIFYING THE AUTHOR'S BELIEFS

DIRECTIONS: The following chart lists examples of **loaded language**. In the right column, describe the connotations that each word has.

Literary Skills Understand the characteristics of an essay.

Reading Skills Identify an author's beliefs.

Loaded words	Connotations
preposterous	1.
destructive	2.
angelic	3.
exhausting	4.

Skills Review

Collection 11

LANGUAGE COACH

The letter *c* can be sounded like a hard "k" or like a soft "s," depending on where in a word it is found. The general rule for pronouncing words with the letter *c* is this:

When the *c* appears before the letters *e*, *i* and *y*, it is pronounced with a soft "s" sound. At other times the *c* is pronounced with a hard "k" sound.

DIRECTIONS: Read this list of words containing the letter *c*. Circle the letter *c* where it is pronounced with a soft "s" sound, and underline it where it is pronounced with a hard "k" sound.

1. scant
2. scent
3. since
4. tactical
5. census
6. considerably
7. perspective
8. taciturn
9. disconcerted
10. buoyancy

ORAL LANGUAGE ACTIVITY

DIRECTIONS: Write a short (one or two paragraphs) speech that explains your opinion about a particular subject. It can be about a project; an incident in your neighborhood, town, or school; a political or social event from history; or something else. In your speech, try to persuade your audience to see your point of view. Use both **logical appeals** and **emotional appeals**. When you are finished, read your speech to the class.

Collection 12

Modern and Contemporary Poetry

Eye, 2000 by Howard Hodgkin/Private Collection/The Bridgeman Art Library/Alan Cristea Gallery, London

Preparing to Read

The Hollow Men

by T. S. Eliot

LITERARY FOCUS: ALLUSION

An **allusion** is a reference to a person, a place, an event, or a quotation that is known from literature, history, mythology, politics, religion, sports, science, and other subjects. Readers must recognize allusions in order to fully understand the meaning of a text. Here are some of the allusions that T. S. Eliot uses in "The Hollow Men":

- The first line, "Mistah Kurtz—he dead," is an allusion to the main character of Joseph Conrad's novel *Heart of Darkness*. Kurtz journeys to the interior of Africa and rapidly loses his humanity. This allusion sets a bleak tone for the poem.
- Eliot's next line, "A penny for the Old Guy," refers to the notorious Gunpowder Plot, an event from British history. On November 5, 1605, a group of assassins led by Guy Fawkes tried to kill King James I and other leaders by setting off an explosion in the cellar of the Parliament building. The plot failed, and Guy Fawkes was executed.

  Even today, every November scarecrow-like images of Guy Fawkes (the "stuffed men" of the poem) are thrown into bonfires all over England. Children join the fun by carrying small "guys" and begging passersby to give them "a penny for the guy" so they can buy fireworks.
- "The Hollow Men" also contains allusions to Shakespeare's *The Tragedy of Julius Caesar* and to Dante's epic *The Divine Comedy*. Be on the lookout, too, for an allusion to the Lord's Prayer and an allusion to a familiar children's rhyme.

READING FOCUS: DRAWING INFERENCES

Writers often expect readers to "read between the lines" of what they write. Readers must use evidence from the text, along with their own knowledge and experiences, to **draw inferences** (make educated guesses).

As you read, make inferences about the hollow men and analyze their character traits to understand how they represent Eliot's view of human history.

Literary Skills
Understand allusion.

Reading Skills
Draw inferences.

Vocabulary Development

The Hollow Men

SELECTION VOCABULARY

supplication (SUHP LUH KAY SHUHN) *n.:* humble plea.

The priest prayed for his supplication to be heard.

perpetual (PUHR PEHCH OO UHL) *adj.:* lasting forever.

He gloomily predicted perpetual suffering.

conception (KUHN SEHP SHUHN) *n.:* the originating of something.

The conception of the new book began with an elaborate vision.

potency (POH TUHN SEE) *n.:* strength; power.

The potency of the vitamins was tested by seeing if people felt better after taking them.

WORD STUDY

DIRECTIONS: Pair each vocabulary word in the first column with its synonym (word with a similar meaning) in the second column. Write the letter of each synonym on the correct line.

_________	**1.** supplication	**a.** beginning
_________	**2.** perpetual	**b.** request
_________	**3.** conception	**c.** effectiveness
_________	**4.** potency	**d.** continual

THE HOLLOW MEN

by T. S. Eliot

BACKGROUND
T. S. Eliot was one of the most influential poets of the twentieth century. Eliot published "The Hollow Men" in 1925. At the time, he believed that humanity was suffering from a loss of will and faith. The complex poem describes a world filled with despair and empty of religion or the promise of salvation.

Mistah Kurtz—he dead.
A penny for the Old Guy

I

We are the hollow men[1]
We are the stuffed men
Leaning together
Headpiece filled with straw. Alas!
Our dried voices, when
We whisper together
Are quiet and meaningless
As wind in dry grass
Or rats' feet over broken glass
In our dry cellar.

Shape without form, shade without color,
Paralyzed force, gesture without motion; (A)
Those who have crossed

1. **hollow men:** allusion to Shakespeare's *Julius Caesar* (Act IV, Scene 2, lines 23–27): "hollow men . . . sink in the trial" (that is, fail when put to the test).

(A) READING FOCUS

A paradox is an apparent contradiction that is actually true. Lines 11–12 list four paradoxes. Based on these paradoxes, what **inferences** can you draw about the hollow men?

With direct eyes, to death's other Kingdom[2]
Remember us—if at all—not as lost
Violent souls, but only
As the hollow men
The stuffed men.

II

Eyes I dare not meet in dreams
In death's dream kingdom
These do not appear:
There, the eyes are
Sunlight on a broken column
There, is a tree swinging
And voices are
In the wind's singing
More distant and more solemn **A**
Than a fading star.

Let me be no nearer
In death's dream kingdom
Let me also wear
Such deliberate disguises
Rat's coat, crowskin, crossed staves[3]
In a field
Behaving as the wind behaves
No nearer—

Not that final meeting
In the twilight kingdom **B**

III

This is the dead land
This is cactus land

A VOCABULARY

Word Study

Solemn means "grave; sober." Think of a synonym (word with a similar meaning) for *solemn*. Use a thesaurus if you need help. Does the synonym have the same effect on the poem as *solemn*? Why or why not?

B READING FOCUS

Draw inferences about why the speaker wants to wear disguises and avoid "that final meeting/In the twilight kingdom."

2. **Those . . . Kingdom:** Those with "direct eyes" have crossed from the world of the hollow men into Paradise. The allusion is to Dante's *Paradiso*.
3. **staves:** rods or staffs; "crossed staves / In a field" form a scarecrow.

Alberto Giacometti (1901-1966) ©ARS, NY; City Square (La Place), 1948. Bronze, 8 1/2" x 25 3/8" x 17 1/4"/The Museum of Modern Art, New York, NY, U.S.A. © 2005 Artists Rights Society (ARS), New York/ADAGP, Paris/ Digital Image/Licensed by SCALA/Art Resource, NY

Here the stone images
Are raised, here they receive
The supplication of a dead man's hand **C**
Under the twinkle of a fading star.

Is it like this
In death's other kingdom
Waking alone
At the hour when we are
Trembling with tenderness
Lips that would kiss
Form prayers to broken stone.

IV

The eyes are not here
There are no eyes here
In this valley of dying stars **D**
In this hollow valley
This broken jaw of our lost kingdoms

In this last of meeting places
We grope together
And avoid speech
Gathered on this beach of the tumid river[4]

4. **tumid river:** Hell's swollen ("tumid") river, the Acheron (AK UH RAHN), in Dante's *Inferno*. The damned must cross this river to enter the land of the dead.

C VOCABULARY

Selection Vocabulary

Supplication means "humble plea." How can a dead man's hand make a humble plea? What do you think Eliot meant by this?

D LITERARY FOCUS

The image of the star is an **allusion** to Dante's use of a star to represent God. What do you think the speaker means by the phrases "a fading star" and "dying stars" (lines 44 and 54).

A LITERARY FOCUS

This stanza is an **allusion** to an old children's rhyme. In it, children dance around a mulberry bush, not a prickly pear. The mulberry bush was a traditional symbol of fertility. What makes going around a prickly pear—a cactus—so strange?

B LANGUAGE COACH

Conception ends in the suffix *–ion*, meaning "the act of." The suffix changes the verb *conceive* into a noun. What other words on this page end in *–ion*? What are the words' original verb forms?

Sightless, unless
The eyes reappear
As the perpetual star
Multifoliate rose[5]
Of death's twilight kingdom
The hope only
Of empty men.

V

Here we go round the prickly pear[6]
Prickly pear prickly pear
Here we go round the prickly pear
At five o'clock in the morning. **A**

Between the idea
And the reality
Between the motion
And the act[7]
Falls the Shadow
For Thine is the Kingdom[8]

Between the conception **B**
And the creation
Between the emotion
And the response
Falls the Shadow
Life is very long

Between the desire
And the spasm
Between the potency

5. **multifoliate rose:** Dante describes Paradise as a rose of many leaves (*Paradiso*, Canto 32).
6. **prickly pear:** cactus.
7. **between . . . act:** reference to Shakespeare's *Julius Caesar:* "Between the acting of a dreadful thing / And the first motion, all the interim is / Like a phantasma or a hideous dream" (Act II, Scene 1, lines 63–65).
8. **For . . . Kingdom:** closing lines of the Lord's Prayer: "For thine is the kingdom, and the power, and the glory, forever and ever."

And the existence
Between the essence
And the descent[9]
Falls the Shadow

For Thine is the Kingdom

For Thine is
Life is
For Thine is the

This is the way the world ends
This is the way the world ends
This is the way the world ends
Not with a bang but a whimper. C D

9. **between . . . descent:** The Greek philosopher Plato defined "the essence" as an unattainable ideal and "the descent" as its imperfect expression in material or physical reality.

C LITERARY FOCUS

The last four lines of the poem continue the **allusion** to the children's rhyme. The original words are "This is the way we clap our hands." What does it mean for the world to end with a "whimper" instead of with a "bang"?

D VOCABULARY

Academic Vocabulary

Although the poem has a bleak atmosphere, do you think it *exhibits*, or demonstrates, hope for the future? Why or why not?

The Hollow Men

VOCABULARY DEVELOPMENT

DIRECTIONS: Complete each sentence with the correct vocabulary word from the Word Box.

Word Box

supplication
perpetual
conception
potency

1. She seemed to have ______________ energy, because she never took a break from her work.
2. We walked near the construction site to see the ______________ of the new bridge.
3. During his ______________, he asked the judge for a light sentence.
4. The brutal dictator had control over all of his citizens, and his ______________ had no limits.

LITERARY FOCUS: ALLUSION

DIRECTIONS: Choose one **allusion** from "The Hollow men" and explain it in the first box. Then, in the second box, describe how the allusion adds to Eliot's overall message in the poem.

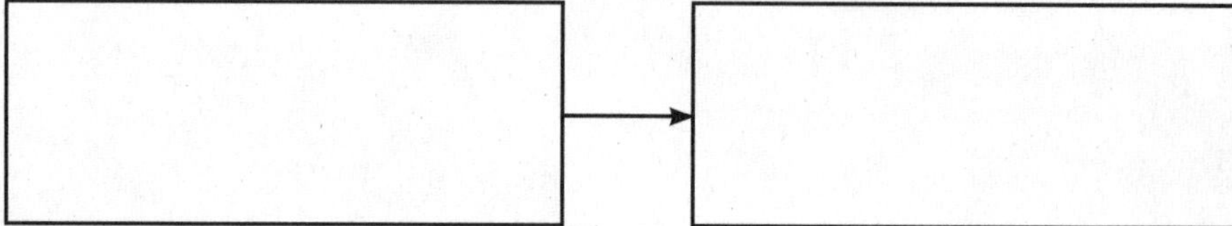

READING FOCUS: DRAWING INFERENCES

DIRECTIONS: The following chart contains **inferences** about Eliot's message in "The Hollow Men." In the second column, provide an example from the text that supports each inference.

Inference	Supporting details from poem
Modern people do not think or feel, and language is meaningless.	1.
Modern people are powerless to take action.	2.

Literary Skills Understand allusion.

Reading Skills Draw inferences.

Preparing to Read

The Second Coming

by William Butler Yeats

LITERARY FOCUS: THEME

The title of William Butler Yeats's poem is an allusion to the Christian prophecy of the Second Coming of Christ that appears in the Book of Revelation in the Bible. An **allusion** is a reference to something that is known from literature, religion, politics, and so on. The Christian idea of the Second Coming is the belief that Jesus will one day return to Earth to usher in an era of peace and justice. The "first coming" was the birth of Jesus in Bethlehem more than two thousand years ago.

The poem's **theme**, or central insight, also relies upon this allusion to the Second Coming, but Yeats turns it inside out. As you read, think about why Yeats reverses the Christian prophecy to portray an end-time of chaos and bloodshed.

READING FOCUS: VISUALIZING IMAGERY

Language that appeals to the senses is called **imagery**. Although most images are visual, imagery can also appeal to the senses of hearing, touch, taste, or smell. Pay attention to the details the poet uses to create a picture in your mind.

Use the Skill To visualize the poem's central image, note elements of its description in the concept web below. In the web's center, write the word "beast." In the surrounding ovals, describe images that relate to the beast.

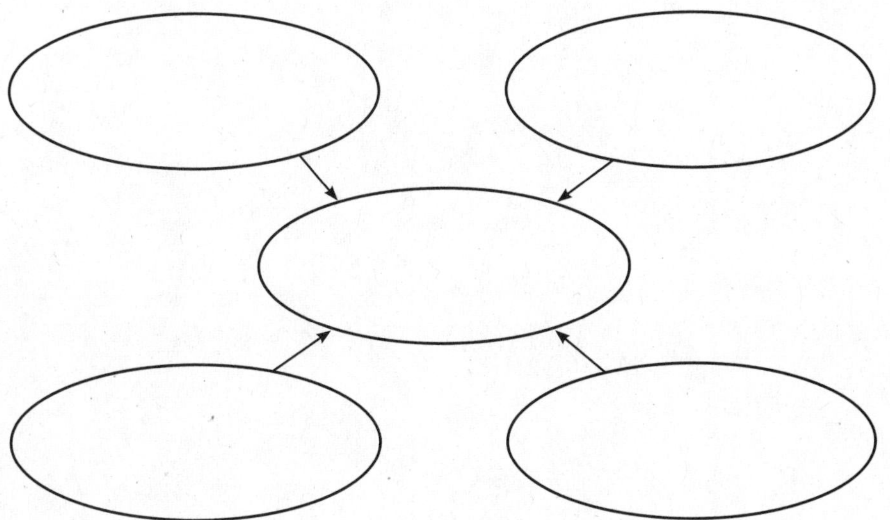

Literary Skills Understand theme.

Reading Skills Visualize imagery.

Vocabulary Development

The Second Coming

SELECTION VOCABULARY

anarchy (AN UHR KEE) *n.:* disorder and confusion.
Anarchy prevailed during the Russian Revolution.

conviction (KUHN VIHK SHUHN) *n.:* firm belief.
She was firm in her conviction that Ireland should be independent.

intensity (IHN TEHN SUH TEE) *n.:* great vigor.
He embraced the task with intensity.

revelation (REHV UH LAY SHUHN) *n.:* act of making known.
The people await a revelation that will confirm their hopes.

vexed (VEHKST) *v.:* troubled.
The outbreak of violence vexed the peace seekers.

WORD STUDY

DIRECTIONS: Pair each vocabulary word in the first column with its antonym (word with the opposite meaning) in the second column. Write the letter of each antonym on the correct line.

________	**1.** anarchy	**a.** indifference
________	**2.** conviction	**b.** uncertainty
________	**3.** intensity	**c.** concealment
________	**4.** revelation	**d.** content
________	**5.** vexed	**e.** organization

THE SECOND COMING

by William Butler Yeats

BACKGROUND

"The Second Coming" addresses Yeats's personal view of history. He saw human history as cyclical. Each cycle, known as a gyre, begins in a rational state and then dissolves into chaos and irrationality. The poem repeats a question that Yeats asks in his book *A Vision:* "What if the irrational returns?" Yeats wrote this poem in 1921, after the horrors of World War I and the Russian Revolution of 1917. He wonders if—like the falconer who can't control his falcon—humankind is spinning out of control and into chaos.

Turning and turning in the widening gyre
The falcon cannot hear the falconer;
Things fall apart; the center cannot hold;
Mere anarchy is loosed upon the world,
The blood-dimmed tide is loosed, and everywhere
The ceremony of innocence is drowned;
The best lack all conviction, while the worst
Are full of passionate intensity. **A**

Surely some revelation is at hand;
Surely the Second Coming is at hand.
The Second Coming! Hardly are those words out
When a vast image out of Spiritus Mundi[1]
Troubles my sight: somewhere in sands of the desert
A shape with lion body and the head of a man,
A gaze blank and pitiless as the sun,

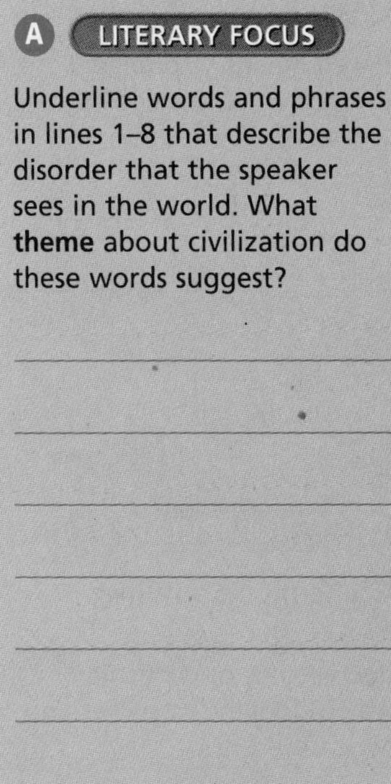

A LITERARY FOCUS

Underline words and phrases in lines 1–8 that describe the disorder that the speaker sees in the world. What **theme** about civilization do these words suggest?

1. **Spiritus Mundi:** Latin for "the world's soul or spirit"; for Yeats, the collective reservoir of human memory from which artists draw their images.

Is moving its slow thighs, while all about it A
Reel shadows of the indignant desert birds. B
The darkness drops again; but now I know
That twenty centuries of stony sleep
Were vexed to nightmare by a rocking cradle, C
And what rough beast, its hour come round at last,
Slouches towards Bethlehem to be born? D

 READING FOCUS

Circle **imagery** that describes the shape the speaker sees in the desert.

 VOCABULARY

Word Study

Reel ("to unwind") and *real* ("actual") are homophones—they have the same pronunciation but different meanings and spellings. Think of two other words that are homophones.

 VOCABULARY

Selection Vocabulary

Vexed means "troubled." Who or what is vexed? By what?

 VOCABULARY

Academic Vocabulary

What is the speaker's *perspective*, or particular way of looking at something, about the future?

The Second Coming

USE A VISUALIZING CHART

DIRECTIONS: The poem's main ideas are listed in the left column below. In the right column, list **imagery** from the text that support these ideas.

Ideas	Imagery
People can't control events happening around them.	
The world is in a state of chaos during times of war. War is bloody and violent and destroys innocence.	
There is no hope of future salvation, because the Second Coming won't be the return of Christ but of some awful beast.	

Applying Your Skills

The Second Coming

VOCABULARY DEVELOPMENT

DIRECTIONS: Complete each sentence with the correct vocabulary word from the Word Box.

Word Box

anarchy
conviction
intensity
revelation
vexed

1. The ________________ that the character was not who she said she was is a surprise twist in the story.
2. His ________________ while discussing the football game told me that he was very interested in sports.
3. I will stick with my ________________ that all animals should be treated with respect.
4. The story was disturbing because the fictional town was filled with ________________ and chaos.
5. We were ________________ by the news that tuition costs were going to rise.

LITERARY FOCUS: THEME

DIRECTIONS: On a separate sheet of paper, write a paragraph in which you describe what you believe is the central **theme** of "The Second Coming." Include examples from the text to support your claim.

READING FOCUS: VISUALIZING IMAGERY

DIRECTIONS: Read the lines from the poem in the first column. In the second column, describe what **imagery** you visualize.

Lines from poem	What I visualize
"Turning and turning in the widening gyre" (line 1)	1.
"The blood-dimmed tide is loosed" (line 5)	2.

Literary Skills Understand theme.

Reading Skills Visualize imagery.

Preparing to Read

Fern Hill

by Dylan Thomas

LITERARY FOCUS: LYRIC POETRY

Lyric poetry focuses on expressing emotions or thoughts, rather than on telling a story. "Fern Hill" is an example of a lyric poem that uses **sound effects** and **figures of speech** (expressive language, such as metaphors, similes, or personification, in which words are used in a way other than their literal sense). This language is used to describe vivid memories of a young boy's enchanted life in the countryside of Wales in Great Britain. The enthusiasm of Thomas's feelings makes a strong impact on the reader.

READING FOCUS: ANALYZING DETAILS

The details that a writer includes in his or her work are carefully chosen to express thoughts, feelings, and impressions. In poetry, many of the details are **sensory details**—details that appeal to the senses of sight, sound, smell, taste, and touch. **Analyzing details** can help you fully understand the author's message.

Use the Skill As you read, jot down details that help you imagine the scene. Use the graphic organizer below to record these details. One detail has been provided.

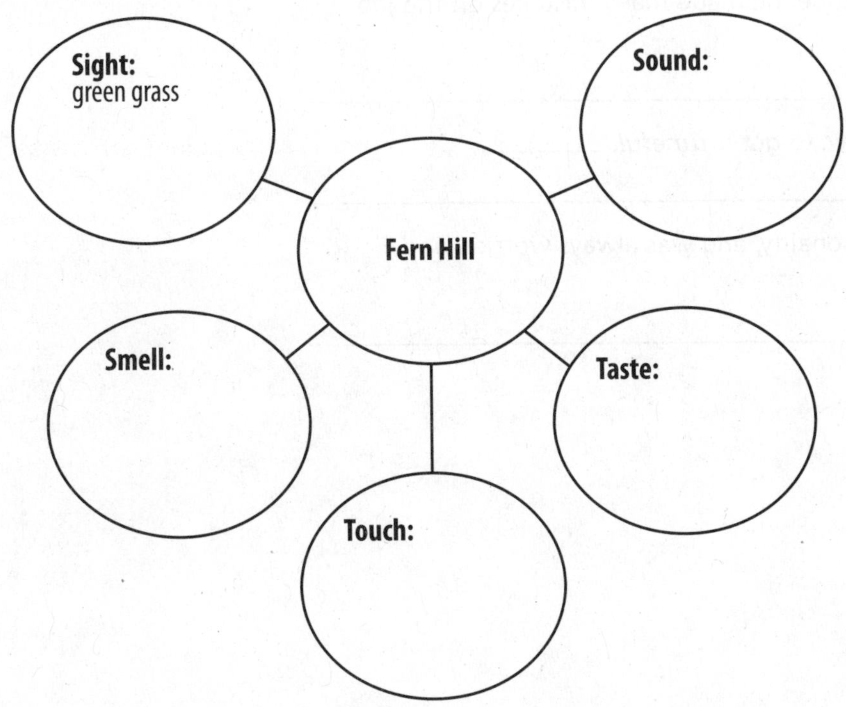

Literary Skills
Understand the characteristics of lyric poetry.

Reading Skills
Analyze details.

Vocabulary Development

Fern Hill

SELECTION VOCABULARY

lilting (LIHLT ING) *v.* used as *adj.:* singing or speaking with a gentle rhythm.
The child's lilting voice expressed his joy.

carefree (KAIR FREE) *adj.:* without worry; happy.
The speaker in "Fern Hill" recalls the peaceful, carefree days he spent outdoors as a child.

heedless (HEED LIHS) *adj.:* careless.
He ran heedless through the fields, unmindful of any threats or dangers.

tuneful (TOON FUHL) *adj.:* musical; melodious.
The tuneful song of the birds filled the sky.

WORD STUDY

DIRECTIONS: For each sentence, write "Yes" if the vocabulary word is being used correctly. Write "No" if it is used incorrectly, and rewrite the sentence so the word is used correctly.

1. The painting on the wall was *lilting* to one side, so I adjusted it.
____
____

2. Because of his *heedless* attitude, he made many mistakes on the job.
____
____

3. I took my car to the mechanic to get it *tuneful.* _________
____

4. She had a very *carefree* personality, and was always worried and anxious. _________
____

FERN HILL

by Dylan Thomas

BACKGROUND

As a child, Dylan Thomas spent summers with relatives who worked on a farm that he calls "Fern Hill" in this poem. The farmhouse is made of the whitewashed stucco typical of Wales and is set in an apple orchard. There are several outlying barns for livestock and hay storage. Not far from the sea, the farm looks down upon huge tidal flats that provide good habitat for thousands of water birds.

"Fern Hill" is a memory of childhood joy. It describes an earthly paradise, a playground for a boy for whom every day is a magical adventure. Yet this joy has a dark side, which is typical of Thomas's poetry. At first, "time" holds the speaker "green and growing." Toward the end of the poem, however, "time" holds him "green and dying."

Now as I was young and easy under the apple boughs
About the lilting house and happy as the grass was green, **A**
The night above the dingle[1] starry,
Time let me hail and climb
Golden in the heydays of his eyes,
And honored among wagons I was prince of the apple towns
And once below a time I lordly had the trees and leaves
Trail with daisies and barley
Down the rivers of the windfall light.

And as I was green and carefree, famous among the barns
About the happy yard and singing as the farm was home,
In the sun that is young once only,
Time let me play and be

1. **dingle:** little wooded valley, nestled between steep hills.

A VOCABULARY

Selection Vocabulary

Lilting means "singing or speaking with a gentle rhythm." How can a house be lilting? What does this suggest is going on inside the house?

VOCABULARY

Word Study

Rode has multiple meanings. Look up the word in a dictionary and tell which meaning you think is used here. Why do you think Thomas used the phrase "rode to sleep" instead of "fell asleep"?

READING FOCUS

What **sensory details** on this page appeal to the sense of hearing?

© Jeff Towns

Golden in the mercy of his means,
And green and golden I was huntsman and herdsman, the calves
Sang to my horn, the foxes on the hills barked clear and cold,
And the sabbath rang slowly
In the pebbles of the holy streams.

All the sun long it was running, it was lovely, the hay
Fields high as the house, the tunes from the chimneys, it was air
And playing, lovely and watery
And fire green as grass.
And nightly under the simple stars
As I rode to sleep the owls were bearing the farm away, A
All the moon long I heard, blessed among stables, the nightjars[2]
Flying with the ricks,[3] and the horses
Flashing into the dark. B

---

2. **nightjars:** common, gray-brown nocturnal birds named for their jarring cries.
3. **ricks:** haystacks.

And then to awake, and the farm, like a wanderer white
With the dew, come back, the cock on his shoulder: it was all
Shining, it was Adam and maiden,
The sky gathered again
And the sun grew round that very day.
So it must have been after the birth of the simple light
In the first, spinning place, the spellbound horses walking
warm C
Out of the whinnying green stable
On to the fields of praise. D

And honored among foxes and pheasants by the gay house
Under the new made clouds and happy as the heart was long,
In the sun born over and over,
I ran my heedless ways,
My wishes raced through the house high hay
And nothing I cared, at my sky blue trades, that time allows
In all his tuneful turning so few and such morning songs
Before the children green and golden
Follow him out of grace,

Nothing I cared, in the lamb white days, that time would take me
Up to the swallow thronged loft by the shadow of my hand,
In the moon that is always rising,
Nor that riding to sleep
I should hear him fly with the high fields
And wake to the farm forever fled from the childless land.
Oh as I was young and easy in the mercy of his means,
Time held me green and dying
Though I sang in my chains like the sea.  F

C **LANGUAGE COACH**

Spellbound means "entranced or fascinated by." Think of an antonym (word with the opposite meaning) for the word *spellbound*.

D **READING FOCUS**

Underline **sensory details** in this stanza that suggest that the speaker sees Fern Hill as a kind of Garden of Eden.

E **LITERARY FOCUS**

Personification is a **figure of speech** in which a nonhuman thing or quality is talked about as if it were human. Circle details in the last two stanzas that personify time.

F **VOCABULARY**

Academic Vocabulary

What is happening to the boy in the last two stanzas? What does the speaker suggest is *inevitable*, or unavoidable?

Applying Your Skills

Fern Hill

VOCABULARY DEVELOPMENT

DIRECTIONS: Decide whether the word pairs are antonyms (words with opposite meanings) or synonyms (words with similar meanings). Write "antonyms" or "synonyms" on the blank lines.

1. lilting; lyrical ____________________
2. carefree; troubled ____________________
3. heedless; focused ____________________
4. tuneful; melodic ____________________

LITERARY FOCUS: LYRIC POETRY

DIRECTIONS: On a separate sheet of paper, write a brief paragraph that describes how Dylan Thomas's use of **figures of speech** in "Fern Hill" helps to convey emotions, thoughts, and feelings in the poem.

READING FOCUS: ANALYZING DETAILS

DIRECTIONS: The chart below includes passages from "Fern Hill." In the second column, tell what sense or senses (sight, sound, smell, taste, or touch) each **sensory detail** appeals to.

Passages from poem	Sense(s)
"the calves/Sang to my horn, the foxes on the hills barked clear/and cold" (lines 15–16)	1.
"Nothing I cared, in the lamb white days, that time would take me/Up to the swallow thronged loft by the shadow of my hand,/In the moon that is always rising" (lines 46–47)	2.

Literary Skills Understand the characteristics of lyric poetry.

Reading Skills Analyze details.

Skills Review

Collection 12

LANGUAGE COACH

DIRECTIONS: An **antonym** is a word that means the opposite of another word. On the blank lines below, write an antonym for each word. The first antonym has been given.

1. anarchy order
2. scary ______
3. secretive ______
4. gain ______
5. potency ______
6. polite ______
7. worrisome ______
8. serious ______
9. conception ______
10. lonely ______

WRITING ACTIVITY

DIRECTIONS: In "Fern Hill," Dylan Thomas writes about happy childhood experiences. Write a short poem (one or two stanzas) that describes a happy childhood memory of your own. In the poem, express your emotions, thoughts, and feelings at the time. Try to include as many **sensory details** (details that appeal to the senses of sight, sound, touch, smell, and taste) as possible.

Collection

13

Expectation and Reality

The Evil Genius of a King. Paris, 1914-15 by Giorgio de Chirico/The Museum of Modern Art, NY/© ARS, NY/ Digital Image/licensed by Scala/Art Resource, NY

Preparing to Read

Araby

by James Joyce

LITERARY FOCUS: EPIPHANY

An **epiphany** is a moment of insight or revelation. Before James Joyce applied the term to literature, the word *epiphany* referred to a religious experience in which a person learns a spiritual truth. Although Joyce gave the word a modern, literary meaning, you will see that the main character's epiphany in "Araby" is described with religious language and imagery.

READING FOCUS: COMPARING AND CONTRASTING

In "Araby," the main character has a vivid imagination that leads him to misunderstand the realities of his life. As a result, the way he imagines things is at times different from the way things really are. **Comparing and contrasting** (finding similarities and difference between) his imaginings and reality will help you understand his epiphany at the end of the story.

Use the Skill As you read the story, use the chart below to list differences between the way the character imagines things to be and the way they actually are.

Imagination	Reality
1.	
2.	
3.	
4.	
5.	

Literary Skills Understand epiphany.

Reading Skills Compare and contrast aspects of a story.

Vocabulary Development

Araby

SELECTION VOCABULARY

imperturbable (IHM PUHR TUHRB UH BUHL) *adj.:* calm, impassive.
The man was imperturbable in the face of the boy's excitement.

somber (SAHM BUHR) *adj.:* gloomy.
The dark, dirty street where he lived was somber.

impinge (IHM PIHNJ) *v.:* strike; touch.
The rays of light from the street lamp impinge on the dark, empty building.

annihilate (UH NY UH LAYT) *v.:* destroy; make nonexistent.
Failure can annihilate a person's hopes.

monotonous (MUH NAHT UH NUHS) *adj.:* unvarying.
The boy found his classwork monotonous.

garrulous (GAR UH LUHS) *adj.:* talkative.
The boy became impatient listening to the garrulous ladies as he tried to read his book in peace.

improvised (IHM PRUH VYZD) *v.* used as *adj.:* made for the occasion with whatever is handy.
Although the tent was improvised, it was good enough to cover the vendor's wares.

pervades (PUHR VAYDZ) *v.:* spreads throughout.
Gloom pervades the entire neighborhood.

WORD STUDY

DIRECTIONS: Write sentences of your own that correctly use each vocabulary word listed above.

1. ______________________________
2. ______________________________
3. ______________________________
4. ______________________________
5. ______________________________
6. ______________________________
7. ______________________________
8. ______________________________

by James Joyce

BACKGROUND

James Joyce's "Araby" is built around scenes from his childhood in Ireland. The narrator's house in the story is based on one where his family lived in Dublin. The Joyces' house, like the one in the story, was located on the same street as the Christian Brothers' School, which Joyce himself attended. The bazaar called *Araby* that the narrator visits was a five-day charity event. The name *Araby* referred to Arabia, which is known for its bazaars, or markets, with long rows of shops. The reference to Arabia, with its deserts and bazaars, would have seemed mysterious and exotic to the children of Ireland, half a world away.

North Richmond Street, being blind, was a quiet street except at the hour when the Christian Brothers' School set the boys free. **A** An uninhabited house of two stories stood at the blind end, detached from its neighbors in a square ground. The other houses of the street, conscious of decent lives within them, gazed at one another with brown imperturbable faces.

The former tenant of our house, a priest, had died in the back drawing-room. Air, musty from having been long enclosed, hung in all the rooms, and the waste room behind the kitchen was littered with old useless papers. Among these I found a few paper-covered books, the pages of which were curled and damp: *The Abbot*, by Walter Scott, *The Devout Communicant*, and *The Memoirs of Vidocq*.[1] I liked the last best because its leaves were yellow. The wild garden behind the house contained a central apple-tree and a few straggling bushes under one of

A LANGUAGE COACH

Here, *blind* means "a dead-end street." *Blind* is a homograph—a word that can have different meanings but is always spelled the same way. What else can *blind* mean? Think of another homograph and write it along with two of its meanings on the lines below.

____

____

____

____

____

1. ***The Abbot . . . Vidocq*** (VEE DUHK): in order, a historical romance about Mary, Queen of Scots, by Sir Walter Scott; an 1813 religious manual written by a Franciscan friar; and the memoirs (though not actually written by François Vidocq) of a French criminal who later became a detective.

A LITERARY ANALYSIS

Circle details in this paragraph that refer to light and dark. How does this imagery affect the story's mood?

B VOCABULARY

Word Study

In medieval monasteries, monks were required to keep silent at certain times. One room, however, was set aside for conversation. This room, the *parlor*, took its name from the Old French word *parleor*, meaning "to speak." How does this relate to today's definition of the word *parlor*? Use a dictionary if you need help.

which I found the late tenant's rusty bicycle-pump. He had been a very charitable priest; in his will he had left all his money to institutions and the furniture of his house to his sister.

When the short days of winter came dusk fell before we had well eaten our dinners. When we met in the street the houses had grown somber. The space of sky above us was the color of ever-changing violet and toward it the lamps of the street lifted their feeble lanterns. The cold air stung us and we played till our bodies glowed. Our shouts echoed in the silent street. The career[2] of our play brought us through the dark muddy lanes behind the houses where we ran the gauntlet[3] of the rough tribes from the cottages, to the back doors of the dark dripping gardens where odors arose from the ashpits, to the dark odorous stables where a coachman smoothed and combed the horse or shook music from the buckled harness. When we returned to the street light from the kitchen windows had filled the areas. If my uncle was seen turning the corner we hid in the shadow until we had seen him safely housed. Or if Mangan's sister came out on the doorstep to call her brother in to his tea we watched her from our shadow peer up and down the street. We waited to see whether she would remain or go in and, if she remained, we left our shadow and walked up to Mangan's steps resignedly. She was waiting for us, her figure defined by the light from the half-opened door. Her brother always teased her before he obeyed and I stood by the railings looking at her. Her dress swung as she moved her body and the soft rope of her hair tossed from side to side. **A**

Every morning I lay on the floor in the front parlor watching her door. **B** The blind was pulled down to within an inch of the sash so that I could not be seen. When she came out on the doorstep my heart leaped. I ran to the hall, seized my books, and followed her. I kept her brown figure always in

2. **career:** course; path.
3. **gauntlet** (GAWNT LIHT): series of challenges. Derived from *gatlopp*, Swedish for "running down a lane," the term originally referred to a form of military punishment in which a wrongdoer had to run between two rows of soldiers who struck him as he passed.

my eye and, when we came near the point at which our ways diverged, I quickened my pace and passed her. This happened morning after morning. I had never spoken to her, except for a few casual words, and yet her name was like a summons to all my foolish blood.

Her image accompanied me even in places the most hostile to romance. On Saturday evenings when my aunt went marketing I had to go to carry some of the parcels. We walked through the flaring streets, jostled by drunken men and bargaining women, amid the curses of laborers, the shrill litanies[4] of shop-boys who stood on guard by the barrels of pigs' cheeks, the nasal chanting of street-singers, who sang a *come-all-you* about O'Donovan Rossa,[5] or a ballad about the troubles in our native land. These noises converged in a single sensation of life for me: I imagined that I bore my chalice[6] safely through a throng of foes. Her name sprang to my lips at moments in strange prayers and praises which I myself did not understand. **C** My eyes were often full of tears (I could not tell why) and at times a flood from my heart seemed to pour itself out into my bosom. I thought little of the future. I did not know whether I would ever speak to her or not or, if I spoke to her, how I could tell her of my confused adoration. But my body was like a harp and her words and gestures were like fingers running upon the wires.

One evening I went into the back drawing-room in which the priest had died. It was a dark rainy evening and there was no sound in the house. Through one of the broken panes I heard the rain impinge upon the earth, the fine incessant needles of water playing in the sodden beds. **D** Some distant lamp or lighted

---

4. **litanies:** repeated sales cries. Literally, a litany is a prayer composed of a series of specific invocations and responses.
5. ***come-all-you* . . . Rossa:** A come-all-you is a type of Irish ballad that usually begins "Come all you [young lovers, rebels, Irishmen, and so on]." O'Donovan Rossa was Jeremiah O'Donovan (1831–1915) from County Cork. He was active in Ireland's struggle against British rule in the mid–nineteenth century.
6. **chalice** (CHAL IHS): cup; specifically, the cup used for Holy Communion wine. Joyce's use of the term evokes the image of a young man on a sacred mission.

C READING FOCUS

Circle the details that describe what the boy sees in his imagination. **Compare and contrast** this image with the images describing the market.

D VOCABULARY

Selection Vocabulary

Impinge comes from the Latin word *impingere*, meaning "drive into; strike against." Knowing this, what do you think *impinge* means?

A LITERARY ANALYSIS

What does the boy do in the back drawing-room? Why do you think he does this?

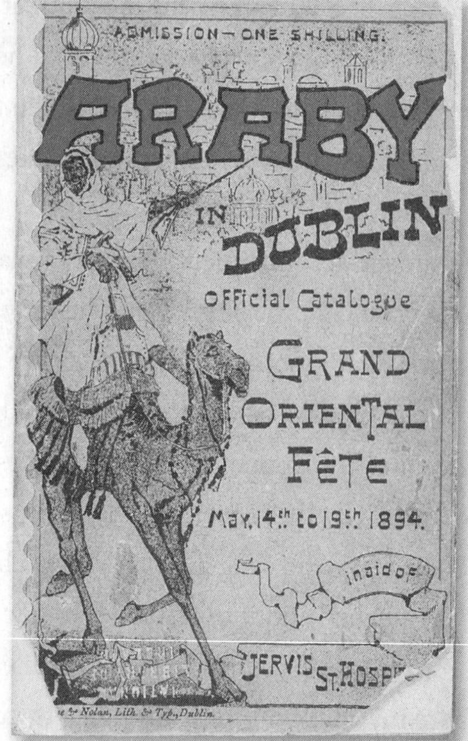

Courtesy of the National Library of Ireland

window gleamed below me. I was thankful that I could see so little. All my senses seemed to desire to veil themselves and, feeling that I was about to slip from them, I pressed the palms of my hands together until they trembled, murmuring: *O love! O love!* many times. **A**

At last she spoke to me. When she addressed the first words to me I was so confused that I did not know what to answer. She asked me was I going to *Araby*. I forget whether I answered yes or no. It would be a splendid bazaar, she said; she would love to go.

—And why can't you? I asked.

While she spoke she turned a silver bracelet round and round her wrist. She could not go, she said, because there would be a retreat that week in her convent.[7] Her brother and two other boys were fighting for their caps and I was alone at the railings. She held one of the spikes, bowing her head toward me. The light from the lamp opposite our door caught the white curve of her neck, lit up her hair that rested there and, falling, lit up the hand

---

7. **retreat . . . convent:** temporary withdrawal from worldly life by the students and teachers at the convent school, to devote time to prayer, meditation, and studies.

upon the railing. It fell over one side of her dress and caught the white border of a petticoat, just visible as she stood at ease.

—It's well for you,[8] she said.

—If I go, I said, I will bring you something.

What innumerable follies laid waste my waking and sleeping thoughts after that evening! I wished to annihilate the tedious intervening days. I chafed against the work of school. At night in my bedroom and by day in the classroom her image came between me and the page I strove to read. The syllables of the word *Araby* were called to me through the silence in which my soul luxuriated and cast an Eastern enchantment over me. I asked for leave to go to the bazaar on Saturday night. My aunt was surprised and hoped it was not some Freemason[9] affair. I answered few questions in class. I watched my master's face pass from amiability to sternness; he hoped I was not beginning to idle. I could not call my wandering thoughts together. I had hardly any patience with the serious work of life which, now that it stood between me and my desire, seemed to me child's play, ugly monotonous child's play. **B** **C**

On Saturday morning I reminded my uncle that I wished to go to the bazaar in the evening. He was fussing at the hallstand, looking for the hat-brush, and answered me curtly:

—Yes, boy, I know.

As he was in the hall I could not go into the front parlor and lie at the window. I left the house in bad humor and walked slowly toward the school. The air was pitilessly raw and already my heart misgave me.

When I came home to dinner my uncle had not yet been home. Still it was early. I sat staring at the clock for some time and, when its ticking began to irritate me, I left the room. I mounted the staircase and gained the upper part of the house.

---

8. **It's well for you:** "You're lucky" (usually said enviously).
9. **Freemason:** The Freemasons are a secret society whose practices were originally drawn from those of British medieval stonemasons' guilds; its members, almost exclusively Protestant, were often hostile to Catholics. The aunt apparently associates the exotic bazaar with the mysterious practices of Freemasonry.

B READING FOCUS

Contrast the boy's everday life with his thoughts of *Araby*.

C VOCABULARY

Selection Vocabulary

Monotonous means "unvarying." Given the meaning and the context, what connotations (associations or feelings) does *monotonous* have for you?

A QUICK CHECK

What things are making the boy increasingly irritable?

B VOCABULARY

Academic Vocabulary

How does the boy *exhibit,* or show, displeasure with his uncle? Why is he upset with his uncle?

The high cold empty gloomy rooms liberated me and I went from room to room singing. From the front window I saw my companions playing below in the street. Their cries reached me weakened and indistinct and, leaning my forehead against the cool glass, I looked over at the dark house where she lived. I may have stood there for an hour, seeing nothing but the brown-clad figure cast by my imagination, touched discreetly by the lamplight at the curved neck, at the hand upon the railings and at the border below the dress.

When I came downstairs again I found Mrs. Mercer sitting at the fire. She was an old garrulous woman, a pawnbroker's widow, who collected used stamps for some pious purpose. I had to endure the gossip of the tea-table. The meal was prolonged beyond an hour and still my uncle did not come. Mrs. Mercer stood up to go: She was sorry she couldn't wait any longer, but it was after eight o'clock and she did not like to be out late, as the night air was bad for her. When she had gone I began to walk up and down the room, clenching my fists. **A** My aunt said:

—I'm afraid you may put off your bazaar for this night of Our Lord.

At nine o'clock I heard my uncle's latchkey in the halldoor. I heard him talking to himself and heard the hallstand rocking when it had received the weight of his overcoat. I could interpret these signs. When he was midway through his dinner I asked him to give me the money to go to the bazaar. He had forgotten.

—The people are in bed and after their first sleep now, he said.

I did not smile. **B** My aunt said to him energetically:

—Can't you give him the money and let him go? You've kept him late enough as it is.

My uncle said he was very sorry he had forgotten. He said he believed in the old saying: *All work and no play makes Jack a dull boy*. He asked me where I was going and, when I had told him a second time he asked me did I know *The Arab's Farewell to his Steed.*[10] When I left the kitchen he was about to recite the opening lines of the piece to my aunt.

I held a florin[11] tightly in my hand as I strode down Buckingham Street toward the station. The sight of the streets thronged with buyers and glaring with gas recalled to me the purpose of my journey. I took my seat in a third-class carriage of a deserted train. After an intolerable delay the train moved out of the station slowly. It crept onward among ruinous houses and over the twinkling river. At Westland Row Station a crowd of people pressed to the carriage doors; but the porters moved them back, saying that it was a special train for the bazaar. I remained alone in the bare carriage. In a few minutes the train drew up beside an improvised wooden platform. I passed out on to the road and saw by the lighted dial of a clock that it was ten minutes to ten. In front of me was a large building which displayed the magical name.

I could not find any sixpenny entrance and, fearing that the bazaar would be closed, I passed in quickly through a turnstile, handing a shilling to a weary-looking man. I found myself in a big hall girdled at half its height by a gallery. Nearly all the stalls were closed and the greater part of the hall was in darkness. I recognized a silence like that which pervades a church after a service. I walked into the center of the bazaar timidly. A few people were gathered about the stalls which were still open. Before a curtain, over which the words *Café Chantant*[12] were written in colored lamps, two men were counting money on a salver.[13] I listened to the fall of the coins. **C**

Remembering with difficulty why I had come I went over to one of the stalls and examined porcelain vases and flowered tea-sets. At the door of the stall a young lady was talking and

C READING FOCUS

The narrator finally arrives at *Araby*. **Compare and contrast** what he sees there with what he had imagined it to be like earlier in the story.

---

10. ***The Arab's . . . Steed:*** popular sentimental poem by the English writer Caroline Norton (1808–1877).
11. **florin:** British coin worth at the time the equivalent of about fifty cents.
12. ***Café Chantant*** (KA FEY SHAHN TAHN): The name refers to a coffeehouse with musical entertainment.
13. **salver** (SAL VUHR): serving tray.

A READING FOCUS

The boy watches a young woman flirt with two young men. How does this scene **contrast** with the conversation the boy had with Mangan's sister?

Courtesy of the National Gallery of Ireland

laughing with two young gentlemen. I remarked their English accents and listened vaguely to their conversation.

—O, I never said such a thing!

—O, but you did!

—O, but I didn't!

—Didn't she say that?

—Yes. I heard her.

—O, there's a . . . fib! **A**

Observing me the young lady came over and asked me did I wish to buy anything. The tone of her voice was not encouraging; she seemed to have spoken to me out of a sense of duty. I looked humbly at the great jars that stood like eastern guards at either side of the dark entrance to the stall and murmured:

—No, thank you. (B)

The young lady changed the position of one of the vases and went back to the two young men. They began to talk of the same subject. Once or twice the young lady glanced at me over her shoulder.

I lingered before her stall, though I knew my stay was useless, to make my interest in her wares seem the more real. Then I turned away slowly and walked down the middle of the bazaar. I allowed the two pennies to fall against the sixpence in my pocket. I heard a voice call from one end of the gallery that the light was out. The upper part of the hall was now completely dark.

Gazing up into the darkness I saw myself as a creature driven and derided by vanity; and my eyes burned with anguish and anger. (C)

B QUICK CHECK

Why doesn't the narrator buy anything at the young woman's stall?

C LITERARY FOCUS

What **epiphany** does the narrator experience at the end of the story?

Applying Your Skills

Araby

VOCABULARY DEVELOPMENT

DIRECTIONS: Complete the following paragraph with words from the Word Box. Some words will not be used.

Word Box

- imperturbable
- somber
- impinge
- annihilate
- monotonous
- garrulous
- improvised
- pervades

Ordinary, everyday life can become (1) ________________ when the same events always happen the same way. Boredom (2) ________________ our routine, spreading throughout our entire daily schedule. If it is not changed occasionally, an everyday routine can (3) ________________ our sense of fun, destroying our ability to be spontaneous. Daily routines can become (4) ________________ or gloomy. (5) ________________ parties or trips can bring new energy and focus to your work.

LITERARY FOCUS: EPIPHANY

DIRECTIONS: On a separate sheet of paper, write a brief paragraph discussing the narrator's **epiphany**. What brings about this revelation?

READING FOCUS: COMPARING AND CONTRASTING

DIRECTIONS: Complete the chart below by **comparing and contrasting** the narrator's perceptions with the realities of his life.

Imagination	Reality
The boy thinks that Araby will be a place of "Eastern enchantment." He imagines that he will get a present for Mangan's sister at the bazaar and then have the opportunity to speak to her again.	

Preparing to Read

No Witchcraft for Sale

by Doris Lessing

LITERARY FOCUS: THEME

Most fiction can be categorized as one of two types: escape fiction or interpretive fiction. **Escape fiction** is pure entertainment. It gives us pleasure, and helps us temporarily escape from the world. **Interpretive fiction,** on the other hand, isn't meant to help us escape from the world, but rather to help us understand it better. Even if it is fantasy, interpretive fiction gives us a sense of what it means to be human. This truth about life revealed in a story is called **theme**. "No Witchcraft for Sale" is an example of interpretive fiction. As you will see, a powerful theme does not have to come from a complex story. Lessing's tale is simple but has a forceful and timely theme.

READING FOCUS: IDENTIFYING HISTORICAL CONTEXT

Historical context refers to the time, place, and events that influence a writer's work, even if the work itself is set in a different time or place. Understanding the atmosphere in which an author writes a story can help you better understand its message. This tale takes place in Southern Rhodesia, a former colony in Africa, during a time of racial and political struggles. Here are some historical connections to keep in mind as you read:

- The story is set at the time when Southern Rhodesia was still part of the British Empire. When Lessing wrote the story in 1964, however, Southern Rhodesia was demanding independence from Britain.
- When the British established the colony, they took the best farmland for themselves. The Rhodesian people were removed from their ancestral homes and sent to lands with poor soil that made raising crops difficult. As a result, those who had previously made a living on the land became a source of cheap labor in cities and were more dependent upon the white minority.
- After Southern Rhodesia declared independence from Britain in 1965, the white minority was eager to establish its own government—a government that would continue the policy of denying rights to black citizens.

Use the Skill As you read the story, look for references to the Rhodesian language, culture, and history. In addition, pay close attention to sections that describe interactions between black and white Rhodesians. Consider how the political climate during which Lessing wrote this story may have influenced her portrayal of the earlier time period.

Literary Skills Understand theme.

Reading Skills Identify historical context.

Vocabulary Development

No Witchcraft for Sale

SELECTION VOCABULARY

reverently (REHV UH RUHNT LEE) *adv.:* with deep respect or awe, as for something sacred.
Gideon reverently held the shiny hair of the child, who looked like an angel.

efficacy (EHF IH KUH SEE) *n.:* ability to produce a desired effect.
Mrs. Farquar had heard of the efficacy of native herbs.

perfunctory (PUHR FUHNGK TUH REE) *adj.:* halfhearted; disinterested.
The scientist was somewhat perfunctory as he explained the benefits of the new drug.

annulled (UH NUHLD) *v.:* erased; cancelled.
The Farquars' anger annulled the guilt they felt towards Gideon.

perversely (PUHR VUHRS LEE) *adv.:* disagreeably; contrarily.
Because the family did not understand Gideon's culture, they considered him to be perversely stubborn.

WORD STUDY

DIRECTIONS: In each sentence below, circle the words or phrases that give a clue to the meaning of the underlined vocabulary word.

1. The Farquars adored their new baby, whom they believed was blessing, and treated him reverently.
2. The efficacy of the drug was plain to see; it was so effective that the child began to recover within hours.
3. We hoped his response to the offer would be enthusiastic, but he gave only a perfunctory reply.
4. We annulled our reservations at the restaurant because we decided not to go out after all.
5. The strong-willed child perversely ignored her parents' order not to play outside in the rain.

No Witchcraft for Sale

by Doris Lessing

BACKGROUND
Doris Lessing was born in 1919 and grew up on a three-thousand-acre farm in Southern Rhodesia, now the country of Zimbabwe. Her family employed about fifty black African workers who earned the equivalent of $1.50 per month and lived in mud huts with no sanitation. Southern Rhodesia was a colony of Great Britain, but both its black and its white residents wanted independence. The white minority wanted to establish a government that continued to limit black citizens' political participation. Black citizens wanted a government in which the black majority would rule. Civil war broke out in the country after it declared independence from Britain in 1965, and more than 25,000 people were killed before the country gained self-rule in 1980.

The Farquars had been childless for years when little Teddy was born; and they were touched by the pleasure of their servants, who brought presents of fowls and eggs and flowers to the homestead when they came to rejoice over the baby, exclaiming with delight over his downy golden head and his blue eyes. They congratulated Mrs. Farquar as if she had achieved a very great thing, and she felt that she had—her smile for the lingering, admiring natives was warm and grateful. **A**

Later, when Teddy had his first haircut, Gideon the cook picked up the soft gold tufts from the ground, and held them reverently in his hand. Then he smiled at the little boy and said: "Little Yellow Head." That became the native name for the child. Gideon and Teddy were great friends from the first. When Gideon had finished his work, he would lift Teddy on his shoulders to the shade of a big tree, and play with him there, forming curious little toys from twigs and leaves and grass, or shaping animals from wetted soil. When Teddy learned to

A LITERARY ANALYSIS
What do we learn about the relationship between the Farquars and their servants?

A QUICK CHECK

How would you describe Gideon's feelings for Teddy?

B READING FOCUS

What does this description of Gideon's living arrangements reveal about the **historical context** of the story?

C LITERARY ANALYSIS

What idea about servants and masters does the discussion in this paragraph convey?

walk it was often Gideon who crouched before him, clucking encouragement, finally catching him when he fell, tossing him up in the air till they both became breathless with laughter. Mrs. Farquar was fond of the old cook because of his love for her child. **A**

There was no second baby; and one day Gideon said: "Ah, missus, missus, the Lord above sent this one; Little Yellow Head is the most good thing we have in our house." Because of that "we" Mrs. Farquar felt a warm impulse toward her cook; and at the end of the month she raised his wages. He had been with her now for several years; he was one of the few natives who had his wife and children in the compound and never wanted to go home to his kraal,[1] which was some hundreds of miles away. **B** Sometimes a small piccanin[2] who had been born the same time as Teddy, could be seen peering from the edge of the bush, staring in awe at the little white boy with his miraculous fair hair and Northern blue eyes. The two little children would gaze at each other with a wide, interested gaze, and once Teddy put out his hand curiously to touch the black child's cheeks and hair.

Gideon, who was watching, shook his head wonderingly, and said: "Ah, missus, these are both children, and one will grow up to be a baas,[3] and one will be a servant"; and Mrs. Farquar smiled and said sadly, "Yes, Gideon, I was thinking the same." She sighed. "It is God's will," said Gideon, who was a mission boy.[4] The Farquars were very religious people; and this shared feeling about God bound servant and masters even closer together. **C**

Teddy was about six years old when he was given a scooter, and discovered the intoxications of speed. All day he would fly around the homestead, in and out of flowerbeds, scattering squawking chickens and irritated dogs, finishing with a wide

---

1. **kraal** (KRAHL): South African village.
2. **piccanin** (PIH KUH NIHN): black African child. Derived from *pequeño* (PAY KAY NYOH), Portuguese for "small," the term is often considered offensive.
3. **baas** (BAHS): Afrikaans for "master." Afrikaans, a language developed from seventeenth-century Dutch, is spoken in South Africa.
4. **mission boy:** one educated by Christian missionaries.

dizzying arc into the kitchen door. There he would cry: "Gideon, look at me!" And Gideon would laugh and say: "Very clever, Little Yellow Head." Gideon's youngest son, who was now a herdsboy, came especially up from the compound to see the scooter. He was afraid to come near it, but Teddy showed off in front of him. "Piccanin," shouted Teddy, "get out of my way!" And he raced in circles around the black child until he was frightened, and fled back to the bush.

"Why did you frighten him?" asked Gideon, gravely reproachful.

Teddy said defiantly: "He's only a black boy," and laughed. **D** Then, when Gideon turned away from him without speaking, his face fell. Very soon he slipped into the house and found an orange and brought it to Gideon, saying: "This is for you." He could not bring himself to say he was sorry; but he could not bear to lose Gideon's affection either. Gideon took the orange unwillingly and sighed. "Soon you will be going away to school, Little Yellow Head," he said wonderingly, "and then you will be grown up." He shook his head gently and said, "And that is how our lives go." He seemed to be putting a distance between himself and Teddy, not because of resentment, but in the way a person accepts something inevitable. The baby had lain in his arms and smiled up into his face: The tiny boy had swung from his shoulders and played with him by the hour. Now Gideon would not let his flesh touch the flesh of the white child. He was kind, but there was a grave formality in his voice that made Teddy pout and sulk away. Also, it made him into a man: With Gideon he was polite, and carried himself formally, and if he came into the kitchen to ask for something, it was in the way a white man uses toward a servant, expecting to be obeyed. **E**

But on the day that Teddy came staggering into the kitchen with his fists to his eyes, shrieking with pain, Gideon dropped the pot full of hot soup that he was holding, rushed to the child, and forced aside his fingers. "A snake!" he exclaimed. Teddy had been on his scooter, and had come to a rest with his foot on the side of a big tub of plants. A tree snake, hanging by its tail from the

D READING FOCUS

How does Teddy's response reflect the **historical context** of this story?

E LITERARY FOCUS

What details in this paragraph tell you that this story is an example of **interpretive fiction**?

© John King/Alamy

roof, had spat full into his eyes. Mrs. Farquar came running when she heard the commotion. "He'll go blind," she sobbed, holding Teddy close against her. "Gideon, he'll go blind!" Already the eyes, with perhaps half an hour's sight left in them, were swollen up to the size of fists: Teddy's small white face was distorted by great purple oozing protuberances.[5] Gideon said: "Wait a minute, missus, I'll get some medicine." He ran off into the bush. **A**

Mrs. Farquar lifted the child into the house and bathed his eyes with permanganate.[6] She had scarcely heard Gideon's words; but when she saw that her remedies had no effect at all, and remembered how she had seen natives with no sight in their eyes, because of the spitting of a snake, she began to look for the return of her cook, remembering what she heard of the efficacy of native herbs. **B** She stood by the window, holding the terrified, sobbing little boy in her arms, and peered helplessly into the bush. It was not more than a few minutes before she saw Gideon come bounding back, and in his hand he held a plant.

"Do not be afraid, missus," said Gideon, "this will cure Little Yellow Head's eyes." He stripped the leaves from the plant, leaving a small white fleshy root. Without even washing it, he put the root in his mouth, chewed it vigorously, and then held the spittle there while he took the child forcibly from Mrs. Farquar. **C** He

5. **protuberances** (PROH TOO BUHR UHNS IHZ): swellings; bulges.
6. **permanganate** (PUHR MANG GUH NAYT): dark purple chemical compound used as a disinfectant.

A QUICK CHECK

Why are Gideon and Mrs. Farquar so concerned about Teddy's eyes?

B VOCABULARY

Selection Vocabulary

Efficacy means "ability to produce a desired effect." What kind of efficacy does the permanganate have on Teddy's eyes?

C LANGUAGE COACH

The suffix *–ly* can be added to some adjectives to form an adverb. The adjective *vigorous* means "energetic." Adding *–ly* creates the adverb *vigorously*, which means, "in an energetic way." Underline another word in this sentence that ends in the suffix *–ly*. What does this word mean?

gripped Teddy down between his knees, and pressed the balls of his thumbs into the swollen eyes, so that the child screamed and Mrs. Farquar cried out in protest: "Gideon, Gideon!" But Gideon took no notice. He knelt over the writhing child, pushing back the puffy lids till chinks of eyeball showed, and then he spat hard, again and again, into first one eye, and then the other. He finally lifted Teddy gently into his mother's arms, and said: "His eyes will get better." But Mrs. Farquar was weeping with terror, and she could hardly thank him: It was impossible to believe that Teddy could keep his sight. In a couple of hours the swellings were gone: The eyes were inflamed and tender but Teddy could see. **D** Mr. and Mrs. Farquar went to Gideon in the kitchen and thanked him over and over again. They felt helpless because of their gratitude: It seemed they could do nothing to express it. They gave Gideon presents for his wife and children, and a big increase in wages, but these things could not pay for Teddy's now completely cured eyes. Mrs. Farquar said: "Gideon, God chose you as an instrument for His goodness," and Gideon said: "Yes, missus, God is very good."

Now, when such a thing happens on a farm, it cannot be long before everyone hears of it. Mr. and Mrs. Farquar told their neighbors and the story was discussed from one end of the district to the other. The bush is full of secrets. No one can live in Africa, or at least on the veld,[7] without learning very soon that there is an ancient wisdom of leaf and soil and season—and, too, perhaps most important of all, of the darker tracts of the human mind—which is the black man's heritage. Up and down the district people were telling anecdotes, reminding each other of things that had happened to them. **E**

"But I saw it myself, I tell you. It was a puff-adder bite. The kaffir's[8] arm was swollen to the elbow, like a great shiny black bladder. He was groggy after a half a minute. He was dying. Then suddenly a kaffir walked out of the bush with his hands full of

7. **veld:** in South Africa, open country with very few bushes or trees; grassland. *Veld*, also spelled *veldt*, is Afrikaans for "field."
8. **kaffir's** (KAF UHRZ): *Kaffir* is a contemptuous term for a black African, derived from *kāfir*, Arabic for "infidel."

D LITERARY ANALYSIS

What do we learn about Gideon's character from the way he helps Teddy?

E VOCABULARY

Word Study

Anecdote comes from the Greek word *anekdota*, meaning "unpublished things." Based on this and what you have read, what do you think *anecdotes* are?

A LITERARY FOCUS

The title of a story often hints at its **theme.** Think about this story's title, "No Witchcraft for Sale." Why wouldn't Africans want to share their secrets about native medicines?

© Juhan Kuus/SIPA Press

green stuff. He smeared something on the place, and next day my boy was back at work, and all you could see was two small punctures in the skin."

This was the kind of tale they told. And, as always, with a certain amount of exasperation, because while all of them knew that in the bush of Africa are waiting valuable drugs locked in bark, in simple-looking leaves, in roots, it was impossible to ever get the truth about them from the natives themselves. **A**

The story eventually reached town; and perhaps it was at a sundowner party,[9] or some such function, that a doctor, who happened to be there, challenged it. "Nonsense," he said. "These things get exaggerated in the telling. We are always checking up on this kind of story, and we draw a blank every time."

Anyway, one morning there arrived a strange car at the homestead, and out stepped one of the workers from the laboratory in town, with cases full of test tubes and chemicals.

Mr. and Mrs. Farquar were flustered and pleased and flattered. They asked the scientist to lunch, and they told the

9. **sundowner party:** British colloquial term for "cocktail party." The term derives from the British custom of gathering for drinks at sunset.

story all over again, for the hundredth time. Little Teddy was there too, his blue eyes sparkling with health, to prove the truth of it. The scientist explained how humanity might benefit if this new drug could be offered for sale; and the Farquars were even more pleased: They were kind, simple people, who liked to think of something good coming about because of them. But when the scientist began talking of the money that might result, their manner showed discomfort. Their feelings over the miracle (that was how they thought of it) were so strong and deep and religious, that it was distasteful to them to think of money. The scientist, seeing their faces, went back to his first point, which was the advancement of humanity. He was perhaps a trifle perfunctory: It was not the first time he had come salting the tail of a fabulous bush secret.[10] **B**

Eventually, when the meal was over, the Farquars called Gideon into their living room and explained to him that this baas, here, was a Big Doctor from the Big City, and he had come all that way to see Gideon. At this Gideon seemed afraid; he did not understand; and Mrs. Farquar explained quickly that it was because of the wonderful thing he had done with Teddy's eyes that the Big Baas had come.

Gideon looked from Mrs. Farquar to Mr. Farquar, and then at the little boy, who was showing great importance because of the occasion. At last he said grudgingly: "The Big Baas want to know what medicine I used?" He spoke incredulously, as if he could not believe his old friends could so betray him. **C** Mr. Farquar began explaining how a useful medicine could be made out of the root, and how it could be put on sale, and how thousands of people, black and white, up and down the continent of Africa, could be saved by the medicine when that spitting snake filled their eyes with poison. Gideon listened, his eyes bent on the ground, the skin of his forehead puckering in discomfort. When Mr. Farquar had finished he did not reply. The scientist, who all

10. salting . . . bush secret: allusion to the ironic advice given to children about catching a bird by putting salt on its tail. In other words, the scientist knows his search may be futile.

B QUICK CHECK

How does the scientist's motivation for finding out the cure compare with that of the Farquars?

C LANGUAGE COACH

The adjective *incredulous* means "skeptical." Knowing this, write a definition for the adverb *incredulously*. Then, use the word in a sentence of your own.

A LITERARY ANALYSIS

Based on what you know about Gideon, how do you think he will reply to the Farquars and the scientist? Explain.

B READING FOCUS

What do the details in lines 202–210 tell about the **historical context** of the story?

this time had been leaning back in a big chair, sipping his coffee and smiling with skeptical good humor, chipped in and explained all over again, in different words, about the making of drugs and the progress of science. Also, he offered Gideon a present. **A**

There was silence after this further explanation, and then Gideon remarked indifferently that he could not remember the root. His face was sullen and hostile, even when he looked at the Farquars, whom he usually treated like old friends. They were beginning to feel annoyed; and this feeling annulled the guilt that had been sprung into life by Gideon's accusing manner. They were beginning to feel that he was unreasonable. But it was at that moment that they all realized he would never give in. The magical drug would remain where it was, unknown and useless except for the tiny scattering of Africans who had the knowledge, natives who might be digging a ditch for the municipality in a ragged shirt and a pair of patched shorts, but who were still born to healing, hereditary healers, being the nephews or sons of the old witch doctors whose ugly masks and bits of bone and all the uncouth properties of magic were the outward signs of real power and wisdom. **B**

The Farquars might tread on that plant fifty times a day as they passed from house to garden, from cow kraal to mealie[11] field, but they would never know it.

But they went on persuading and arguing, with all the force of their exasperation; and Gideon continued to say that he could not remember, or that there was no such root, or that it was the wrong season of the year, or that it wasn't the root itself, but the spit from his mouth that had cured Teddy's eyes. He said all these things one after another, and seemed not to care they were contradictory. He was rude and stubborn. The Farquars could hardly recognize their gentle, lovable old servant in this ignorant, perversely obstinate African, standing there in front of them with lowered eyes, his hands twitching his cook's apron, repeating over

11. mealie: corn.

and over whichever one of the stupid refusals that first entered his head. **C**

And suddenly he appeared to give in. He lifted his head, gave a long, blank angry look at the circle of whites, who seemed to him like a circle of yelping dogs pressing around him, and said: "I will show you the root."

They walked single file away from the homestead down a kaffir path. It was a blazing December afternoon, with the sky full of hot rain clouds. Everything was hot: The sun was like a bronze tray whirling overhead, there was a heat shimmer over the fields, the soil was scorching underfoot, the dusty wind blew gritty and thick and warm in their faces. It was a terrible day, fit only for reclining on a veranda with iced drinks, which is where they would normally have been at that hour.

From time to time, remembering that on the day of the snake it had taken ten minutes to find the root, someone asked: "Is it much further, Gideon?" And Gideon would answer over his shoulder, with angry politeness: "I'm looking for the root, baas." **D** And indeed, he would frequently bend sideways and trail his hand among the grasses with a gesture that was insulting in its perfunctoriness. He walked them through the bush along unknown paths for two hours, in that melting destroying heat, so that the sweat trickled coldly down them and their heads ached. They were all quite silent: the Farquars because they were angry, the scientist because he was being proved right again; there was no such plant. His was a tactful silence.

At last, six miles from the house, Gideon suddenly decided they had had enough; or perhaps his anger evaporated at that moment. He picked up, without an attempt at looking anything but casual, a handful of blue flowers from the grass, flowers that had been growing plentifully all down the paths they had come.

He handed them to the scientist without looking at him, and marched off by himself on the way home, leaving them to follow him if they chose.

When they got back to the house, the scientist went to the kitchen to thank Gideon: He was being very polite, even

C LITERARY ANALYSIS

The Farquars hardly recognize Gideon because, to them, his behavior is "ignorant" and "stupid." Why has Gideon's behavior changed?

D VOCABULARY

Academic Vocabulary

Why do you think the search for the root is taking *considerably* longer, or longer by a large amount, than before?

though there was an amused look in his eyes. Gideon was not there. Throwing the flowers casually into the back of his car, the eminent visitor departed on his way back to his laboratory.

Gideon was back in his kitchen in time to prepare dinner, but he was sulking. He spoke to Mr. Farquar like an unwilling servant. It was days before they liked each other again.

The Farquars made inquiries about the root from their laborers. Sometimes they were answered with distrustful stares. Sometimes the natives said: "We do not know. We have never heard of the root." One, the cattle boy, who had been with them a long time, and had grown to trust them a little, said: "Ask your boy in the kitchen. Now, there's a doctor for you. He's the son of a famous medicine man who used to be in these parts, and there's nothing he cannot cure." Then he added politely: "Of course, he's not as good as the white man's doctor, we know that, but he's good for us." **A**

After some time, when the soreness had gone from between the Farquars and Gideon, they began to joke: "When are you going to show us the snake root, Gideon?" And he would laugh and shake his head, saying, a little uncomfortably: "But I did show you, missus, have you forgotten?" **B**

Much later, Teddy, as a schoolboy, would come into the kitchen and say: "You old rascal, Gideon! Do you remember that time you tricked us all by making us walk miles all over the veld for nothing? It was so far my father had to carry me!"

And Gideon would double up with polite laughter. After much laughing, he would suddenly straighten himself up, wipe his old eyes, and look sadly at Teddy, who was grinning mischievously at him across the kitchen: "Ah, Little Yellow Head, how you have grown! Soon you will be grown up with a farm of your own. . . ."

A READING FOCUS

In this paragraph, we find out that Gideon is the son of a famous medicine man. What does the cattle boy's "polite" comment reveal about the **historical context** of the story?

B LITERARY ANALYSIS

Why do you think the Farquars are now able to joke about the matter that had previously angered them?

No Witchcraft for Sale

USE A HISTORICAL CONTEXT CHART

DIRECTIONS: Use the chart below to analyze the **historical context** of "No Witchcraft for Sale." The first column shows passages from the story. In the second column, explain what the passages tell you about the historical context of the story.

Passages	Historical context
"With Gideon he was polite, and carried himself formally, and if he came into the kitchen to ask for something, it was in the way a white man uses toward a servant, expecting to be obeyed." (lines 75–78) →	
"And Gideon would double up with polite laughter . . . " "Ah, Little Yellow Head, how you have grown! Soon you will be grown up with a farm of your own . . .") (lines 285–290) →	

Applying Your Skills

No Witchcraft for Sale

Word Box

- reverently
- efficacy
- perfunctory
- annulled
- perversely

VOCABULARY DEVELOPMENT

DIRECTIONS: Complete the sentences below with the correct vocabulary words from the Word Box. Some words will not be used.

1. Malcolm says the ______________________ of this new study method is amazing; his grades have improved dramatically.
2. Zoë ______________________ read the passage from the religious manuscript.
3. In order to save some money, Claire ______________________ her magazine subscriptions.

LITERARY FOCUS: THEME

DIRECTIONS: On a separate sheet of paper write a paragraph that describes the **theme** of "No Witchcraft for Sale."

READING FOCUS: IDENTIFYING HISTORICAL CONTEXT

DIRECTIONS: Match each passage from the story in the first column with information it reveals about life in Southern Rhodesia during the period of British rule in the second column. Write the correct letters on the blank lines.

Story passages	Historical information
a. ". . .Mrs. Farquar felt a warm impulse toward her cook . . . he was one of the few natives who had his wife and children in the compound and never wanted to go home to his kraal . . ." (lines 26–30)	______ **1.** After colonization, black Rhodesians were expected to abandon their traditional beliefs and values.
b. "He was rude and stubborn. The Farquars could hardly recognize their . . . servant in this ignorant, perversely obstinate African . . ." (lines 220–222)	______ **2.** During colonization, many black citizens were made to leave their ancestral homes so that the white minority could take over the most productive farmland for themselves.
c. "'Ask your boy in the kitchen . . . he's the son of a famous medicine man . . .'" (lines 270–272)	______ **3.** European settlers in Africa did not understand or trust the colony's black citizens.

Literary Skills Understand theme.

Reading Skills Identify historical context.

Preparing to Read

Games at Twilight

by Anita Desai

LITERARY FOCUS: IMAGERY

Imagery is language that creates pictures in your mind. Imagery usually focuses on visual details, but it can also appeal to the other senses (hearing, touch, taste, and smell). Almost all writers use imagery to help readers picture settings, characters, and actions. In this story, Anita Desai drenches us in the smells, textures, sounds, and colors of a summer afternoon in India. Desai helps us to experience the world through the eyes and ears of her characters, from the bursting open of a door to the crushed silence of a defeated child.

READING FOCUS: ANALYZING DETAILS

Although one detail may not have much meaning, many details together add depth to a story. Without details, a scene can be bland. For example, the scene, "The children played a game" needs more details. Who are the children, when and where did they play, what happened, and how did they feel about it? As you read the following story, **analyze details** to note how the imagery allows you to see a scene and to share a character's feelings and experiences.

Use the Skill As you read, use a chart like the one below to analyze details and imagery in the story. One example of this process is provided below.

Details from the story	My analysis
"Their faces were red and bloated with the effort, but their mother would not open the door, everything was still curtained and shuttered in way that stifled the children, made them feel that their lungs were stuffed with cotton wool and their noses with dust and if they didn't burst out into the light and see the sun and feel the air, they would choke." (lines 4–10)	The heat sounds unbearable. The vividness of the author's language helps me better understand India's climate. It also makes me wonder why the mother is keeping her children inside. I'll keep reading to determine her motivation.

Literary Skills Understand imagery.

Reading Skills Analyze details.

Vocabulary Development

Games at Twilight

SELECTION VOCABULARY

maniacal (MUH NY UH KUHL) *adj.:* crazed; wildly enthusiastic.
The boy's maniacal laughter revealed his enjoyment of the game.

stridently (STRY DUHNT LEE) *adv.:* harshly; sharply.
The boy yelled stridently at the disobedient dog.

superciliously (SOO PUHR SIHL EE UHS LEE) *adv.:* disdainfully; scornfully.
The girl superciliously rejected her sister's request to play.

temerity (TUH MEHR UH TEE) *n.:* reckless boldness.
The girl had the temerity to stand up on her bike seat.

intoxicating (IHN TAHK SUH KAYT IHNG) *v.* used as *adj.:* causing wild excitement, often beyond the point of self-control.
The child found the game hide–and–seek to be intoxicating.

dogged (DAWG IHD) *adj.:* stubbornly persistent.
The boy was dogged in his determination to win the game.

lugubrious (LUH GOO BREE UHS) *adj.:* solemn or mournful, especially in an excessive way.
The children made a lugubrious sound when they were forced to come in for the night.

ignominy (IHG NUH MIHN EE) *n.:* shame; disgrace.
He could hardly stand the ignominy of having lost the game.

WORD STUDY

DIRECTIONS: Use your knowledge of the vocabulary words to note whether the following word pairs are synonyms (words with similar meanings) or antonyms (words with opposite meanings).

1. maniacal; calm ____________________
2. stridently; jarringly ____________________
3. superciliously; contemptuously ____________________
4. temerity; audacity ____________________
5. intoxicating; dull ____________________
6. dogged; determined ____________________
7. lugubrious; elated ____________________
8. ignominy; pride ____________________

Games at Twilight

by Anita Desai

BACKGROUND
This story takes place shortly after India won its independence from Britain in 1947. During the long British rule in India, many upper-class Indian families adopted Western values, behaviors, and customs, including games such as the one played in the story.

It was still too hot to play outdoors. They had had their tea, they had been washed and had their hair brushed, and after the long day of confinement in the house that was not cool but at least a protection from the sun, the children strained to get out. Their faces were red and bloated with the effort, but their mother would not open the door, everything was still curtained and shuttered in a way that stifled the children, made them feel that their lungs were stuffed with cotton wool and their noses with dust and if they didn't burst out into the light and see the sun and feel the air, they would choke. A

"Please, ma, please," they begged. "We'll play in the veranda and porch—we won't go a step out of the porch."

"You will, I know you will, and then—"

"No—we won't, we won't," they wailed so horrendously that she actually let down the bolt of the front door so that they burst out like seeds from a crackling, overripe pod into the veranda, with such wild, maniacal yells that she retreated to her bath and the shower of talcum powder and the fresh sari that were to help her face the summer evening. B

They faced the afternoon. It was too hot. Too bright. The white walls of the veranda glared stridently in the sun. The

A LITERARY FOCUS

Underline **imagery** in the first paragraph that helps you understand the effect of the heat on the children.

B LANGUAGE COACH

Words that contain the same root are in the same **word family**. Notice that the word *maniacal*, meaning "crazed" or "wildly enthusiastic," contains the root *maniac*. Identify the root of another word in this sentence. Write the two words below.

___

___

A READING FOCUS

Analyze details in this paragraph. What senses do these details and images appeal to?

B QUICK CHECK

Compare the actions of the children and the parrots.

C QUICK CHECK

What is the cause of the conflict between the children?

bougainvillea[1] hung about it, purple and magenta, in livid balloons. The garden outside was like a tray made of beaten brass, flattened out on the red gravel and the stony soil in all shades of metal—aluminum, tin, copper, and brass. No life stirred at this arid time of day—the birds still drooped, like dead fruit, in the papery tents of the trees; some squirrels lay limp on the wet earth under the garden tap. The outdoor dog lay stretched as if dead on the veranda mat, his paws and ears and tail all reaching out like dying travelers in search of water. He rolled his eyes at the children—two white marbles rolling in the purple sockets, begging for sympathy—and attempted to lift his tail in a wag but could not. It only twitched and lay still. **A**

Then, perhaps roused by the shrieks of the children, a band of parrots suddenly fell out of the eucalyptus tree, tumbled frantically in the still, sizzling air, then sorted themselves out into battle formation and streaked away across the white sky.

The children, too, felt released. They too began tumbling, shoving, pushing against each other, frantic to start. Start what? Start their business. The business of the children's day which is—play. **B**

"Let's play hide-and-seek."

"Who'll be It?"

"You be It."

"Why should I? You be—"

"You're the eldest—"

"That doesn't mean—"

The shoves became harder. Some kicked out. The motherly Mira intervened. She pulled the boys roughly apart. There was a tearing sound of cloth, but it was lost in the heavy panting and angry grumbling, and no one paid attention to the small sleeve hanging loosely off a shoulder. **C**

"Make a circle, make a circle!" she shouted, firmly pulling and pushing till a kind of vague circle was formed. "Now clap!" she roared, and, clapping, they all chanted in melancholy

1. **bougainvillea** (BOO GUHN VEEL EE UH): woody, tropical vine with showy, purplish leaves.

unison: "Dip, dip, dip—my blue ship—" and every now and then one or the other saw he was safe by the way his hands fell at the crucial moment—palm on palm, or back of hand on palm—and dropped out of the circle with a yell and a jump of relief and jubilation. **D**

Raghu was It. He started to protest, to cry "You cheated—Mira cheated—Anu cheated—" but it was too late, the others had all already streaked away. There was no one to hear when he called out, "Only in the veranda—the porch—Ma said—Ma *said* to stay in the porch!" No one had stopped to listen, all he saw were their brown legs flashing through the dusty shrubs, scrambling up brick walls, leaping over compost heaps and hedges, and then the porch stood empty in the purple shade of the bougainvillea, and the garden was as empty as before; even the limp squirrels had whisked away, leaving everything gleaming, brassy, and bare. **E**

Only small Manu suddenly reappeared, as if he had dropped out of an invisible cloud or from a bird's claws, and stood for a moment in the center of the yellow lawn, chewing his finger and near to tears as he heard Raghu shouting, with his head pressed against the veranda wall, "Eighty-three, eighty-five, eighty-nine, ninety . . ." and then made off in a panic, half of him wanting to fly north, the other half counseling south. Raghu turned just in time to see the flash of his white shorts and the uncertain skittering of his red sandals, and charged after him with such a bloodcurdling yell that Manu stumbled over the hosepipe, fell into its rubber coils, and lay there weeping, "I won't be It—you have to find them all—all—All!" **F**

"I know I have to, idiot," Raghu said, superciliously kicking him with his toe. "You're dead," he said with satisfaction, licking the beads of perspiration off his upper lip, and then stalked off in search of worthier prey, whistling spiritedly so that the hiders should hear and tremble.

Ravi heard the whistling and picked his nose in a panic, trying to find comfort by burrowing the finger deep—deep into that soft tunnel. He felt himself too exposed, sitting on an

D LITERARY ANALYSIS

Judging from her actions, what kind of person is Mira?

E LITERARY FOCUS

Underline the **imagery** that describes the emptiness after everyone but Raghu runs away.

F READING FOCUS

Analyze details in this paragraph. Then, describe in your own words the tension that Manu feels.

A VOCABULARY

Academic Vocabulary

Describe Raghu from Ravi's *perspective,* or way of looking at something.

B VOCABULARY

Word Study

Mortuary orignates from the Latin word *mori,* meaning "to die." Knowing this, what do you think a mortuary is?

upturned flowerpot behind the garage. Where could he burrow? He could run around the garage if he heard Raghu come—around and around and around—but he hadn't much faith in his short legs when matched against Raghu's long, hefty, hairy footballer legs. Ravi had a frightening glimpse of them as Raghu combed the hedge of crotons and hibiscus, trampling delicate ferns underfoot as he did so. Ravi looked about him desperately, swallowing a small ball of snot in his fear. **A**

The garage was locked with a great heavy lock to which the driver had the key in his room, hanging from a nail on the wall under his workshirt. Ravi had peeped in and seen him still sprawling on his string cot in his vest and striped underpants, the hair on his chest and the hair in his nose shaking with the vibrations of his phlegm-obstructed snores. Ravi had wished he were tall enough, big enough to reach the key on the nail, but it was impossible, beyond his reach for years to come. He had sidled away and sat dejectedly on the flowerpot. That at least was cut to his own size.

But next to the garage was another shed with a big green door. Also locked. No one even knew who had the key to the lock. That shed wasn't opened more than once a year, when Ma turned out all the old broken bits of furniture and rolls of matting and leaking buckets, and the white anthills were broken and swept away and Flit sprayed into the spider webs and rat holes so that the whole operation was like the looting of a poor, ruined, and conquered city. The green leaves of the door sagged. They were nearly off their rusty hinges. The hinges were large and made a small gap between the door and the walls—only just large enough for rats, dogs, and, possibly, Ravi to slip through.

Ravi had never cared to enter such a dark and depressing mortuary of defunct household goods seething with such unspeakable and alarming animal life but, as Raghu's whistling grew angrier and sharper and his crashing and storming in the hedge wilder, Ravi suddenly slipped off the flowerpot and through the crack and was gone. **B** He chuckled aloud with astonishment at his own temerity so that Raghu came out of the hedge, stood

© Jon Hicks/eStock Photo

silent with his hands on his hips, listening, and finally shouted, "I heard you! I'm coming! *Got* you—" and came charging round the garage only to find the upturned flowerpot, the yellow dust, the crawling of white ants in a mud hill against the closed shed door—nothing. Snarling, he bent to pick up a stick and went off, whacking it against the garage and shed walls as if to beat out his prey.

Ravi shook, then shivered with delight, with self-congratulation. Also with fear. It was dark, spooky in the shed. It had a muffled smell, as of graves. Ravi had once got locked into the linen cupboard and sat there weeping for half an hour before he was rescued. But at least that had been a familiar place, and even smelled pleasantly of starch, laundry, and, reassuringly, of his mother. But the shed smelled of rats, anthills, dust, and spider webs. Also of less definable, less recognizable horrors. And it was dark. Except for the white-hot cracks along the door, there was no light. (C) The roof was very low. Although Ravi was small,

C QUICK CHECK

How does being in the shed compare to Ravi's previous experience of being trapped in a cupboard?

A READING FOCUS

Analyze details in this paragraph. What kind of atmosphere does the author create with her decription of the shed?

B LITERARY FOCUS

Underline **imagery** in lines 140–159 that appeals to the senses of sight, smell, hearing, and touch. What is most frightening to Ravi about being in the shed?

he felt as if he could reach up and touch it with his fingertips. But he didn't stretch. He hunched himself into a ball so as not to bump into anything, touch or feel anything. What might there not be to touch him and feel him as he stood there, trying to see in the dark? Something cold, or slimy—like a snake. Snakes! He leapt up as Raghu whacked the wall with his stick—then, quickly realizing what it was, felt almost relieved to hear Raghu, hear his stick. It made him feel protected. **A**

But Raghu soon moved away. There wasn't a sound once his footsteps had gone around the garage and disappeared. Ravi stood frozen inside the shed. Then he shivered all over. Something had tickled the back of his neck. It took him a while to pick up the courage to lift his hand and explore. It was an insect—perhaps a spider—exploring *him*. He squashed it and wondered how many more creatures were watching him, waiting to reach out and touch him, the stranger. **B**

There was nothing now. After standing in that position—his hand still on his neck, feeling the wet splodge of the squashed spider gradually dry—for minutes, hours, his legs began to tremble with the effort, the inaction. By now he could see enough in the dark to make out the large solid shapes of old wardrobes, broken buckets, and bedsteads piled on top of each other around him. He recognized an old bathtub—patches of enamel glimmered at him, and at last he lowered himself onto its edge.

He contemplated slipping out of the shed and into the fray. He wondered if it would not be better to be captured by Raghu and be returned to the milling crowd as long as he could be in the sun, the light, the free spaces of the garden, and the familiarity of his brothers, sisters, and cousins. It would be evening soon. Their games would become legitimate. The parents would sit out on the lawn on cane basket chairs and watch them as they tore around the garden or gathered in knots to share a loot of mulberries or black, teeth-splitting *jamun*[2] from the garden trees. The gardener would fix the hosepipe to the water tap, and water would fall lavishly through the air to the ground, soaking

2. ***jamun*** (JAH MUHN): plumlike fruit.

the dry yellow grass and the red gravel and arousing the sweet, the intoxicating scent of water on dry earth—that loveliest scent in the world. Ravi sniffed for a whiff of it. He half-rose from the bathtub, then heard the despairing scream of one of the girls as Raghu bore down upon her. There was the sound of a crash, and of rolling about in the bushes, the shrubs, then screams and accusing sobs of "I touched the den—" "You did not—" "I did—" "You liar, you did *not*" and then a fading away and silence again.

Ravi sat back on the harsh edge of the tub, deciding to hold out a bit longer. **C** What fun if they were all found and caught—he alone left unconquered! He had never known that sensation. Nothing more wonderful had ever happened to him than being taken out by an uncle and bought a whole slab of chocolate all to himself, or being flung into the soda man's pony cart and driven up to the gate by the friendly driver with the red beard and pointed ears. To defeat Raghu—that hirsute,[3] hoarse-voiced football champion—and to be the winner in a circle of older, bigger, luckier children—that would be thrilling beyond imagination. He hugged his knees together and smiled to himself almost shyly at the thought of so much victory, such laurels. **D**

There he sat smiling, knocking his heels against the bathtub, now and then getting up and going to the door to put his ear to the broad crack and listening for sounds of the game, the pursuer and the pursued, and then returning to his seat with the dogged determination of the true winner, a breaker of records, a champion.

It grew darker in the shed as the light at the door grew softer, fuzzier, turned to a kind of crumbling yellow pollen that turned to yellow fur, blue fur, gray fur. Evening. Twilight. The sound of water gushing, falling. The scent of earth receiving water, slaking its thirst in great gulps and releasing that green scent of freshness, coolness. Through the crack Ravi saw the long purple shadows of the shed and the garage lying still across the yard. Beyond that, the white walls of the house. The bougainvillea had lost its lividity, hung in dark bundles that quaked and twittered

3. **hirsute** (HUHR SOOT): hairy; shaggy.

C QUICK CHECK

What makes Ravi decide to remain in hiding a while longer?

D LITERARY ANALYSIS

Why does Ravi want to win the game so badly? Based on what has happened so far, how do you think the game will end?

A READING FOCUS

Analyze the details in this paragraph and describe how you think Ravi feels.

B LITERARY ANALYSIS

Why does Ravi start crying?

and seethed with masses of homing sparrows. The lawn was shut off from his view. Could he hear the children's voices? It seemed to him that he could. It seemed to him that he could hear them chanting, singing, laughing. But what about the game? What had happened? Could it be over? How could it when he was still not found? **A**

It then occurred to him that he could have slipped out long ago, dashed across the yard to the veranda, and touched the "den." It was necessary to do that to win. He had forgotten. He had only remembered the part of hiding and trying to elude the seeker. He had done that so successfully, his success had occupied him so wholly, that he had quite forgotten that success had to be clinched by that final dash to victory and the ringing cry of "Den!"

With a whimper he burst through the crack, fell on his knees, got up, and stumbled on stiff, benumbed legs across the shadowy yard, crying heartily by the time he reached the veranda so that when he flung himself at the white pillar and bawled, "Den! Den! Den!" his voice broke with rage and pity at the disgrace of it all, and he felt himself flooded with tears and misery. **B**

Out on the lawn, the children stopped chanting. They all turned to stare at him in amazement. Their faces were pale and triangular in the dusk. The trees and bushes around them stood inky and sepulchral, spilling long shadows across them. They stared, wondering at his reappearance, his passion, his wild animal howling. Their mother rose from her basket chair and came toward him, worried, annoyed, saying, "Stop it, stop it, Ravi. Don't be a baby. Have you hurt yourself?" Seeing him attended to, the children went back to clasping their hands and chanting, "The grass is green, the rose is red. . . ."

But Ravi would not let them. He tore himself out of his mother's grasp and pounded across the lawn into their midst, charging at them with his head lowered so that they scattered in surprise. "I won, I won, I won," he bawled, shaking his head so that the big tears flew. "Raghu didn't find me. I won, I won—"

It took them a minute to grasp what he was saying, even who he was. They had quite forgotten him. Raghu had found all the others long ago. There had been a fight about who was to be It next. It had been so fierce that their mother had emerged from her bath and made them change to another game. Then they had played another and another. **C** Broken mulberries from the tree and eaten them. Helped the driver wash the car when their father returned from work. Helped the gardener water the beds till he roared at them and swore he would complain to their parents. The parents had come out, taken up their positions on the cane chairs. They had begun to play again, sing and chant. All this time no one had remembered Ravi. Having disappeared from the scene, he had disappeared from their minds. Clean.

"Don't be a fool," Raghu said roughly, pushing him aside, and even Mira said, "Stop howling, Ravi. If you want to play, you can stand at the end of the line," and she put him there very firmly.

The game proceeded. Two pairs of arms reached up and met in an arc. The children trooped under it again and again in a lugubrious circle, ducking their heads and intoning

"The grass is green,
The rose is red;
Remember me
When I am dead, dead, dead, dead . . ." **D**

And the arc of thin arms trembled in the twilight, and the heads were bowed so sadly, and their feet tramped to that melancholy refrain so mournfully, so helplessly, that Ravi could not bear it. He would not follow them, he would not be included in this funereal game. He had wanted victory and triumph—not a funeral. But he had been forgotten, left out, and he would not join them now. The ignominy of being forgotten—how could he face it? He felt his heart go heavy and ache inside him unbearably. He lay down full length on the damp grass, crushing his face into it, no longer crying, silenced by a terrible sense of his insignificance. **E**

C QUICK CHECK

Why are the other children confused by Ravi's celebration?

D VOCABULARY

Selection Vocabulary

Use context clues from the children's rhyme to write a definition of *lugubrious*.

E READING FOCUS

Analyze details in the last paragraph that describe how Ravi feels. Why is Ravi so sad?

Applying Your Skills

Games at Twilight

VOCABULARY DEVELOPMENT

DIRECTIONS: Complete the word analogies below by writing the words from the Word Box on the correct blanks. Some words will not be used. One analogy has been completed and explained as an example.

Word Box

- maniacal
- stridently
- superciliously
- temerity
- intoxicating
- dogged
- lugubrious
- ignominy

CIRCUS : HAPPY :: funeral : lugubrious

A circus is a happy event, as a funeral is a lugubrious, or mournful, event.

1. DOG : LOYAL :: donkey : ____________
2. SUCCEED : PRIDE :: fail : ____________
3. ACCEPT : WARMLY :: reject : ____________
4. DRIVING THE SPEED LIMIT : CAUTION :: driving recklessly : ____________

LITERARY FOCUS: IMAGERY

DIRECTIONS: Complete the chart below by listing the senses that the following examples of **imagery** appeal to.

Images	Senses
"No life stirred at this arid time of day—the birds still drooped, like dead fruit, in the papery tents of the trees; some squirrels lay limp on the wet earth under the garden tap." (lines 25–28)	1.
"Ravi shook, then shivered with delight, with self-congratulation. Also with fear. It was dark, spooky in the shed. It had a muffled smell, as of graves." (lines 134–136)	2.

READING FOCUS: ANALYZING DETAILS

DIRECTIONS: Write a brief paragraph discussing how **analyzing details** helped you find insights into the characters and plot of "Games at Twilight."

____

____

____

____

____

Literary Skills Understand imagery.

Reading Skills Analyze details.

Skills Review

Collection 13

LANGUAGE COACH

DIRECTIONS: The following words are homographs. **Homographs** are words that have the same spelling but different meanings, and may or may not have different pronunciations. On the blank lines, write two definitions for each word. Use a dictionary for help. Be sure to include the part of speech (noun, adverb, adjective, or verb) for each definition.

1. refuse

   ____

   ____

2. minute

   ____

   ____

3. address

   ____

   ____

4. wound

   ____

   ____

5. desert

   ____

   ____

ORAL LANGUAGE ACTIVITY

DIRECTIONS: In "Games at Twilight," you learned how the use of **imagery** can help readers feel like they are part of a story. On a separate sheet of paper, write a short essay (about two paragraphs) that describes a typical day for you at school. Try to use imagery that appeals to all five senses (hearing, touch, taste, smell, and sight). Read your essay in front of the class. Have your classmates tell which details helped them best imagine the scenes you described.

Vocabulary Review

Unit 6

DIRECTIONS: Match each vocabulary word in the first column with its correct definition in the second column. Write the letter of each definition next to the correct vocabulary word.

	Word		Definition
______	**1.** perspective	**a.**	adjust for a new purpose
______	**2.** carefree	**b.**	destroy
______	**3.** suppressed	**c.**	widely but unfavorably known
______	**4.** potency	**d.**	kinship; bond
______	**5.** sordid	**e.**	troubled
______	**6.** dogged	**f.**	without worry
______	**7.** buoyancy	**g.**	kept from being known
______	**8.** somber	**h.**	filthy; foul
______	**9.** supplication	**i.**	gloomy
______	**10.** anarchy	**j.**	disorder and confusion
______	**11.** annihilate	**k.**	humble plea
______	**12.** affinity	**l.**	a particular way of looking at something
______	**13.** notorious	**m.**	crazed; wildly enthusiastic
______	**14.** reverently	**n.**	stubbornly persistent
______	**15.** lamentable	**o.**	regrettable; unfortunate
______	**16.** vexed	**p.**	lightness of spirit; cheerfulness
______	**17.** maniacal	**q.**	strength; power
______	**18.** adapt	**r.**	with great respect or awe, as for something sacred

Applying the Key Concepts

Unit 6

DIRECTIONS: Review the Key Concepts at the beginning of this unit. Then answer the following questions:

WORLD WAR I: THE GREAT WAR

- When T. S. Eliot wrote "The Hollow Men," British people were feeling the lingering effects of World War I, and many predicted a bleak future. Describe how Eliot's poem reflects these feelings of hopelessness.

WORLD WAR II AND ITS AFTERMATH

- How might Primo Levi's book "Survival in Auschwitz" affect how people think about governments' limits on individual freedoms?

IDENTITY AND DIVERSITY

- In what way is the story "No Witchcraft for Sale" by Doris Lessing a voice for the people who struggled against colonial powers after World War II?

Index of Authors and Titles